The Triple Helix: The Soul of Bioethics

Also by Lisa Bellantoni

MORAL PROGRESS: A Process Critique of MacIntyre

The Triple Helix: The Soul of Bioethics

Lisa Bellantoni
Associate Professor of Philosophy, Albright College, USA

Montante Family Library
D'Youville College

© Lisa Bellantoni 2011

All rights reserved. No reproduction, copy or transmission of this publication may be made without written permission.

No portion of this publication may be reproduced, copied or transmitted save with written permission or in accordance with the provisions of the Copyright, Designs and Patents Act 1988, or under the terms of any licence permitting limited copying issued by the Copyright Licensing Agency, Saffron House, 6–10 Kirby Street, London EC1N 8TS.

Any person who does any unauthorized act in relation to this publication may be liable to criminal prosecution and civil claims for damages.

The author has asserted her right to be identified as the author of this work in accordance with the Copyright, Designs and Patents Act 1988.

First published 2011 by
PALGRAVE MACMILLAN

Palgrave Macmillan in the UK is an imprint of Macmillan Publishers Limited, registered in England, company number 785998, of Houndmills, Basingstoke, Hampshire RG21 6XS.

Palgrave Macmillan in the US is a division of St Martin's Press LLC,
175 Fifth Avenue, New York, NY 10010.

Palgrave Macmillan is the global academic imprint of the above companies and has companies and representatives throughout the world.

Palgrave® and Macmillan® are registered trademarks in the United States, the United Kingdom, Europe and other countries.

ISBN: 978–0–230–30099–6

This book is printed on paper suitable for recycling and made from fully managed and sustained forest sources. Logging, pulping and manufacturing processes are expected to conform to the environmental regulations of the country of origin.

A catalogue record for this book is available from the British Library.

Library of Congress Cataloging-in-Publication Data

Bellantoni, Lisa, 1969–
   The triple helix : the soul of bioethics / Lisa Bellantoni.
     p. cm.
   Includes bibliographical references and index.
   ISBN 978–0–230–30099–6
    1. Bioethics. I. Title.

QH332.B445 2011
174.2—dc23   2011020962

10 9 8 7 6 5 4 3 2 1
20 19 18 17 16 15 14 13 12 11

Printed and bound in the United States of America

Contents

Introduction: What Good Is Philosophical Bioethics?		1
1	The Wages of Grief	8
	1.1 What grief teaches	8
	1.2 Keeping time	19
2	Getting Too Personal?	30
	2.1 What good are persons?	30
	2.2 What's new with you?	39
3	Where do Bioethicists Come From?	49
	3.1 Do utilitarians do it better?	49
	3.2 Life as we know it?	54
	3.3 What's love got to do with it?	60
	3.4 What good is life?	64
4	Invasion of the Body Snatchers	74
	4.1 We young immortals?	74
	4.2 The duty to live?	79
	4.3 Death be not proud?	84
	4.4 Was it good for you?	91
5	Are We Good Enough?	99
	5.1 Dehumanizing human dignity	99
	5.2 Disabling persons	103
	5.3 No additives, preservatives, or fillers?	113
	5.4 We can rebuild him …?	119
6	Engineering Bioethics	126
	6.1 Biofallacies	126
	6.2 The indignity of human dignity	136
	6.3 Is dying a moral project?	142
	6.4 The sanctity of power	145
7	Who Do Bioethicists Think They Are?	152
	7.1 The object of my affection?	152
	7.2 Getting too personal again?	160
	7.3 My right to your life?	166
	7.4 The privacy paradox	171

8	A Culture of Living	179
	8.1 What good is happiness?	179
	8.2 Feeling too good?	186
	8.3 Bringing transcendence to life	193
9	The Triple Helix: Time, Love, and Memory	202
	9.1 What wondrous love is this?	203
	9.2 A life cycle bioethic?	212
	9.3 Bringing transcendence back to life	216

Notes	224
Bibliography	227
Index	229

Introduction: What Good Is Philosophical Bioethics?

What ails philosophical bioethics? That may seem an odd query. No field within contemporary philosophic practice is more widely debated or more fraught with practical implications beyond the discipline's narrow academic pursuits. Today, philosophers-cum-bioethicists serve on ethics boards, consult with advisory committees, and seek to influence public policy on a broad range of biomedical practices, from stem cell research to end-of-life care. Yet even a cursory examination of the research articles and textbooks produced by these bioethicists reveals nothing distinctively philosophical about their evaluations. Their ethical analyses emphasize the same range of practical considerations as those offered by physicians, psychologists, nurses, and even political scientists and theologians – themselves all turned would-be bioethicists. Analyses which apply a specific type of philosophical ethics – for example utilitarian, or virtue-based, or deontological, or pragmatic – too, typically involve not matters of grand philosophical import, but the more mundane and narrowly confounding questions of how to apply generic moral principles such as beneficence and justice to specific cases.

Absent from these investigations is any sustained, substantive attention to the questions which most capture public attention. They exclude discussion of the human soul, of mortality, and of what makes human lives distinctively human and valued as such. These are, of course, the antique metaphysical concerns that were forcibly expelled from philosophical analysis nearly a century ago, by those who insisted that such ideas, lacking empirically identifiable referents, were inadmissible in proper philosophical discussion. On this view, philosophy grew up, and ceased addressing quaint queries such as what we are made of, and what happens to us when we die. For many philosophical bioethicists, the methodological exclusion of such concerns properly divorces it not only from sectarian religious beliefs, but also from any metaphysical presumptions that cannot be empirically defended. This effectively privatizes such questions, leaving to individual discretion beliefs about the ultimate good of human persons.

For philosophical bioethicists, privatizing such beliefs prevents some persons from imposing their beliefs upon others. Predictably, however, some of those excluded from rational debate often pursue alternative means to introduce their commitments into the arena of public policy, by force of law or majority vote, or even through intimidation or violence. The bombing of abortion clinics, perpetrated to defend the sanctity of human life, underscores the purchase of such ethereal ideals. Yet to note that contemporary philosophical bioethics lacks soul, methodologically, expresses a broader concern relating to the scope of philosophical discourse. Traditionally, philosophical investigation has deemed considerations of the soul, the relation of soul and body, and our proper path in our preparation for death, as worthy of rational discussion and admissible of non-sectarian debate.

Into this fray step some theologians insisting that we are not mere cells, not mere animals, but creatures of a divine order. These theorists claim to espouse a culture of life, in defense of its absolute sanctity. The very absoluteness of their claims, however, in practice devalues that life. It fosters not a culture of life, I will argue, but a cult of life, a cult that idolizes not human living – not human individual human lives as we know them – but an idealized specter that degrades the human dignity they otherwise aspire to protect at every turn. In the face of this cult, many philosophers cum academic bioethicists adopt a stance of broad refusal to engage with presuppositions they deem beyond the scope of reasoned debate. These ideas are instead dismissed as metaphysical miasma, long since abandoned by philosophers. If that's the case, however, then on what basis may bioethicists engage ill-founded metaphysical or theological presuppositions? That question is critical because however aggressively these beliefs are excluded from public debate, they remain no less evocative, no less influential, and no less seductive to their adherents.

Privatizing such convictions does nothing to make public debate less polarized. Instead, it reinforces the charge against philosophical bioethics that it poses a no less substantively metaphysical, and no better founded, view of human life and human dignity. That view, foreshadowed by philosophers as diverse as Immanuel Kant and Jean-Paul Sartre, depicts human persons as autonomous, as self-legislating, or even self-creating in their moral capacity, and as defined in opposition to any natural constraints. Autonomous ends, as Kant describes humans, have as their chief moral mandate the task of making themselves better than nature made them. Agents as Sartre describes them are even more self-authoring, as they are defined neither by nature nor by divine behest, but as precisely what they make of themselves, and nothing else. What I will here deem the cult of rights, then, takes its inception from a metaphysical anthropology. That anthropology, no less than the cult of life's, leaves it as mysterious how autonomous ends, any more than the transcendent souls that the cult of life depicts, bear bodies that might either warrant, or even need, moral protection. The souls described by the cult of life, like the agents depicted by the cult of rights, are what they are, metaphysically and morally, independently of and precisely in opposition to the vagaries of biological living – of procreating and living and ailing and aging and dying – which they wholly transcend as conditions of their moral worth.

Persons as both cults describe them do none of these things, I will argue; thus the very project of ascribing bioethical norms to them poses a paradox. We are not, on either view, persons in our transient particulars – our pleasures and pains and loves and desires and preferences – but only in our metaphysical status as souls or ends. Both cults insist that we are essentially our persons, and only incidentally, only epiphenomenally, only temporarily, our individual bodily and psychic affects. Yet how, as essentially disembodied persons, secure in our inviolable dignity, could the fortunes of our bodies or psyches then affect us morally, such that they might require bioethical norms? And how might we identify such norms, if we are valuable only insofar as we are not our bodies? Both cults identify as valuable only the transcendent autonomous ends or souls that all persons bear in common. In this manner, both cults strip any moral authority from the privacy, subjectivity, or interiority of individuals as individuals. For the cult of life, for example, we should not pursue physician-assisted suicide, even to relieve grave afflictions, because we would thereby devalue human life in itself. For the cult of rights, such pursuits are only permissible when they prove fully autonomous, unconstrained by the individual grief and pain and terror which, they insist – apparently without irony – might prevent us from acting as any rational person might under such circumstances, and thereby as ourselves.

Despite our inviolable dignity, then, we seem for the cult of life to have a mysterious means of violating that transcendent worth, through what we do to our quite undignified bodies. Despite our inalienable autonomy, we seem for the cult of rights to countenance an equally mysterious capacity to imperil that autonomy, again, by acting at the behest of a merely animal body. Both cults thereby license wholesale incursions into how others live their bodies and psyches. Yet on neither account do persons, in their persons, die; nor are they born, nor do they age, or ail, or even change, in their essence – so much so that the entire human life cycle should be a matter of moral indifference to them. Persons so conceived, moreover, are entirely independent of others, in their persons. For the cult of life, our birth signals the emergence of a transcendent soul. For the cult of rights, our birth signals the equally miraculous occurrence of a transcendent end. Souls and ends accrue their worth *a priori*, independently of any human agency. Nor can souls or ends affect that transcendent worth though the merely empirical adventures of their bodies, or through their agency. Our absolute worth as persons, rather, is both unearned and inalienable. We can neither enhance nor diminish it no matter what we do to our own or others' bodies or psyches or agent capacities.

As disembodied persons, moreover, we are immune to the vagaries of time, age, and illness; as transcendent ends or souls we do not traffic in ailing or aging or pro-creating or grieving or living or dying in their particulars. Unsurprisingly, these themes – of time, love and memory – are largely absent from contemporary bioethical discussions as both cults conduct them. For the cult of life, the life they profess to love, to venerate, to sanctify, has little to do with biological living. It attends instead to a speculative, supernatural ideal. The suffering, aging, and dying of particular persons, like their desiring, pleasing and enjoying, are mere epiphenomena. For the cult of life, the transcendent ideal, rather than our experience, forges the stuff of human life, the primary datum commanding our moral allegiance. This ideal is deeply biophobic. It dignifies human life only by ascribing to it the utter transcendence of human living. This cult deems human life to be absolutely sanctified only by disembodying persons, by alienating their transcendent dignity from their biological lives. It then leaves no recourse for dignifying living in its biological complexities. If we are who they say we are, of course, that point is irrelevant, since we neither ail nor age nor pro-create nor grieve nor die, really. Yet it then seems that we can love human life only by making it something entirely other than life as we know it.

This, of course, is the cult of life's ultimate objection to the cult of rights: that the latter asserts the dominion of human will over human life, undertaking to liberate us from nature's provenance. Yet in this endeavor, they join forces. For the cult of rights, our absolute moral worth attends our unfettered autonomy. Such an account, however, is no more amenable to human living. If we can make whatever we wish of our bodily estate, its health or function matters not at all, metaphysically or morally. If we can make of time, of finitude, of grief whatever we wish, they alike have no substantive metaphysical or moral claim upon us. Persons fully liberated from the vagaries of human living neither yield nor warrant any intelligible bioethic we can scarcely enhance the care of human persons, of the living and the dying, if we have no substantive conceptions of health or illness. Nor can caring for embodied persons be a moral requirement if our actions or inactions leave their autonomy, finally, untouched. Only if persons are embodied, I suggest, can the treatment of their bodies matter morally. Moreover, only if persons can affect other persons, in their persons, can we exhibit substantive moral agency.

To identify bioethical norms in particular, we must affirm that some substantive moral goods attend the particulars of human living, such that we might literally embody a bioethic. The claim that human bodies matter, morally, resists not only both cults' accounts of human persons, but also the vast bulk of Western metaphysics and ethics. That history includes a long legacy of fear and shame and disgust attaching to the empirical particulars of human embodiment: our unseemly dependencies on others, all manner of needs and desires, of pleasures and pains, of hopes and fears, all coursing through us against a back-drop of finitude: of illness, aging and death. Given that legacy, it is understandable that the cult of rights asserts our utter independence of such potential impingements upon our autonomy, and a love of liberty that transcends our more local and transient affections, all of which are finally its creatures. It is equally understandable that the cult of life counsels us to resist animal pleasures, as more befitting our dignity. Perhaps it makes more sense to valorize life ever-lasting and a love divine, regnant over the vagaries of human affection and beneficence. But these loves are difficult to envision in human terms: in their utter indifference to the fates and fortunes of one's fellows, in their invulnerability to pain or pleasure, or grief. They are loves which do not traffic in the realities of human living, of pro-creating, ailing, dying and grieving.

A human love properly conceived, I suggest, does not liberate human persons from our finite embodiments and personalities. Quite the contrary, it brings those particulars to life. Persons are born of embodied persons, I will argue, and embody others' genes, others' histories, others' values, and others' affects. Such is the elemental form of human procreation; yet we view that procreativity too narrowly if we confine the term to relations between parents and children. All of us are, I suggest, person makers, not merely in our capacity to produce biological issue, but also in our capacity to render others both objects of our valuations, and subjects to those valuations – as we are to theirs. I mean here to resist the basic premise shared by both cults: that we are, in our persons, mutually transcendent substances. I mean to advance instead, as a literal metaphysical thesis, that we are constituted in our persons by others, and that only in mutually personalizing persons may we dignify or degrade them. Only as objects of others' creative powers are we rendered subjects, and only in that mutual dependence is the specific interiority of our persons accessible and thus vulnerable to others' actions. To say that we dignify or degrade others through our actions implies strictly that we bring them into being in ways that are morally salutary or morally destructive.

Taken together these points imply that whatever good resides in human living must itself be finite and transitory, such that we are morally enjoined to cultivate it. We are, then, human organisms not only in our biological finitude, but also in our mutual constitution of each other. Only on these bases, as mutually accessible in our persons, does it matter morally how we regard each other. At the same time, I will argue, whatever proves to be of intrinsic value in human living will equally prove to be a creature and embodiment of human living in its finitude. If we are to love not life or liberty or persons, but living individuals, we cannot espouse any bioethic that enjoins us, finally, to love not living persons but abstract ideals. When assaying moral value, we must first acknowledge our own capacity to elevate or degrade, to humanize or to dehumanize persons. I emphasize that contrast because we dignify nothing, least of all ourselves, by valorizing grand ideals of human life that bear no resemblance to, and ultimately are hostile to, human life as we know it.

In the mutual making of persons, conversely, I mean to depict the cultivation of individual human lives in their particulars – their bodily interiority, their psychic subjectivity, their agency – particulars apart from which persons would require no more defense. For both cults, persons are mutually transcendent specters, inviolable, unreachable and timeless. Yet what we grieve in the ailing, aging and dying of specific persons, and what we celebrate in procreation – the stuff of any bioethic humanely conceived – asserts precisely the contrary: that something of novel, substantive, irreplaceable value attends the arrival of a new person, and that something of substantive worth perishes with his or her passage.

That worth, I argue, is rooted not in transcendent properties, but in the bodily and psychic interiority and agency through which persons constitute one another in their particulars, and thereby, in their persons. Accordingly, for any bioethic to prove humane and dignifying, it must take the cultivation of such metaphysical and moral subjectivity or privacy as its proper end. Both cults, in their combating paternalisms, are morally toxic not only in diminishing the quality of empirical living, but in their quest to usurp moral authority from the individual interiority and agency without which grand moral bromides like human dignity or the sanctity of human life are meaningless. In contrast, I suggest, only by cultivating the privacy and agency of persons – through our moral practices – does bioethics pose any prospect of dignifying persons, by bringing transcendence quite literally to life.

1
The Wages of Grief

1.1 What grief teaches

We have a gift for making virtue of necessity; our propensity to do this may prove our curse. When we cannot forestall endless successions of pregnancies, we deem them gifts of God or Fortune or nature's bounty. When we can do nothing to forestall aging and physical decline, we speak in hushed tones of revered elders and their hard won wisdom. When we cannot repel death, we invoke the language of theodicy, assuring ourselves that everything happens for a reason. These bromides, however, have scarcely discouraged our efforts to wrest greater control over our embodiment. To the contrary, as our reproductive practices become more optional, any particular pregnancy become less a reflexive joy or sorrow, and more a matter of individual choice. When we can defer signs of physical decline, by cosmetic surgery or therapeutic or enhancement-oriented medical treatments, aging becomes less a relentless inevitability to be embraced and more itself a medical malady to be resisted. When death can be better managed and timed, it becomes less an inerrant feature of the human condition, and more a matter of individualized, substantive choice. Indeed, this growing autonomy in the face of natural necessity is at the heart of the conflict between the cult of life and the cult of rights. For the cult of life, liberating ourselves from that necessity dehumanizes us, stripping us of our dignity and catapulting us into a Brave New World, a post-human future. For the cult or rights, conversely, that autonomy underwrites our dignity, which resides in our capacity to transcend any ostensible natural necessity.

So conceived, these contrasting positions seem to begin their analyses from rationally incommensurable premises, from accounts of human dignity, and indeed of human personhood, that are in principle irreconcilable. For the cult of life, any future predicated on such outsized expansions of human autonomy tends inexorably towards some kind of dystopia: clones run amok, spare-parts harvesting, replacement or designer children, two hundred year old parents, death on demand, and a gaggle of transgenic hybrid horrors all populate this cult's overheated imagination. For the cult of rights, in contrast, the basic issue is not what persons are, or will make of themselves through such biological interventions, but the autonomous capacity that underlies those developments and is thus the proper locus and end of our ethical queries. As such, while the cult of rights allies itself with such innovations insofar as they evince individual choice, the cult of life opposes such innovations on precisely the same basis. This fundamental contrast provokes some ethicists to regard these cults' ensuing disputes not only as rationally incommensurable, but as illustrating the impossibility of any epistemic or meta-ethical basis for supporting practical claims in bioethics.[1] As such claims appeal to no publicly available facts, moral or otherwise, the argument goes, they are essentially emotive, voicing arbitrary preferences enforceable, finally, not by force of reason, but by force of law, or fraud, or power. On that view, not only can we make no rational public decisions about how best to use – or not use – emerging biotechnologies, but such decisions – when made by individuals as individuals – admit neither any rational basis nor any possibility of rational adjudication.

If that's the case – if bioethics is nothing more than an arena for competing sects seeking to impose their preferred styles of living upon one another by any means available – then philosophical bioethics is an oxymoron, for philosophy in any traditional guise aspires to truth. Moreover, philosophers can add nothing substantive to such debates if appeals to reason or to fact have no claim upon the subjects engaging in them. Nor would such appeals have any use, shorn as such of any motive force. They would lack, that is, not only rational but practical warrant. Yet so too, on that analysis, would any claim advanced within this arena, on any basis: Assertions that we ought to defend life, or defend autonomy, would prove simply that: assertions, whose only defense would reside in the power of their defenders to impose those claims on others. Those impositions, however, would make nonsense of the transcendent moral capacity that both cults ascribe to persons. At the same time, I will argue that this shared ascription of transcendence – rather than the competing ways that the cults depict this transcendence – undercuts any intelligible bioethic. It does so not by posing incommensurable premises, but by divorcing those premises – about human dignity and human autonomy – from the lived realities of procreating, maturing, ailing, aging and dying, from live as we know it.

I begin, then, by seeking not to resolve these cults' incommensurability, but to refer them jointly to a more basic premise: We are born, we age, and we die. Botox injections and heart surgery not-withstanding, neither our human dignity, nor our autonomy, elides these facts of human living. For many of us, biomedical practices will make these processes no less difficult – and perhaps even harder – than they were in ages past. Certainly, public health measures and the broad availability of medical services have indisputably enhanced millions of lives. Yet in the debates that most vividly exercise would-be bioethicists of all stripes – those concerning the beginning and ending of human lives – we seem to have traded one range of concerns (over an untimely death – too soon, too unhealthy, too worn down) for another (too late, too unhealthy, too worn down). The cult of rights frames this challenge as one of potentially diminished quality of life. On that basis, it yields to individuals' extensive control over the timing and manner of their deaths, including, in some cases, a right to assistance in dying. While such control marks for the cult of rights an ultimate defense of human autonomy and dignity, for the cult of life it abrogates that dignity by asserting our dominion over human life – a life which is not finally our own, but God's or nature's. For the cult of rights, dying poses one instance of the generic moral injunction to defend human autonomy; for the cult of life, dying poses one instance of the generic moral injunction to sustain our place in a natural or divinely ordained order, not by opposing but by subordinating our will to that order.

Both approaches thereby commend ways of managing the dying process. Yet they do so by rationalizing it, far afield of the grief that attends it. The cult of rights offers living wills, do-not-resuscitate orders, rights to refusal of futile medical treatment, even a choice of places and times and ways to do one's dying. The moral import of the process is that it reflects the dying person's choices, that it is individual and autonomous, that it respects the person's wishes. The proper terminus is a good enough death, a dignified death, adequately controlled and timed and managed, preserving as much of the patient's autonomy as possible. As noble as this aspiration may be, it grossly misstates the degree of autonomy available to dying persons, and disavows the reality of the dying process and the grief that trails in its wake. Most know too well that death is often a messy, ugly, painful business, however well planned and managed. Many bear daily witness – in themselves or in some intimate others – to the relentless dissolution of self that attends a body's dissolution. We may well be, or wish ourselves to be, transcendent ends. But no such wish escapes the laws of physics and chemistry – whose ineluctable entropy pulls us apart cell by cell, dissolving each person whose body ultimately collapses in upon itself. For the cult of rights, the bodily and emotional and social responses that attend dying are subjective epiphenomena, private materials upon which we may overlay any meaning of our choosing in rendering the process meaningful, dignified, and uniquely ours. Yet that very insistence negates the reality of dying, with its relentless stripping away not merely of autonomy and dignity, but finally of the self pushed quite literally to its vanishing point.

While the cult of rights devalues the suffering and grief that attend these losses in this way, rendering them subjective epiphenomena of which we may make entirely what we will, the cult of life idolizes such suffering. It affirms both the natural necessity that we suffer in dying as an inescapable feature of the human condition, and a moral injunction that we endure such suffering as the proper subordination of human will to that natural or divinely appointed order. For the cult of life, then, we are to witness in our dying signatures of grace; persons properly willing to endure insufferable suffering affirm the dignity of human life in itself. Indeed, so transcendent is that worth that persons are enjoined to endure such suffering, even against their wishes, to preserve their human dignity – even if their continued living appears to them to have lost its worth. To impose this gift of life on unwilling persons, however, seemingly affirms less the dignity of this particular person – in his or her own moral capacity – than an abstract ideal of human dignity. While the cult of rights reduces bodily dissolution to a set of biological epiphenomena, the cult of life elevates enduring that suffering to a moral mandate. For the cult of rights, autonomous persons transcend and lend meaning to their biological dissolution; for the cult of life, dignified persons alike transcend that dissolution. Neither autonomous agents nor dignified persons die in any substantive sense. The latter transcend their bodies, entering into eternal life; the former, too, retain their autonomy, however mysteriously – precisely because it is defined in opposition to any bodily epiphenomena.

On neither account are persons essentially embodied, essentially temporal; nor does it make any sense to mourn their passing, as nothing of substantive metaphysical or moral import is lost thereby. Dying persons should not bemoan their fates, for they endure eternally, whether as disembodied souls or as transcendent ends. Nor should the living grieve their passage. Indeed, grief among the living is but the obverse to grief among the dying, as both are metaphysical misfits. They embody comparable epiphenomena, attaching not to real losses, but to private, arbitrary and transitory preferences. In grief, however, it would seem that both the living and the dying undergo a shared metamorphosis: as a dying body stills to a corpse, it unfurls that person's bindings to a social life and a social reality. The dying person does not merely fade from the scene, but is wrenched away cell by cell, moment by moment. For both cults, such a description would prove not merely metaphorically but metaphysically muddled. Persons, as souls or ends, are not only atemporal, but asocial, are wholly self-subsistent in their dignity or autonomy. On both views, any grief we endure at another's passing would be our own doing, a creature of our misguided resistance to the natural order of things. Moreover, the task of grief management or grief work at this point is precisely to still our heated imaginations, to acclimatize to this new reality, to get on with our lives.

We have an entire grief industry prepared to help us do just that – to get a grip on ourselves. Grief, they assure us, is as individual, as potentially autonomous and self-directed as the death or failure that provoked it. There are stages and guide-posts, but these are flexible and varied, not one size fits all. If these fail to restore us, we have diagnostic criteria for complicated grief, treatment protocols and counseling, workbooks and support groups, all aimed at the management of grief. Yet for those enduring the process, the very term grief management may seem an almost comical oxymoron. How do we get a grip on ourselves when we no longer feel like ourselves – when the social bonds that once seemed so vitally to constitute our projects and self-definitions, our persons, are unraveling before our eyes? How can we accede to these new found states of affairs, when the subjects grasping the facts – namely you and I – have changed irrevocably – as a condition of those states of affairs being facts? How do we stage our responses, when grief comes crashing down around us like a tidal wave? How do we talk ourselves into acclimatizing to a world that we do not wish to be born, a world in which the deceased continue only in our memories, in a few prized artifacts. Worse, how can we acclimatize to that world when those very memories so often intrude themselves obsessively upon us, as unbidden interlopers from which we seek escape? The haunting reality to which we must adapt is not the person's death, but the enduring absence that death portends: the past that can no longer be altered, fixed, improved, reconciled; the future that looms so barren, a bastard present that gapes open at the seams, stuffed to the breaking point with pasts that we wish were not, and futures that we long for but that cannot be.

More sober-thinking philosophers would point out at this point that these *feelings* – emphasis added – are after all the creatures of our minds, thoughts and intentions that refer to states of affairs that are quite impossible. Indeed, grief is an exercise in counter- factuals, in our resistance to the inevitable, our refusal to accept unalterable facts. On this count, its perpetuation would seem quite plainly irrational, an emotive response that tells us less about how the world is than about how we process it – in this case, improperly. Moreover, these feelings will become manageable with time, when reason re-asserts itself, and we return to the practical affairs of living. We will be told that it is irrational, unhealthy, pointless to torture ourselves with such thoughts, and unreasonable to seek definitive answers to the inevitable – and inevitably ill-formed questions – that death raises. We will hear that the deceased himself or herself would not have wished this for our future, and that as time passes we will see matters more accurately, more truthfully, more rationally. The physical symptoms of grief will resolve – in the preferred clinical terminology – and the felt absence of the person, the echoes in mind and body, the physical discomfiture and disease will pass into equanimity. Now, if all of this were true – if the physical discomfiture were internally produced and the psychic anguish sustained by our thoughts, then it would make perfect sense to say that grief teaches us little about the world or ourselves, that it has little if any truth-value. The above insistences, alas are not true, and succeed only in misrepresenting what we are on the most basic of measures – how we live and how we die.

The point that grief contains little or no truth value encompasses two mistaken ideas: that our minds, sans emotion and bodily affect, provide us with our principle path to truth, and that those minds, which are, finally, our persons, are self-subsistent. Philosophers have long denied that emotions accurately render an objective world, or in contemporary terms, that they house and convey information. Against their subjective deliverances, rather, our minds must strive to secure the objectivity, the public availability, held to disclose truths about the world we inhabit. Despite its prominence, however, the view that our minds wholly transcend our bodily and emotional states founders on the simplest observations. Brain injury retards our thinking, and brain death extinguishes any evidence of it. We have no evidence that such autonomous minds obtain within comatose bodies, and strong evidence that physical machines are better at purely rational calculations than we are. We may even associate patterns of failed reasoning with specific brain impairments. These points count so strongly against the mind-body dualism that both cults embrace that many contemporary philosophers reject even its possibility. Yet even those who grant that minds are essentially embodied maintain that emotions yield subjective data at best contingently referent to an objective world obtaining beyond the observer's mind. If, however, our thinking capacities are essentially embodied, we have no *a priori* basis for dismissing emotions as a potential source of truthful information, not merely about us but about the world we inhabit.

I wish to maintain here not the broad thesis that all thinking has an emotional component, but the narrower thesis that emotion yields factual information about the world. Emotions obtain in the objective world, after all, even if only as housed within and among their apprehenders – who, of course, inhabit that ostensibly objective world as conditions of their mutual presence. Moreover, it is a sophistical conceit to hold that what exists for real must obtain for all apprehenders under all circumstances, and even when it is not thus apprehended. We have no affirmation, for example, that the mood in this room is somber or jovial, and can readily adduce evidence for that claim in the reports of other apprehenders. We are, of course, well schooled in the habit of identifying as merely subjective, or ultimately unreal, those apprehensions that attach to bodily or emotional states that we cannot share or render fully publicly available. We cannot, for instance, feel one another's pain or pleasure immediately, though we can gain varying degrees of access to those feelings through words, gestures, physical responses and the like. The epistemic bias against regarding such experiences as factual, and their social communications as informative, as instances of knowledge generation, reflects the epistemic intuitions of both the cult of rights and the cult of life that emotions are not a source of knowledge but are to be evaluated by rational, knowledge-producing practices.

This bias would seem to be of extra-ordinary import to philosophical bioethicists – if they are, for example, to make substantive judgments about quality of life issues. For the cult of rights, such judgments underwrite individuals' liberty to decide for themselves when they have suffered enough, or suffered excessively, even to the point of claiming their right to assistance in dying. That right, however, is not absolute on their own account, but is restricted to those who not only choose wholly autonomously, but who have legitimate reasons for their choices, such as intractable pain. To defend the publicly claimed right of persons to make such decisions for themselves, these ostensible defenders of autonomy insist, such reasons must be premised on publicly assessable facts, not on mere subjective whims or arbitrary or transitory preferences. The cult of rights, however, precludes both bodily states and emotional affects as reasons precisely insofar as they deem such affects to compromise an agent's ability to choose autonomously. Agents, for example, must be screened for depression, and counseled repeatedly on their alternatives. Their bodily and psychic states, that is, yield neither definitive data about how the agent is, nor have any evaluative force in determining that agent's good. That ultimate power, rather, resides in his or her autonomous will. As wholly autonomous agents, however, we are supposedly unaffected by bodily and emotional states, whereas if afflicted by such subjective and arbitrary data, we surrender the capacity to act autonomously. We have, then, no basis for such making such quality of life judgments as individuals, precisely because our private bodily and emotional states, on this account, yield no public information.

For the cult of rights, the very basis for our claim on a right to make quality of life judgments – our disembodied autonomy – undercuts any legitimate basis for making such judgments. An analogous point holds equally for the cult of life, which depicts bodily and psychic suffering as moral goods. While such goods are publicly available, however, the dignified person who ostensibly endures them is wholly distinct from his or her bodily and emotional states, which are subjective, arbitrary and transitory. On that count, it would make no more sense to validate suffering as a moral good than it would to valorize breathing or digestion, as they would all alike prove mere bodily ephemera. Indeed, given this cult's espoused dualism, it is unintelligible how suffering – confined to bodily and psychic states – could affect persons at all. Moreover, even if it does so affect them, the cult of life insists that such suffering, attaching to epiphenomena, is itself finally unreal. Such, of course, is the terminal logic of this view's theodicy, its assertion that all such bodily afflictions will be redeemed in the order of things. They yield in themselves, then, neither facts nor truths. Indeed, this position – against the cult of rights – rejects quality of life considerations as morally suspect precisely because it excludes bodily and psychic suffering, and the grief attending them, from persons in their transcendent dignity. To that extent, however, such suffering can prove finally no good at all, because it never attaches to persons as persons. Transcendent souls, like autonomous agents, neither suffer nor die, really; they simply entertain bodily and psychic epiphenomena for a time.

Those epiphenomena, moreover, lack epistemic relevance and moral content: they teach us nothing about the lived body because there is nothing to learn – we are not our bodies, but our transcendent souls or autonomous wills. More strikingly, our bodily and psychic states bear no moral content because our agency and worth – our autonomy and dignity – wholly transcend them. We have, then, not only no basis for a bioethic attaching to embodied persons, since we are as persons disembodied, but also no need for such a bioethic, as our moral worth transcends the un-realities of living and dying. This bizarre result follows directly from both cults' dualisms, which systematically understate both the moral import of suffering and grief within bioethics, and how informative such states are in characterizing persons. The cult of rights espouses a deeply inconsistent dualism: it denies a transcendent soul irreducible to bodily functions, as the cult of life conceives it, and yet asserts our enduring rational, autonomous capacities sustained over against the body even amid the dying process. An autonomous person thus disengaged from his or her body, however, is unlikely to suffer or grieve through aging and dying, such phenomena becoming at best incidental aspects of his or her personhood. The cult of life, on the other hand, embraces a deeply inconsistent dualism of its own. Persons, this view insists, are unions of body and soul, and yet the soul transcends and out-lives the body. More starkly, the soul alone animates the body with its enduring worth: only as ensouled does the human body bear inherent worth or dignity. Conversely, if the soul is the epicenter of such value, we have no basis for ascribing moral worth to the body *qua* living body.

Proponents of the cult of life will object here, of course, that human bodies remain ensouled throughout the dying process. Yet given that soul's transcendence, it makes just as much sense to say that we ensoul our cars or our houses by inhabiting them, and just as little sense to say that we thereby dignify them – any more than we do our bodies. Likewise, proponents of the cult of rights may object that they do acknowledge how bodily and emotional states may affect our rational and autonomous capacities. Indeed, they regard such states as potential constraints upon our autonomy. That admission, however, denies that the transcendent capacity asserted as the basis for our status as autonomous agents is, as they otherwise insist, wholly autonomous of our bodily states. Indeed, any such admission of essential embodiment – on either cult's part – unravels their shared presumption that we are transcendent, self-subsistent agents.

Yet persons so conceived – neither pro-creating, nor ailing, nor aging, nor dying in their persons – wholly escape the vagaries of living that bioethicists ostensibly address. Metaphysically self-subsistent, morally secure in their inviolable dignity or autonomy, they neither admit of harm from others, nor injure those others in their persons. On both accounts, then, we must regard even the grief accompanying, say, bereavements as subjective ephemera, neither metaphysically informed – since persons as persons neither age nor ail nor die – nor morally apt – since persons as persons are self-subsistent. At the same time, however, the lived reality of such grief is palpable: the longing for another moment with the lost person, for second chances; the inexplicable anger, perhaps at the deceased person for dying, perhaps at oneself for real or imagined failings, or at the world for allowing this particular death to occur, and its apparent indifference to this death's cosmic import; the odd fussing over artifacts and continuing signs of the deceased's lasting presence, the obsessive considering of what we might have done differently; the lingering wisps of unrealizable futures; the refusal to refashion a future now forever incomplete; the seemingly unending despair, the grasp of what religious authors have euphemistically described as the dark night of the soul, as if it were but one night. And through it all the restless searching, the groping – less for some semblance of a future purpose than for some hope that the deceased remains. This searching, more than anything else, I suggest, reveals the first important truth that such grief uncovers: we are constituted through and through by those we love – their histories, their projects, their hopes and expectations – and with their deaths, the person we are dies as well.

I suggest, then, that just as the dying process takes the deceased apart cell by cell, so too does it unravel those left behind. Nor do I hold that that point is metaphorical, but metaphysically accurate. The well-documented physical changes that accompany intense grief – diminished immune function, disrupted sleeping and eating patterns, changes in blood chemistry – all attest to a biological distillation, a re-organization of the bodily habits by which we live our world. Equally striking, the characteristic emotional patterns that such grief evokes portend our essential sociality – that we are in our persons constituted by other persons, that they are quite literally parts of us. It is, I suggest, not an exaggeration but a factual assertion that with that person a world, our world, has died – a world where we were known, a world we knew how to navigate – a world where past and present and future follow as naturally as night follows day. Grief is the physical and psychic dissolution of that world, of a shared past, a mutually enjoyed present, a mutually anticipated future. To describe this process as the dissolution of one world and the remaking of another is literally apt. And in that process, we are slowed by our inability to locate the deceased in that new world, and by our reluctance to enter it – to continue – in the person's absence. That enduring absence, I suggest, indicates that that person is not extrinsically related to us, but is a component of who we are, or better, who we were, but can no longer be. To envision such a new world, after all, is to envision a future forever unpopulated, not because it is empty, but because the loved person does not, cannot, reside there, any more than the person that we used to be can.

In grief, then, time heals nothing; it is time itself that must be healed. Facile observers may note that perhaps our grief is sharper because it reminds us of our mortality, that time runs short for all of us. Yet a grieving person has infinitely too much time, a jumble of pasts, intrusive and vexing, regrets for things done and left undone, all tumbling into a fun-house vision of bizarre futures, stretching into an endless, unimaginable horizon. We may sift through these times, all run together, groping in vain for some familiar point of reference, some trajectory – only to find no such direction, but merely the cold necessity of charting anew paths at once familiar and newly alienated. We cannot go home in that sense, not because the place is no longer there in that space or in that time, but because we are alike no longer us, no longer who we were at that space and time. We may review continually our last interactions with the deceased, stained with guilt and shame and fear, and run into ourselves not in our idealized versions – but as we were – inescapably and irremediably. It is simply inapt to say that we endure grief from within or without; it is better to say that we embody it, that we make it real in the world as a felt absence. Yet the intense reality of this grief, of this enduring absence, limns equally the enduring presence of the deceased not just in our past but also in our present, and in whatever future we may cobble together for ourselves henceforth. It is then not metaphorically but factually true that that person was, is, and shall be part of us; that that part of us has died; that our sociality is intrinsic to our persons, such that we are quite literally made up of those we love.

We are not, in other words, self-subsistent souls any more than we are disembodied individuals. Neither in our bodies, nor in our persons, nor even in our temporalities, are we wholly our own. Philosophers of most stripes would deny that point, insisting that the being-toward-death, the recognition of our own mortality, is what most individuates us. Indeed, they suggest, it is the fear of our death that renders our grief so intense; it does the deceased no good, and serves instead to encapsulate our self-concern in the face of our finitude. That point is doubly misleading. Death itself, as Epicurus recognized millennia ago, is nothing to us, an unimaginable abstraction. Our philosophical pretensions notwithstanding, we know nothing of death in itself, and have neither reason, nor experience, nor wisdom to draw on in that regard. What little we know of death, we know through grief. And if grief teaches us anything, it is that even our temporality is not ours alone. We are not each a singular trajectory pointed ineluctably toward our own death. We are rather an inter-weaving with others' times, times that become constitutive of our own. To recognize that point, we need only witness spouses who soon follow each other in death, or parents who would willingly swap places with their deceased children, to see that the time we envision in this fashion is not exclusively – indeed not even extensively – our own, but belongs also to those who constitute us. We fear their deaths as much, and perhaps more, than our own, for we recognize in each such fearsome prospect our own potential extinction. Nor need this recognition, this propensity, be altruistic: we die as much as we love.

1.2 Keeping time

In advancing the previous point, I wish to deny what the cult of life affirms: a metaphysical dualism insisting that persons are souls irreducible to their bodies, and transcending those bodies in a life everlasting. Defenders of the cult of rights typically take an analogous tack, holding that while our autonomy may be functionally irreducible to our embodiment, our personhood dissipates at death, if not well before, when we lose our autonomous capacities. Against the cult of life, such philosophically sophisticated bioethicists might draw upon an extensive history that ascribes to philosophers a distinctive expertise in matters of life and death. That notion echoes Cicero's famous injunction that to philosophize is to learn to die. This contention, as later popularized by 20th century existentialists like Jean-Paul Sartre – for whom our being-towards-death marks our uniquely human grasp of mortality – is palpably false. To be sure, philosophers have had much to say on the matter: For Epicurus, death was nothing to us; for Epictetus, it inhabited a divinely appointed cosmic order to which we should properly be indifferent. For Socrates death marked the soul's liberation from the body; for Aristotle, the terminus of a good life, after which the moral quality of our lives may be assessed in their entirety. Epicurus thus counsels defiance, an absence of fear that may render us akin to gods, who themselves need not fear death; Epictetus counsels indifference; Socrates, tranquility; and Aristotle, acceptance, assurance that one's happiness, ascribed within the boundaries of one's life-span, is secured from life's travails.

This small sampling shows two important facets of philosophical discourse on these matters. First, they are directed at individuals, as individuals, as advice on the means of exerting some measure of mastery over their own deaths. To be sure, recommendations like Epictetus' are generalized beyond that point: we are, he commends, to regard the deaths even of our friends and family members as no different from our own, nor any different than the loss or destruction of common household objects. In this way philosophers, no less than their religious counterparts, engage equally in theodicy, justifying not the ways of god but of the cosmos. Importantly, in both cases the grief that attends these processes, if addressed at all, is depicted as an epiphenomenon, as something to be understood and accepted amid a broader eschatology or cosmology. Any remaining suffering is self-induced, exhibiting either a misapprehension of our place in the cosmos, or insufficient faith in providence.

Such grief is a creature of our imagination rather than our reason, whose proper response is detachment and reappraisal. As such, these recommendations require us to turn our attention away from our lived experience, the private bodily symptoms and subjective emotional responses – and toward these explanatory schemes – precisely as a means of understanding what that grief tells us about our insertion in the world. The grief we feel, we're told, while understandable, signals precisely our lack of philosophic understanding: improving our knowledge of the world– of the objective, universal reality of death for us beyond these subjective ephemera – marks our success in learning how to die, and thereby, in learning how to understand ourselves throughout our lives.

This understanding of death, as an individual event rather than a social process, and the individualization of subjective grief, however, distorts what death can teach us – not only about human nature, but also about our prospects for moral agency. This issue would seem especially salient to bioethicists, who aim to asses the moral tenor of our practices of dying and caring for the dying. Yet even philosophers turned bioethicists have had little to say that would be philosophically distinctive about these issues. They defend human autonomy – as an ideal – just as do those philosophically trained ethicists who work in legal or media or business ethics, using the same conceptual formulations and the same philosophical presuppositions, among them that persons are in principle individuals, isolable from their social networks. Moreover, the autonomous agents they describe, no less than the transcendent souls depicted by the cult of life alike, elide any markings of temporality, any substantive embodiment in – or perhaps better, of – the vagaries of living and dying. On neither account, after all, are such vagaries metaphysically real. For the cult of rights, they prove to be subjective ephemera, of which agents may make whatever they will. For the cult of life, they become transitory afflictions, offered up in service to an abstract ideal, the value of human life – apart from any specific living person. Any grief attending these processes is thus also unreal, a subjective spark that either disavows the cult of life's grand theodicy, or signals nothing whatsoever about how the cult of rights' autonomous agents obtain in their autonomy.

Such accounts, however, falsify what persons are and undercut the moral implications of this grief for bioethics. I do not wish to hold simply that grief limns our temporality and sociality, but also that it discloses facts about the world that impose a moral order upon us. To speak of the moral facts of grief, or perhaps even of an ethics of grief, might seem strange – especially if grief conveys facts about the world over which we have quite limited influence. Do we properly regard as greedy, or even as excessively delicate, someone who wishes that the deceased had enjoyed a longer life? Do we morally censure the inexplicable anger of a grieving person directed at a world that has come undone at the seams?

Do we properly depict as lust the excessive attention directed by a bereaved person to the deceased's simplest personal artifacts? Do we dismiss as prideful those laments that one should have done something better, something different, something more, somehow? Do we dismiss as envy a longing for futures lost to us but available to others? Do we reject as gluttony the longing that an entire world be restored to its former state? Do we rightly regard as moral failures the despair, the lethargy that attend enduring, unremitting, crushing grief? Indeed, if we hold even the mildest form of the traditional ethical injunction that ought implies can, may we justifiably object that it is unjust, unwise, unprincipled, uncharitable, to impose moral standards on a process of bereavement over which we seemingly have so little control? Does it make any more sense to insist that we should be able to resist unbidden feelings of despair and grief than to say that we should be able to resist hunger of thirst?

The problem with that latter query, and indeed, with that entire catalogue of the traditional seven deadly sins, is that grief imposes its own moral order – and resists us when we violate it – precisely because it reveals a factual world. The personal artifacts we lust after and jealously guard prove no magic talisman in sustaining the presence of the deceased. Envy proves fruitless: those who retain their loved ones have theirs, not ours: no one else had precisely what, precisely who, we had prior to their death, and what they have is not wanted precisely because it is not, can never be, ours as the deceased was. Our greed to have that particular life, and none other, restored, passes futilely into gluttony. Anger and despair issue more properly neither at the deceased nor at what world has done or allowed to befall us, but at our own shortcomings – things we did and things we failed to do – and under whose burden pride gives way. We can no more make ourselves better in the past – with the passage of time – than we can change the deceased's fate. Indeed, the latter's presence remains obdurate in death, as a fulcrum around which our past and future precariously pivot.

The bulk of grief work, I suggest, is a matter of this keeping time: not, that is, of keeping a past alive, nor even of re-envisioning a future, but of rewriting a personal narrative irrevocably changed because who we were has also ceased (branching points). The initial shock of grief leaves some frozen in the past, wishing futilely to be who they once were, in the world they shared with the deceased. That shock catapults others head-long into a far future, a future so far removed from the deceased's lingering presence that the survivor can at least pretend to remain who he or she was, as if nothing had changed. But the work of grief permits neither of these alternatives. Rather, it demands that we revive time. If death and grief teach us anything, it is that the time is the most valuable of our resources, the condition of anything else we may do. That temporality is written into our cells – which recapitulate our inheritances, and limn our life cycles. It shapes equally the projects we undertake, the aims they serve, and the measures and marks of their enduring success. Most vitally, I suggest, it underlies our social relations, whose quality and depth we convey largely in how we spend our time, which is to say, in how we spend our lives. Metaphysically, socially, biologically – on all levels, we are the sum total of the time that has been invested into us by others, and the time we have re-invested into others as a result. We come to be biologically, through our inheritances, we survive through parental and other time investments, and we endure by embodying ourselves amid the projects and activities and persons that comprise our lives.

This inter-twining of temporality and sociality conditions our moral lives as neither immortal souls nor individual autonomy could. It is our temporal nature, not merely as future-directed, but as embodied in others, that comprises the vast bulk of our moral lives. We aim to resolve our own habits, and variously succeed or fail. We adopt roles and responsibilities that affirm that we will act in accordance with them, now and in the future. We take vows and oaths, make ourselves predictable, and gauge others' like predictability as grounds of our willingness to invest in those others and their causes.

We come to know persons through their pasts and their aspirations, and form families or friendships predicated on the shared investments of time and energy that come to make up who we are, thereby creating the trajectories of our lives. On these counts, the challenge that grief poses, to our persons and our projects, is starker than either cult envisions, as it is this inter-twining that dying imperils, and it is against its unwitting dissolution that grief protests. Just as we shed our skins as we live, we shed portions of ourselves as we endure grief. It closes off futures no longer available, pasts now unrecoverable, and transgressions now irreparable. Grief, then, cannot help but restructure our persons, morally and metaphysically: it highlights a relation amid which we may have failed, or exceeded, our own ideals – and thereby makes more or less possible some versions of our future selves, rendering some more likely, others unthinkable. In any such case, it irrevocably reshapes our time – how we will live it, and how it will die with us.

And in enduring this grief, we are keeping time with the deceased. As the bond between us unravels before our eyes, we recognize what we shall lose, a shared past now unreachable, a promised future now undeliverable. We have only a bastard present, a hodge-podge of pasts and futures gathered together haphazardly, and the stark gnawing reluctance to fashion them into a future. Whether we wish it or not, the dying take us with them, at least part way. We may assert our autonomy all we wish, even in the face of our own deaths; we may follow Epicurus in insisting that we may live like gods, untouched by our own mortality. Yet even if we elide death, grief comes for all of us, whether through loss, or failure, or regret. On this count, grief is at once the great leveler and the great teacher: a leveler because it comes even to partisans of the cults of life and rights; a teacher because it diagnoses what ails contemporary bioethics. The problem, I suggest, is not an irresolvable culture war, but the commitment of both cults to metaphysical dualisms that negate the lived reality of suffering and grief, and indeed, that void the entirety of human living – in pro-creating, maturing, ailing, grieving, aging and dying – of metaphysical and moral import. Were either dualism true, the disembodied, self-subsistent and transcendent persons so depicted would neither need, nor even admit of a bioethic, secure as they would be from time's dominion. We have no such security – apart from articles of faith on either side – however, but only the sturdy guarantee that we, and more vitally those we love, will ail and age and die. As such, I suggest, what's missing from both cults is any sustained, substantive discussion of how grief and love shadow their debates – debates currently couched in intellectualized abstractions.

It should astonish us that bioethicists – who traffic in pro-creating, ailing, aging, dying - speak so little of love and grief. Or perhaps not, given that they have no purchase on the persons either cult describes. If we are autonomous rational agents, these experiences are properly private, subjective matters of our own concern, and only contingently attach to those surrounding us. If we love anyone, that signifies a willed relation, of which we may make anything we wish. If we are transcendent souls, our value is underwritten by the love of an unfathomable God, and attaches to us precisely in our role as God's creatures.

These points are most striking when the person, *qua* individual, is no longer reachable, being for example in a deep, irreversible coma or a persistent vegetative state (PVS). For the cult of rights, this person may remain an object of love, but that only as an emotive response to what is, properly, a vacant body. The person ceased to be when their cognitive capacities failed; we now mourn rather than love that person, and attend to their body as an extended funeral rite. Conversely, for the cult of life, the person remains, wholly intact, until all biological function ceases, and is an object of love, yet only as an object. Absent reciprocity, the ostensible person retains that status not as the individual he or she is, but in and through a sustained relation with God. To say that we continue to love that person is again, strictly speaking, inapt; it would be more accurate to say that we love persons, not as individuals, but as creatures of God, who are valued on that basis and relation.

Both accounts, however, negate the enduring quality of love amid grief; both deny the irreducible psychic interiority and individuality that is the primary object of human love, and precisely what we grieve losing. More tellingly, both accounts systematically distort the impact of love and grief upon our experiences of living and dying – dissolving the intimate personal investments that tether particular lives together irrevocably. I stress that last point because defenders of both cults depict persons who neither age nor ail nor grieve nor die, and thereby render inexplicable why those persons care so vitally about the vagaries of living. Among the most prominent recent examples of this confusion is the Terri Schiavo saga, already deemed a classic case by both cults' defenders.[2] For the cult of life, removal of this woman's life-sustaining feeding tube, after roughly fifteen years in a PVS state, marked a murder most foul, a negation of her inalienable right to life. For the cult of rights, that removal demonstrated respect for the patient or her medical proxy, in this case her husband, to decide for themselves whether to continue living in such a state. Both cults appeal, moreover, to the person's inalienable dignity: the former to assert her right to continued life, the latter to assert her – or her proxy's - right to self-determination.

For the cult of rights, such self-determination underlies a death with dignity; indeed, we can properly reserve such autonomy to ourselves, even in a PVS state, by codifying a living will, and by thereby timing and managing our dying process. Yet the problem here is plain: however well we control our dying, the process itself signifies an irresistible personal dissolution, a body undone by chemical and physical laws, a person wrenched away from the social bonds that lend structure and purpose to our life. To demand a death with dignity, a death conformal to our wishes, is akin to requiring that we summon rain on order, or reverse the trajectory of the sun.

Even if we actively intervene in timing that death, we do so in accord with biological facts that impose themselves indifferently upon our wishes. Bioethicists serving the cult of life insist famously that we not interfere in nature or God's dominion. Some reject any such efforts to time or control our deaths as unduly liberating people from the existential agonies that properly accompany dying, and that perhaps prepare us for our lives in the afterworld. We ought not, they insist, to control such events, to "play God." Were we to follow this insistence to its logical conclusion, of course, we would have to foreswear all medical intervention, not only that which might hasten, but equally that which might forestall death. That point is important because it issues less from the logic of the argument than from its rhetorical force. But who, in such cases, really plays God? Those who advocate that we decide the value of our lives for ourselves, or those who demand that we prolong our lives even against our wills? Indeed, who in this case reserves to themselves the right to speak for God, to cast moral judgment upon individual choices, to decide for another the value of his or her life? Defenders of the cult of life insist that they do precisely the opposite, respecting and valuing all life equally, over and against those who would play God by deeming some lives not worth living. Yet that position equally reserves to itself divine provenance, the right to play God, to exercise dominion over the lives and consciences of individuals, by legal and political as well as by moral force. To be sure, a broad swath of the bitter public debate attending Terri Schiavo's fate emphasized precisely these terms: the autonomy of individuals to decide the values of their lives for themselves, against the insistence that all lives are equally valuable, are equally gifts of grace whether accepted willingly or by compulsion. Yet missing from this debate, for the most part, is what either cult is defending.

If life is ever-lasting, the temporal passing of the body is if anything to be celebrated, and in no way affects the person's soul. Equally, if our autonomy attends our psychic function, then no person but only a body remains. In neither case is a person in a PVS an object of moral concern: for the latter cult because no longer an autonomous person; for the former cult, because personhood remains wholly unaffected by such biological vagaries.

Indeed, both approaches, in segregating a particular aspect of persons – be it the soul orrational autonomy – from any embodiment – depict dying as itself epiphenomenal, a process or state that leaves persons unaffected as persons. Such is the rationale of the cult of life's theodicy, wherein the soul transcends all trappings of human biological living. Such, also, is the rationale of the cult of right's defense of autonomy, predicated on our complete transcendence of nature's dominion.

We would do well to consider here, however, how costly the stories we tell ourselves about death may be, and how readily, in aiming to transcend the attendant grief, we may unwittingly – and quite cruelly – afflict grievous harm on the dying. One of grief's great gifts, after all, is its insistence, its demand that we be honest with ourselves both about what we lose in others' deaths – and about how losing them shapes us. Evidence for this proposition abounds in narratives describing the deaths of deceased loved ones.

In *How We Die*, for example, physician Sherwin Nuland describes how the death of his mother and brother, early in his career, shaped his ideas of medical practice.[3] He struggled with conveying the reality of his brother's terminal condition to him, believing instead that his obligation as a physician was to sustain his brother's hope for a longer life. Yet, he reports, that baseless hope ultimately sanctioned painful, debilitating, treatments that diminished the quality of his brother's remaining life, and bound the two in an enduring grief clouded by Nuland's regrets and second-guessing. This may be an inevitable and even apt accompaniment of such grief. But two points bear emphasis here.

First, even if that tenor of grief is inevitable, his brother might have received better treatment if that reality had been borne more accurately. The problem is not merely an evasion of medical futility – a cruel redundancy here – but also an evasion of the grief that would attend a terminal diagnosis, for the dying person and for those who love him.

In such situations a grief deferred may well be a noble alternative, sparing both the dying person and his intimates some of the suffering that that dying evokes. We may also admire the tilting-at-windmills spirit of sustaining hope or even defiance in the face of death. Yet is it more dignified to sustain – and cultivate – a groundless hope for what cannot be, than to surrender to the reality of dying? That question is far from rhetorical: Deprivation of hope, admission of futility – perhaps after many difficult alternatives have been pursued, and exhausted – bears its own grave costs, as does initiating the grief process in the dying person and those who accompany him.

Indeed, it may be easier all around to endure futile treatment, but to what end? Nowhere is this query more pressing – and more far afield of contemporary bioethics – than in PVS and like situations. For the cult of life, such lives must be sustained as all others, because persons are absolutely valuable; for the cult of rights, such lives are objects of choice, because persons are, most vitally, autonomous. That autonomy, however, proves significantly more ambivalent than the cult of rights suggests. As medical anthropologist Sharon Kaufman reports, for example, despite decades of familiarity with living wills, powers-of-attorney, informed consent practices and the like, most persons viscerally resist being the agents of their own or others' deaths even if those deaths are in large measure desired by both.[4] Those who previously believed they would resist extra-ordinary care often seek it once confronted with its need. Persons who serve as proxies hesitate to withdraw futile treatments even when they acknowledge that this is what the dying person wanted. Many persons want more rather than fewer such life-sustaining interventions as their conditions worsen, even if these efforts compromise their quality of life. Moreover, the decision to discontinue such lives, Kaufman reports, is made even more tortured, uncertain, and conflicted by medical and institutional practices that incline persons towards life-extending interventions even when their benefits are marginal at best. She cites, for example, funding policies that encourage life-sustaining over palliative care, and institutional policies that make sustaining life the default option of medical procedures in all but the severest cases.

This ambivalence engulfs PVS patients. They flout any conception of how a conscious, self-aware, agent lives. So what do we preserve, in preserving their lives? If we lose nothing of substantive value to or of ourselves amid our biological vagaries, we might draw two equally well-founded conclusions: PVS patients' transcendent souls or autonomous capacities either remain entombed in their bodies, populating such wards, or they elide such embodiment, shedding their skin. If the latter point is true, how we treat those bodies matters neither metaphysically, since they are precisely not the persons in question, nor morally, since the worth of such persons attaches to their transcendent status as souls or ends. If the former point is true, conversely, we can regard persons neither as transcendent souls nor as autonomous agents, but only as essentially embodied, essentially subject to the biological vagaries of living and dying. Both cults, affirming the transcendence of persons, make nonsense of the debates surrounding how persons die. If the cult of life is right, the soul of any dying or PVS person abides, wholly independently of what we do to his or her body. Similarly, if the cult of rights is correct, the autonomy of any dying or PVS person abides, wholly independently of anything we do to his or her body. In neither case should PVS patients warrant the moral interest ascribed to them in cases such as Terri Schiavo's, wherein the person is quite literally beyond help or harm.

That such patients have such a hold both on their intimate others and on public concern, however, suggests that we believe neither in the transcendence that either cult ascribes to us, nor in our individual self-subsistence. Our worlds could neither be unmade, nor imperiled, nor even affected by those others' fates, were the latter point true. Nor would we grieve their absence, if they were still themselves, essentially, in their persons. Indeed, one striking element of cases such as Terri Schiavo's is their capacity to transmute private into public grief. Both cults render such grief nonsensical, mere ephemera surrounding the more vital issue: the Great Culture War between the right to live and the right to die. But we would have no such war if we were the self- subsistent, transcendent beings they aim to defend. To the contrary, I suggest, those beings and the ideals they augur are themselves mere theoretical ephemera, timeless constructs that crumble when we keep time with those we love, both the living and the dead. Bioethicists of both stripes ignore this elemental process of keeping time, deeming us instead, effectively, young immortals, who once born march forth forevermore, un-touched by time. Yet neither in living nor in dying do we evince these powers. We out-live those we love, only to agonize over a lost few moments; we acknowledge that many die too long, too slowly, die many times before their final cessation, and yet so often find it unthinkable to commend hastening that too short time of dying. We argue fruitlessly about that timing – in timeless abstractions – while the specter of time slips through our fingers, forever unreachable, forever unrecoverable. It is this paradox, I suggest, that animates the ferocity with which we debate how to die – and for which bioethicists of both cults have yet to provide a public language. To bridge that chasm – between private grief and public policy – we must begin instead not with the defense of abstract ideals, but with the elucidation of living practices.

2
Getting Too Personal?

For both cults, the challenge posed by embodied living couldn't be starker: persons, after all, are souls or ends, and thereby alone bear self- awareness, an enduring self-identity, and an agential capacity. In distinguishing us from other animals, these capacities simultaneously comprise for both views the central element of human worth. On both views, rejecting metaphysical dualism threatens the transcendence of animality that marks human worth. This case is made extensively by cult of life defenders Moreland and Rae, who argue that only such a dualistic understanding of human persons can serve as normative basis for bioethics.[1] In the emotionally charged public debates surrounding not only euthanasia and PAS but also genetic engineering, cloning, human embryo research, and the like, the nature of personhood most often occupies center stage. This point is illustrated forcefully by the on-going furor over stem-cell research. Proponents deny that fetal tissue research involves human experimentation. Opponents, in contrast, affirm that life begins at conception, and that there is no other way to understand fetal tissue except as embodied humanity. This should be owed the full dignity appropriate to it, and experimentation upon these tissues is seen as putting some lives unconscionably at the service of others. Either view poses a metaphysical quandary: what is the nature of human personhood?

2.1 What good are persons?

Moreland and Rae assert a version of Thomistic creationism, wherein God *ex nihilo* infuses the product of human fertilization with a substantial soul, thereby rendering it a complete person. Even granting the theological trappings, however, their account founders on metaphysical as well as on moral grounds. It begins from the premise that humans are substances essentially identified also as persons, independently or prior to any specific functions or capacities associated with persons. We would not, they insist, be persons with distinctive human capacities like self-identity or agency if we did not have souls as they describe. If we say all humans have such souls, however, even absent any or all of those realized potentials, then we also hold that there is no necessary connection between the occurrence of those capacities and the possession of souls.

This implication of Moreland and Rae's account is deeply inconsistent with the natural law tradition of Thomistic creationism, which insists upon an essential bond between mind, body and soul. Yet this inconsistency is precisely necessary if, as in the case of other cult of life defenders, they are to maintain that embryos, PVS patients, humans born without brains, fully functioning adults, and those sunken into advanced dementia are all equally and fully human persons. Moreover, on that creationist view the divinely created soul instantiates a real potential, i.e. a person, but it does not thereby instantiate a specific individual person. If persons are persons apart from their realization of any particular potential, then their self-identity is entirely generic, signifying an instance of a type. As a metaphysical marker of personhood it can obtain only as an abstract potential: it may subsequently be contingently realized, of course, but not necessarily so. If our absolute self-identity signifies our personhood, nothing about our specific, contingent selves attaches to it, even our individual realization of some human potential.

On this view it's no easier to individuate fully functioning adult human persons than it is to individuate persons in comas, or in Petri dishes, or as pre-conceived vessels of potential in God's mind. In each case we have a set of abstract potentials accidentally related to the person under question. Yet if that is what we are, really, what becomes of the specific individuals we seem to believe ourselves to be? If personhood is essentially a set of abstract potentialities, the real development of those potentialities – being inessential to our personhood – cannot attach organically to that essence. If they were thus related to the essence personhood, then any absence of such development, as in embryos, would negate the claim that those humans qualify as persons. Simply put, were our personhood organically related to the development of those realized potentialities, then any failure to realize those potentials would imperil personhood. Indeed, personhood would prove irremediably vulnerable to all manner of contingencies, such as illnesses, accidents and the like.

At the same time, if mind and body are contingently related to human personhood, nothing that might be done to the psychophysical union per se would touch our personhood. On this view, therefore, in cases like abortion and fetal tissue research, nothing done to the empirical bodies of these creatures, or to their contingently realized potentials, could affect their essential personhood. To insist that fetuses and embryos are already full persons undercuts any moral claims that their factual dependence upon their mothers for gestation might engender. The notion that one self-subsistent soul or substance could or would need to occupy another soul, much less depend upon something extrinsic to it for its unfolding, would seem wholly contradictory. This biological relation makes sense, if at all, only as a contingent relation between two contingent bodies.

If the moral worth of the embryo or fetus attaches only and irremediably to its personhood, which obtains fully independently of the mother's activities, the mother neither discharges a moral obligation by bringing that fetus to term, nor violates any such obligation by aborting that fetus. In either case, the person remains unaffected. As self-subsistent substances, persons have no moral relation: they are at most – and inexplicably – spatially related. Indeed, that fetus as a contingent body has no moral claim either on that specific mother or any other person. As a person, rather, that fetus neither needs nor requires nor warrants parental investment, either from its genetic parents or from other specific persons. Its status as a person is morally inert with respect to specific persons, because that personhood is self-subsistent. Parents as parents, that is, have no impact on persons as persons, either for good or for ill. As such, whether they bring any particular fetus to term is a matter of moral indifference, as they have no power, metaphysically or morally, to harm substances.

This result, strikingly, turns one major defense of the worth of persons exactly on its head. Traditionally, one cult of life defense of the intrinsic worth of persons, as contrasted with non-human animals, has always been that humans alone possess an immortal soul. This premise under-writes cult of life defenders' insistence that practices like physician assisted suicide (PAS) are intrinsically evil, because they subordinate the intrinsic worth of persons to an instrumental goal like avoiding suffering, or exercising human agency. Persons as the cult of life conceives them, however, cannot be thus subordinated regardless of what we, or they, do to their bodies, or even to their wills. Dispatching their bodies leaves persons unaffected, since they are at best contingently related to those bodies. Embodied living in its entirety is wholly extrinsic to the intrinsic value of life. That point may seem puzzling insofar as PAS opponents locate moral value in our willful submission to a painful death. On their own view, persons do not die, really, and biological death bears no moral freight. Not only does the body's fate prove irrelevant, so too does the willing that accompanies it: human will, after all, is also a contingent feature of persons. Whether we kill ourselves, or are killed, we are not affected in our persons. No willed attitude to biological death has moral freight: resistance, embrace, and suicidal impulses are all irrelevant to the person.

One striking implication of this view is that persons as persons essentially exhibit wills no more than they do bodies; those capacities may attain as abstract potentials, but they need not come into being. To that extent, moral agency is itself not an essential but a contingent element of personhood. Persons are fully persons, *in toto*, apart from such capacities. Persons are valuable as matters of metaphysical fact: Even if we try to devalue life, that act is futile because our contingent will has no power to devalue life; equally, we may assert that we value human life absolutely, but that assertion adds nothing to the value of persons if that value already exists *a priori*. Indeed, not only human agency but self-identity, in the sense of enduring personality, inhabits that temporal, finite and contingent, realm, Persons, after all, are fully formed at conception. Our bodies and minds, pleasures and pains, and hopes and fears, are ours only privately, subjectively, transiently. When we speak of persons bearing intrinsic worth, we say both that they are valuable in their immaterial essence and that they are therefore not valuable in their finitudes and contingencies. As persons, we may do anything with respect to them, and vice versa, insofar as they and we refer to bodies and minds and personalities. To say that we value persons thus means equally and only that we value their immaterial essence. Their self-identity attaches only to their metaphysical status as persons; indeed, as persons they are exactly not identical with their bodies, minds and personalities, which have no such intrinsic merit or worth.

Yet that point embeds two contradictions: the persons they defend, in their transcendence, are not recognizably human; conversely, their moral worth neither requires nor even admits any moral defense. In affirming the divine creation of persons, the cult of life renders wholly contingent, wholly inessential, the role of gestation, labor, birth and familial investment in bringing any particular person into being. Indeed, the term "particular person" proves an oxymoron. Moreover, this account paradoxically undercuts any normative claims of family members upon each other. For instance, on any creationist account, every embryo embodies a generic fetus, a person *in toto*, who nonetheless has irrevocable claims upon its mother for care. The basis of that claim, this cult maintains, is that the mother's body is the embryo's natural state. Yet that state has nothing to do with that embryo's person. Whether the biological mother sustains or evicts the embryo, it remains unaffected, its worth inalienable.

On this view, it is flatly contradictory to predicate obligations to the conceived person on the basis of its biological dependence. As a person, it admits no dependencies because it transcends all biological and social contingencies, including its genetic link to any particular person. Personhood thus conceived, I suggest, is not merely a meta- physically suspect but a morally bankrupt entity. If human persons are essentially impregnable – in their worth – then we neither need normative guidelines, nor could they secure anything of value. To be moral patients as persons, the actions of others would have to affect us in our persons; conversely, to be moral agents in any substantive sense, we would need to have the capacity to affect other persons in their intrinsic worth. If we are enjoined to protect that worth in others and in ourselves, that is, then this implies strictly that we can imperil that worth. Yet the cult of life denies that prospect. It insists unintelligibly both that persons bear inalienable worth, and that how persons are brought into being, empirically, can somehow affect that worth.

It may seem odd here to accuse cult of life defenders of ignoring the moral import of how persons come into being. They are, after all, obsessed with defending natural norms of human pro-creation, as over against the cult of right's defense of pro-creative liberty. Yet insofar as God creates inviolable souls *ex nihilo*, natural norms attach not to supernatural persons but only to their embodied contingencies. As such, the means of human pro-creation leave its ostensible end, persons, wholly untouched, and prove void of moral content. To object, for example, that human cloning turns persons into products is nonsensical if persons are unaffected by their biological contingencies. At the same time, however, cult of rights defenders often oppose cloning on analogous grounds, asserting that such a practice reduces children to objects of their parents', rather than their own, design. Here, the objection is less to the means of reproduction than to the intent and likely result. To produce children with one's specific ends in view, they maintain, contravenes the children's autonomy. That charge, however, holds only if the children's autonomy can be affected by genetic modification. Yet the relation they envision between the empirical features of one's agency, such as one's genes, and one's autonomous, self-directing capacity are no less shrouded in mystery. On the one hand, they suggest, our autonomy is constrained by the vagaries of our biological functioning; on the other hand, only insofar as we transcend those vagaries do we act autonomously.

This is hardly a new problem. Kant struggled famously with this paradox: to act autonomously, we must be wholly self-determining, and yet the organic constitution of our being all but precludes that prospect. To act morally, we must have a will that can be affected by inclination; yet that will must be capable of acting wholly independently of any and all such inclinations. Cult of rights defenders thus maintain simultaneously that: our autonomy is cordoned off from all biological and social affections, such that it is self-determining; and that cloning imposes upon the children thereby produced biological or social constraints that undercut their potential autonomy. Yet none of us, whether cloned or not, choose our genotypes. Moreover, the biological constitution of the child, on this view, has no impact on the child's autonomy; nor could parental intentions or expectations. More strikingly, such autonomy is not a biological or social creation: it is not a product of parental investments, but an intrinsic, *a priori* feature of persons. As such, the cult of rights, like the cult of life, finally ascribes that moral worth and capacity to persons by fiat; the latter by divine intervention, the former by the mysterious, and indeed inexplicable, occurrence of autonomy amid our natural impulses. At the same time, while the cult of rights ostensibly ascribes autonomy to persons on the basis of some functions, such as a first-person perspective or self-awareness, the origin of this capacity is no less mysterious than is the soul's origin as posited by the cult of life. If that capacity must transcend our biological nature, not only can its occurrence not be identified with distinctive human capacities such as rationality, but that autonomous capacity also cannot be brought into being, i.e. cannot depend on the agent's development over time.

Importantly, then, if we do speak of defending persons, as in the cloning case, we cannot speak in terms of moral obligations to their empirical prospects. So what remains as the object of moral consideration? For defenders of the cult of life, biological parents are obliged always to be open to the "transmission of life," that is, to be subject to natural and divine dictates. Cloning thwarts that imperative both in subordinating the relevant natural or divine dictates to human control, and in undercutting the moral relations between parents and children. These parental obligations typically arise from two bases: the natural dependence of children on their parents' care, and the parents' role as conduits for nature's or God's decrees. Children, however, are created by God, and their personhood is guaranteed even prior to their natural conception. Yet thereby, parents are not charged with a substantive formative role in their children's development. The children's dependencies are contingent elements of their embodiment, not essential elements of their persons. Their personhood unfolds inviolably, wholly apart from their parents' efforts. Persons are, then, akin to fish, whose fry, from conception, unfold a *telos* they will realize if they're not interfered with. As an analogue to human reproduction, this implication seems patently false, as parenting requires an enormous range of positive, directive, formative inputs; indeed, the position noted above predicates the ostensibly unique parental obligations of human parents upon the children's dependence, on their lack of self-sufficiency, and their need for corresponding care and investment.

Yet on the creationist accounts espoused by the cult of life, the embryo or fetus, from conception, is an independent being with a trajectory distinct from its parents. How can we believe, simultaneously, that the embryo is utterly dependent upon the mother, and that it has an independent trajectory, which together sustain its moral claim upon her? The problem is straightforward: as a person, the disembodied soul unfolds its *telos* wholly apart from parental input. As such, neither parent nor child is essentially or internally related to the other: their mutual dependence, in occupying those biological and social roles, is a contingent matter. Persons are no more parents or children than they are redheads or musicians: persons are, essentially, nothing but persons. To that extent, however, we can say neither that persons as persons are obliged to attend to other persons on the basis of contingent needs, nor that we owe specific others a particular range of obligations. As persons, we need no one, and nothing. Yet if we need nothing, fetal claims upon a mother cannot hinge on the former's dependence; moreover, as a self-subsistent being, it already is, and always will be what it is in its person, inviolable and unaffected regardless of what is done to its embodiment. On this point, the cult of life, so zealous in protecting the fetal body from feared maternal aggression, succeeds too well for its purposes. In wholly denying any substantive maternal contribution to the person's development, it negates any claim that withdrawing those contributions does substantive harm. In placing the inviolable fetus wholly beyond human reach, it thereby places that worth beyond all human obligations.

Indeed, the cult of rights' fetal viability criterion, while equally incoherent, offers a measure of fetal protection closer to what the cult of life seeks. This position asserts that when the fetus can live outside the mother's body, the mother surrenders discretion over its fate. If fetal viability is the transition point to personhood, however, the period prior to that involves no moral relation between embryo and the mother. Moreover, because fetal development, and indeed child development, does not evince autonomy, the entire passage to full-blown autonomy is a baffling metaphysical interlude, through which we miraculously emerge from our subjection to our bodies, social environs and characters, into fully autonomous agents. Such a passage, in fact, would seem no less miraculous than the creationist claim that persons are born *in toto*. For while the cult of rights might then recognize that personhood is an attainment rather than a birthright, it would require, given its insistence that persons are ends in themselves, and thus not the proper objects of moral melioration or construction by others, that such autonomous capacities were self-made. On that account, not only gestation, labor and birth, but the entire range of parental investment would drop away, external accouterments to a personhood which exemplifies not full divinity but full self-creativity. For the cult of life, the proper object of fetal protection is not the fetal body but the disembodied soul that needs or admits no such protection; for the cult of rights, the proper object of protection is not the fetal person but the autonomy that person may mysteriously instantiate apart from any material contingencies. In both cases, personhood is guaranteed apart from parental action: in the first, as created by God; in the second, as created by agents.

If either of these positions is true, however, no reproductive practice, including genetic engineering or cloning, could imperil human nature or dignity or autonomy, all of which would remain beyond human reach. Oddly, both the cult of life and the cult of rights resist human cloning in particular, and the broader impetus parents may have to select genes for their children. For the cult of life, such selection is a gross intrusion of human will into a natural process, rendering the persons thus produced as manufactured rather than pro-created. For the cult of rights, such selections unduly shape the capacities of the resulting children, being instances of parents stacking the deck by attempting to mold their children in particular directions. Yet on both accounts, genetic constitution is irrelevant to the worth of persons; as such, how that constitution is empirically created cannot matter morally, precisely because that's not how persons are created at all. For the cult of life, it makes no more sense to maintain that all genetic constitutions are equally valuable than it does to deny that point, and on precisely the same basis: genetic constitution is irrelevant to personhood.

Indeed, as an empirical and contingent matter, the entirety of human pro-creation obtains apart from matters moral. An analogous point holds for the cult of rights, for whom, properly speaking, genetic potential is wholly independent of potential autonomy. Genetic engineering and cloning cannot, on this view, intrude upon one's autonomy, which must emerge, however inexplicably, wholly apart from one's biological contingencies and social inheritances. An autonomous person cannot be manufactured, because persons are self-created. Nor can a person be the object or product of another human will: for the cult of life, persons are products of God's will; for the cult of rights, persons are self-willed.

For either position to hold that cloning or genetic engineering imperils the dignity or autonomy of the persons thus produced, then, they must affirm what they explicitly deny: that persons are substantively embodied. Yet how bioethicists of either cult reproduce themselves remains one of the great mysteries of modern medicine, and indeed of modern metaphysics. For the cult of life, no necessary relation holds between sexual reproduction and the divine creation of a supernatural soul. Indeed, the biological process of conception unfolds over several days, as distinct from the atemporal creation of the soul, which God authors *ex nihilo*. We have indeed then a miracle of life, precisely because no element of living persons is necessary to transmit that life. Why, then, the proscriptions attending sexual reproduction? The cult of life alleges that marriage is the sole proper relation for life-transmission. But whether the bodies that mysteriously shadow those souls are conceived within or outside of marriage, in human bodies or test tubes or microwave ovens, is incidental to the soul and irrelevant to the treatment of persons as persons. The cult of life, however, aggressively advances the opposite case, lamenting a brave new world where biotechnologies disrupt natural life transmission and confound normative family relations. Natural life transmission is itself a contradiction in terms, however, since the transit of life in its intrinsic worth is wholly supernatural; moreover, as it should remain unaffected by family arrangements, since persons as persons are fully formed at conception.

Strangely, the cult of rights raises similar concerns, albeit on different bases. For the cult of rights, the lone norm guiding sexual reproduction is mutual consent, and family formation follows suit. While championing reproductive liberty against the cult of life, however, it often opposes reproductive practices such as cloning as militating against that liberty. In cloning, the objection runs, parents not only select a genotype but a future they wish to see for their children, depriving them thereby of what some theorists deem their right to an open future. Parents and children, however, are not autonomous at all: only as persons to persons do they enter moral relations. To say that parents thereby unduly influence their children or affect their futures conflates the natural or empirical realms of such influences, and the autonomous realm wherein persons interact as moral agents. Children, moreover, are not shepherded to that autonomy precisely because it must obtain independently of any such causal influences. Both cults, after all, define human moral capacity strictly in opposition to any embodied state. As such, this moral status, whether as disembodied soul or autonomy, cannot be transmitted in and through and thereby tainted by such biological constraints.

Given those conclusions, the relentless moralizing that forever surrounds human reproduction underscores the quandary both cults face. We have no greater evidence of our finitude, of our subjection to animal impulses, of our irremediable dependencies upon others, than sexual reproduction. Against our out-sized pretensions that we are different and better than mere animals, the vicissitudes of human reproduction suggest the exact opposite: that we are our bodies, as constituted by others' genetic contributions, that we are irremediably dependent and social beings, constituted in our persons by those who make personal investments in us, and that we are irremediably finite, and subject to the contingencies that befall our bodies, or personalities, our lives. Strikingly, the cult of rights resists these points no less than does the cult of life. For the cult of life, persons bear inviolable moral worth; for the cult of rights, persons bear inviolable autonomy.

For both approaches, that status is a metaphysical and moral given. Yet if we can neither affect nor be affected by persons in their personhood, what good is this status, morally?

2.2 What's new with you?

That question is vital because among the most heated debates among bioethicists of both cults are those involving genetic engineering, a venue wherein their competing ideals matter least. Whereas these technologies' proponents envision a morally permissible and maybe even obligatory ameliorative project that offers to liberate future persons from some natural vagaries, opponents from both cults see in such projects a denaturing and a dehumanization of human persons. This point was made forcefully by Hans Jonas a generation ago. In his influential work *The Technological Imperative,* Jonas takes to task biological interventions which, he maintains, seize such control over nature, and in particular over the future nature of human beings, that they render persons not the agents but the objects of that technology.[2] These concerns underlie the familiar cult of life objection that we ought not to play God with future persons, designing them to suit our ends. They equally fuel the cult of rights' objection that such efforts commodify persons, making their natures and qualities subject to unfettered parental choices. They alike reflect the insistence that we ought not to engage in positive eugenics: the deliberate selection of traits conducive to health and welfare. While those objections accord fully with those advanced by the cult of life, Jonas' account equally reflects the cult of rights' insistence that we treat persons not as objects of our design, but as agents with their own projects and prospects.

Jonas' objections also underscore both the cult of rights' insistence that these emerging technologies truncate the autonomy of future persons, rendering them the objects of our designs, and the cult of life's insistence that they are intrinsically evil because they dissolve human dignity. The most forceful cult of life critics hold that such biotechnologies sever the naturally normative links between our biological nature and capacities and the ethical practices appropriate to that nature. Biotechnologies, they insist, are unnatural and thus immoral because they both reproduce persons in a technologically mediated way, and sever the naturally normative relations among parents and children. Yet these objections are self-refuting. If our human nature is fixed *a priori*, and inviolable, we could neither change nor imperil that nature in its essence. Some critics hold that cloning deprives children of unique genotypes. Yet even the most theologically conservative of these critics deem cloned children fully human, fully ensouled, fully dignified. Other critics insist instead that how clones are produced imperils the moral status not of the clones themselves but of the activities that produce them. This position, however, renders puzzling how clones, bearing absolute human worth, could be produced through immoral means. For the cult of life, inserting human will into the pro-creative act is immoral, as it flouts the natural normativity of God's supernatural creativity.

To affirm the natural normativity of nature's course would, of course, preclude recourse to biotechnologies such as cloning and gene splicing. But it would no less preclude our use of antibiotics and surgery to prolong human lives. If letting nature take its course is our ultimate guide, the whole of medicine, in intention and in fact, proves *verboten*. Nor will it help such critics to object that antibiotics and vaccines are natural means of life-extension, enhancements of natural products we're already given by nature, whereas cloning and the like are not. Among nature's many gifts, we simply do not find syringes, intravenous drips and the like. Nor should the oft-mentioned recourse to the claim that nature is a pharmacy confuse the issue: knowledge and use of these available compounds and materials requires organized bodies of knowledge at least, and quite often, extensive laboratory processes, refining and other technological interventions. Moreover, while it may be true that the compounds' components occur naturally, so too do the components of a cloned embryo. In both cases, natural givens are synthesized through technological means. If we are to consider cloned embryos unnatural and thus *verboten* given these technological modifications, then we're no less required to regard vaccines and antibiotics as equally suspect. In each case, rather, we're enjoined by this position instead to let nature take its course, to submit to natural or divine necessity.

That demand, moreover, presupposes that we have a biological essence that both underwrites human worth and evokes one and only one means of reproduction in that worth's defense. Biologically, however, the only fixed species are those already extinct; genetic variability is a condition of biological viability, a condition of natural life. To that extent, it is equally implausible that a historically variable human genetic make-up could underwrite metaphysically invariant moral laws. For the cult of life, again, the issue with cloning is that a child's genotype has been selected not by nature but through human will.

Yet properly speaking, neither process affects persons in their persons, precisely because human persons, in their inalienable worth, are not human at all; they retain that worth wholly apart from their genotype, and how that genotype comes to be, biologically. Put more directly, human reproductive practices are only contingently related to the creation of persons, and so have no moral content. Indeed, the very insistence that we have no normative options underscores this point: if we are passive conduits of nature's creativity who can reproduce in only one way, reproduction poses no moral issues because it evokes no human agency. Such issues arise, rather, only when we have such options, i.e. when a fissure obtains between how things are and how things ought to be. Certainly, for the cult of life the issue is less that we have no such options than that we ought not to have them. Given possession of the *capacity* to intervene, however, using or not using that capacity are equally choices. To refuse to use such interventions is no less to impose one's choice or selection upon one's children, i.e. no less an intervention than is choosing to use that technology.

That recognition, conversely, fuels the cult of rights' insistence that the issue here is less how clones are produced biologically, than how parental pressures might shape their development. Their objections, too, however, are unintelligible. They do not, for example, regard the autonomy of naturally occurring twins as imperiled by their shared genotypes. To the contrary, they recognize in such cases that twinned genotypes do not impose identical fates, and that identical twin genotypes, rather, will grow into unique individuals with their own talents and tastes and propensities. This, however, is precisely what such critics fear that clones will lack: an inalienable right to an open future, undecided by their parents or others. Yet that open future attends clones neither more nor less than other identical twins, and the latter neither more nor less than anyone else. However children are produced, they acquire a genotype at someone else's behest: whether it's deliberately designed or naturally ceded to them, it is neither more nor less theirs to do with what they will. Children's genetic inheritances would seal their fate only if we affirm a genetic determinism that even biological fact contravenes – only, that is, if we believe that we are reducible to our genes, replicable at will by ourselves or our heirs should the mood strike. Biologically, no such perfect replication is possible, even if a genotype can be replicated largely intact. More vitally, we could clone a person only if we deny what the cult of rights otherwise affirms: that our autonomy wholly transcends not only our genotypes and bodies, but equally any environmental or social influences.

Such, of course, is the fear of cult of rights critics who worry that while our genes are not our fate, social expectations and pressures might well be. Surely, they suggest, parents who have a hand in designing or even cloning their children, will aim to have an undue influence on how those children develop. Surely, they contend, such an influence, genetic and social, comes perilously close to what the cult of life deems "playing God". To be sure, some parents already seek to impose such influence upon their children, engineering their selection of schools and careers and hopes and aspirations. All of these choices impose parental expectations and pressures on children. Such is the inescapable condition of children who are for so long dependent upon the care of others. On exactly the same basis, moreover, parents equally inescapably impose, whether through random genetic inheritance or deliberate design, a set of genetic potentials upon their children. Whether chosen or left to natural lottery, it is simply false that any child could ever select its range of genetic potentials, or escape parental social impositions. Again, such is the nature of human reproduction that it cedes the constitution of one generation to its progenitors. Not only do those children inherit their genetic and social potentials from their parents, they also face the possibility that their parents will view them as status symbols, as economic assets, or even as objects to satisfy their own whims, rather than as individuals in their own right. Genetic selection, then, may be a venue for the imposition of parental choices, but it is neither new nor different in kind from genetic impositions left to nature.

Those concerns, moreover, can arise only if we maintain what the cult of rights joins the cult of life in denying: that we are our bodies, are our genotypes, such that those biological contingencies can affect our inviolable autonomy or worth as persons. Both cults would not only have to deny, then, that we are transcendent ends, but would also have to affirm that the signs of human transcendence they both posit – our first-person self-awareness, self-identity and agency – matter morally only in their subjection to the vagaries of biological living. For the cult of life, persons are born of supernatural creativity, and bear a transcendent dignity. On this basis, parents are enjoined to be indifferent to the genotype their child bears, and instead to value the person in that personhood. At the same time, the cult of life ascribes enormous moral freight to how children are produced. The biological embodiment of children, however, can matter morally only if parents thereby bring persons into being, and do so not as transcendent ends or disembodied souls, but as particular, living, embodied personalities.

That both cults oppose cloning is unintelligible, I suggest, not only because biological replication leaves persons untouched, but because they both alike advocate cloning by other means. For the cult of life, human reproduction is precisely that, an endless spewing forth of identical souls unaffected by any personalizing vagaries of body or mentality or sociality with like others. Indeed, the demand for relentless sameness rises to become a cardinal virtue: we are and must be always what we have been, and always shall be. We are, as persons, already everything we must be; negation of our inalienable worth is not merely morally *verboten* but metaphysically impossible. As such, our pro-creative acts, like all others, have neither any substantive moral task nor implicate any substantive moral issue. Similarly for the cult of rights, our status as transcendent ends bears an origin that remains forever mysterious. Simultaneously, we are enjoined not to make of future persons objects of our designs, and assured that their autonomy is inalienable, that nothing we do to them can bereft them of their worth. As such, we are morally enjoined not to do the metaphysically impossible, to make of future persons objects of our own ends.

Both accounts, I suggest, are themselves dehumanizing in making transcendent ends or disembodied souls, rather than living, embodied personalities, the sole object of their moral prescriptions. More strikingly, they are depersonalizing, enjoining the bare replication of ends or souls rather than the procreation of novel personalities. That is the moral difference between animal reproduction and human procreation: its aim at substantive novelty as an end, which can succeed only insofar as parents invest their own personalities into their children so cultivated. Only if human procreation is personalizing, if it brings into being new persons, substantively affected in and through their persons, can it bear any moral freight. That this process requires a dyadic, mutually constitutive relation denies explicitly what both cults affirm: that our moral worth resides in a self-subsistent, self-identical, atemporal property mysteriously haunting our bodies and personalities. The cult of life reduces the body and personality of any individual person to a metaphysical accident: it enjoins us to respect that person's worth not as an individual, but as a bearer of human dignity. The cult of rights advances an analogous challenge, as it induces us to respect any individual person not as an individual in his or her embodied personality, but as a bearer of autonomy or dignity. Neither conception of human dignity is distinctively human at all; quite to the contrary dignity is, on both guises, shorn not only of body and personality but also of any human tinctures. We're enjoined to venerate, then, not persons but personhood; not agents, but autonomy.

To locate persons' worth or moral status in abstract conceptions of personhood, autonomy, or dignity offers a specious moral advantage. It affirms the inherent worth and dignity of all persons, but only by de-valuing what is unique, individuating, personalizing in the persons thus valued. These accounts equally locate that worth in a metaphysical realm beyond human reach, such that persons per se are precisely not moral patients, precisely not subject to moral harm in their persons. We are thereby licensed to do anything we wish with respect to their bodies or personalities, or to our own, as we can imperil nothing of moral worth regardless of what we do. As such, we are neither moral patients nor moral agents: we can neither destroy moral worth through our actions, nor create it. To the contrary, our agency attaches to us only contingently, and only in and through contingencies of living.

Whatever our biological or personal or social fates, our souls soar aloft, our autonomy endures unfettered. Whatever moral injunctions we propose, then, are superfluous – because we have nothing of value to lose, or to gain, in their enactment. Missing in both accounts, then, is any prospect for identifying what makes biological living itself a moral good or even a locus for such goods.

In this manner, both cults signal the demise of bioethics, which has neither any substantive moral content nor a substantive moral task. Still, both cults aspire to make of cloning and the like vital moral matters. They cannot do so, insofar as they void human personhood or autonomy of the irreducible first person self-awareness, self-identity and agency that they otherwise venerate. They cannot do so, I suggest, because those elements are signs not of a transcendent moral status, but of the irreducible individuality and novelty that human pro-creation yields, not in the reproduction of a species, but in the mutual cultivation of distinct personalities. The root of our normative relations lies therefore, not in our mutually inviolable intrinsic worth, but in our mutual constitutions and transformations, our dual status both as agents and patients. That first point, the ineradicable sociality of human persons, obtains from conception in the fusion of sperm and egg, through gestation, and through the personalizing investments that parents make in this particular child. Only through such interaction does a new personality come to be. At the same time, only insofar as this pro-creation is mutual can we depict parents and children as internally and integrally related parts. Persons bring persons to life, not extrinsically or contingently, but in their persons.

If persons are mutually constituting, both in bodily and in social investments, then we must deny that our personalizing elements – our first person perspective, self-identity and agency – signify metaphysical properties isolable from our social relations. Rather, I suggest, persons personalize each other through the families, languages and social practices which lend substance to the first-person perspective, self-identity and agency associated with having a soul, or being an end. This dependence upon such conditions of living denies what both cults assert: that persons are essentially independent, self-subsistent, self-sufficient in their persons. Instead, it implies that human persons are, in and for themselves, essentially incomplete, and that this incompleteness underwrites our moral nature. Persons are not born, I suggest, but made: children are living artifacts of those who raise them, both by virtue of their embodied first-person perspectives, and by virtue of the social investments that re made in cultivating the child's self-identity and agency. As the previous discussion of cloning hints, however, such children are no more reducible to the combination of genetic inheritance and environmental impact than to either of those influences taken in isolation. They are not conceived or born as complete persons; rather, there is a gap between what they are, by biological nature and social inheritance and what they might become as fashioned through their own efforts in selecting and pursuing distinctive ends, i.e. through what they make of themselves, and of others in turn.

That we experience such a gap, that we are not *a priori* all that we shall ever be, is a presupposition of our existence as moral beings. It is equally what makes us person-makers, in ourselves and in others, and cedes to us thereby an extraordinary range of responsibilities for cultivating the dignifying social practices through which persons are procreated. Born sanctified, dignified, autonomous, forever transcendent, we would have no such task. We have a substantive moral project, rather, only insofar as we may through our agency bring something of moral worth, or not, into being. To suggest that future persons are both the inevitable and proper objects of present persons' designs in this way, however, runs afoul of both cults. Both locate our inalienable human dignity not in our actions or characters, but in a metaphysical property that we cannot fail to exemplify. Thus inviolable, we are never subject to dignifying or degrading actions in our persons. So inviolable is this property that it cannot function as a normative guideline, as it obtains wholly apart from human action. For the cult of life, we should not design future persons because our procreative task is to provide a passive conduit for divine creativity; for the cult of rights, we should not design future persons lest we imperil their autonomy. Such critics also hold, however, that bioengineering renders the human body an upgradable object, and any children thus produced become commodities, designed to embody a minimum health standard, for example, as a measure of their acceptability to be born. On their own accounts, however, engineering for or against a particular health status leaves human dignity or autonomy unaffected. Nor, importantly, would we select some future persons over others by selecting genotypes, because genotypes are wholly extrinsic to persons.

Moreover, we already use a huge variety of technologies to enhance contingent capacities such as health, intelligence and athletic performance: extensive schooling, athletic, artistic, and musical training, and the like. What makes these interventions less threatening to human dignity or autonomy than genetic interventions? One prospect both cults pose is that genetic enhancement might lessen the ambition of persons so enhanced, or conversely, limit the satisfaction they find in their accomplishments. These objections make sense, however, only if genetic interventions seed ready-made, out of the box, fully functional talents and capacities, which require no further refinement. Yet the prospect of genetic enhancement may pose the opposite challenge if extraordinary endowments prove to require even greater effort and skill to master. Precisely, say other critics, who object that the social practices that surround such genetic potentials will intensify the already undue pressures parents place upon their children to perform to the formers' expectations. This objection, however, assumes that genetic intervention imposes distinctive pressures that nothing else does. It may not be subsequently modifiable by the child, true, but that's true of every genotype a child may receive: we all take what we get. But what of the claim that parents ought to accept the children they get without trying to engineer them? What, such critics ask, happens to the surprise element of procreation, and to the parent's willingness to raise the child as a distinct individual?

In such questions, these critics voice their ultimate concerns about the potential dehumanizing and degrading impact of biotechnologies. Yet these concerns are wholly misplaced. Theoretically, they are incoherent, given the simultaneous insistence that human dignity and autonomy transcend nature. Moreover, those accounts themselves, in separating human persons from human bodies, in disembodying persons, invite us to view human bodies as commodities, as machines comprised of upgradeable parts, and temporarily animated by the immaterial souls or autonomous agents that mysteriously haunt them. It is not modern science or contemporary biotechnology, but these moral anthropologies and the norms they underwrite, that void the human body of moral worth.

In reducing the value of the human body, they thereby devalue the procreative act itself. If human bodies are merely for reproducing themselves according to nature's dictates, this process neither needs nor admits of moral guidance.

Indeed, the vaunted laws of nature become redundant accessories over-lain upon merely biological reproduction. To leave the process unfettered absolves us comfortably of any responsibility for the ultimate dispositions of that life. We instead let nature dispense life and death sans human interference. Far from dignifying human persons, these approaches locate their ethereal status in mere numerical differences among souls, truncating the first-person perspective, self-identity and agency they aim ostensibly to protect. Far from rendering human autonomy an exulted capacity imperiled by biotechnologies, such approaches render that capacity both unintelligible and morally inert. At the same time, they void any human reproductive practices of moral content, precisely because persons simply are, as a matter of metaphysical fact, dignified in being persons.

3
Where do Bioethicists Come From?

3.1 Do utilitarians do it better?

How bioethicists reproduce themselves is one of the great mysteries of modern metaphysics, and perhaps, one of the greatest miracles of modern medicine. Cultists of both varieties, despite their surface disputes, assert unanimously that we are not our bodies. Their moral projects unite not only in opposing human animality, but in wholly disembodying the transcendent souls and autonomous agents they respectively venerate. In this they assert at once the fact of metaphysical dualism, and the moral demand that we transcend any animal accompaniments of human nature. They follow, thereby, the vast bulk of the Western moral tradition in defining human worth and moral capacity wholly in opposition to human animality. Given that heritage, utilitarianism might seem an attractive alternative to either cult, as it harkens back to the Epicureans who defined persons as their bodies. Historically, however, all such efforts have been dismissed, predictably, as animalistic, as degrading, as beneath human dignity. Epicurus himself advocated a life of comparatively simple pleasures, a life predicated on enjoying experiences in themselves, experiences identified as pleasurable and thus good, or not pleasurable and thus not good, by the human body. Eschewing references to any transcendence beyond our embodied sensibilities, he recommended instead that we seek contentment in easily attained enjoyments, in the time available to us across our natural lifespan. For this he has endured centuries of moral censure, most notably at the behest even of those ethicists who might seem most ostensibly open to his account.

Even theorists such as Mill, for example, whose utilitarianism defines moral good and ill by reference to pleasures and pains, evokes that historical presumption. He famously rejects any straightforward hedonic calculus of pleasures and pains, and dismisses any such proposed ethic as fit only for swine. Better to be a man dissatisfied than a pig satisfied, he famously intones. Following a long moral tradition of slandering the porcine community, Mill holds that simple bodily pleasures, because easily attainable, prove repetitive, and are too easily sated to satisfy a human being's more properly complex aspirations. As such, one central basis for distinguishing simple from complex pleasures is how their pursuit affects the agents who pursue them. Complex pleasures are qualitatively superior to simple pleasures, Mill insists, because they aim not at mere animal happiness or contentment, but at the development of distinctively human powers. To this extent, for Mill we must emphasize complex over simple pleasures in order to self-actualize, to develop what Aristotle regarded as powers of the distinctively human soul. Apart from such self-development, Mill maintains, echoing Aristotle, we will endure the perpetual discomfiture of what the ancients described as a disease of the soul, the thwarting of human potential that precludes any prospect of human happiness.

Two points bear emphasis here. First, while utilitarians like Mill identify happiness with pleasure, the pleasure that they commend, as a product of deliberate human activity, transcends the comparative passivity of simple animal, bodily enjoyments. Indeed, to that end, the utilitarian calculus Mill proposes systematically favors long-term over short-term pleasures, and emphasizes delayed gratification precisely because animal immediacy is not an over-riding moral consideration. That trajectory is critical because this approach requires us to convert simple natural pleasures into more complex desires and tastes if we are to self-actualize. We are enjoined, in fact, to make happiness more difficult to attain by pursuing satisfactions that require greater activity. Only amid comparative scarcity – of time, resources, talents and the like – do rarer, more complex satisfactions come to the fore. Indeed, on this account, those least satisfied with what they have developed or attained may well prove happiest, as the primary moral value of our activity resides in the struggle to self-actualize. Indeed, these complex satisfactions, unlike their simple predecessors, are effectively insatiable. With simple bodily enjoyments, we have a natural terminus: we can only imbibe so much before the body asserts itself. Consuming complex satisfactions, in contrast, has no natural constraint apart from our time and resources; our ambitions may well prove endless. This point exemplifies the extent to which the history of ethics is itself best by unintended consequences. Greed, avarice and gluttony, for example, are deemed by moralists the world over as creatures of the human body contrary to ethical imperatives. Those imperatives, however, in divorcing human aspirations from natural constraints, breed the gluttony, greed and avarice they excoriate. Epicurus himself recognized this basic tenet of human psychology millennia ago, and counseled against pursuits of luxury that sought satisfactions beyond the simplest and most readily attained. He identified thereby the locus of gluttony and the like not in an animal body easily sated, but in an insatiable will and its creatures: ceaseless desire for acquisition, and delicacies and avarices of all variety, trailing perpetual discontent in their wake. His point is hardly new, but his emphasis on rooting moral norms in how we live our bodies could scarcely be more alien to contemporary bioethicists. All unite against the prospect that a mere animal body might yield moral data; that, for example, pleasure and pain might mark distinctive moral values or disvalues in their own right, or that the human body might yield some moral authority of its own. While the cults of life and rights explicitly define our moral worth and agency in opposition to our bodies, and indeed take disembodying us to be a primary moral task, utilitarians follow suit in their efforts to elevate and to purify properly human enjoyments. We distill those enjoyments precisely by detaching them from simple animal need or bodily intentionality and redirecting them to greater ends: eating becomes a complex ritual, drinking a gourmand event, sex a servant to romantic ideals. In this way, we beautify or purify natural enjoyments by purging them of any animal elements. Conversely, we come to regard simply sated pleasures as morally inferior if not morally suspect, insofar as they may then entice us away from distinctively humanizing achievement.

That would seem a peculiar result for an ethic that takes pleasure and pain as its benchmark, except that the pleasure and pain so described are not essentially referent to the human body, but at most to that body as recast by human intellect and imagination. We are, after all, entirely capable of converting pleasure into pain and pain into pleasure – in the service of greater goods – precisely because we can divorce pleasure and pain from their bodily roots. Self-denial can pass over into self-fulfillment, as it often does among ethicists. That point is critical here because the utilitarianism of Mill joins with both cults in refusing any conception of bodily epistemic or normative authority, or even of bodily integrity. All three approaches, for example, deny that health is a natural good. The cult of life maintains, albeit inconsistently, both that all health statuses are equally good, and that absence of health may be a means to our moral improvement because it demands our endurance. For utilitarians, similarly, ill-health can prove morally edifying, and thereby, a source of self-actualization. For the cult of rights, we may make what we wish of our health status, as it leaves our autonomy unaffected. On none of these accounts is the enjoyment of health, in itself, a moral good. Whereas for Epicurus health per se offered a passive pleasure to be properly enjoyed as such, for all three approaches above we must make something of our health to endow it with moral significance.

More strikingly, on none of these accounts can biological health be an intrinsic good. For the cult of life, life is equally valuable regardless of its contingent quality; for the cult of rights, autonomous persons are valuable wholly apart from their bodily states; for utilitarians, we may self-actualize regardless of our health status. On all three accounts, not only is our health status wholly irrelevant to our moral worth, but we have no basis for seeing the body per se as a source of normative authority. For the cult of life, all bodily estates are equally good. For the cult of rights, all bodily estates are matters of indifference. For utilitarians, any bodily estate can enable self-actualization. On none of these accounts, that is, does the body per se assert any moral claims of its own: if I wish to cut off my limbs, or add random organs, I do no moral harm, as I imperil nothing of value. On this count, one irony of bioethics is the complaint often voiced by partisans of all three approaches that modern medicine reduces the human body to an object of technological manipulation. The vast bulk of the western ethical tradition, of course, does precisely the same thing by rendering the body an inert object requiring manipulation by the will.

That point may prove unsurprising, insofar as most such accounts regard the body as an ever-present threat to our transcendence, a reminder of our animality. Less explicable, however, is the longstanding tendency to ally morals and medicine. The human body so conceived cannot be a moral object, I suggest, because all three accounts deny it any authority as a moral subject. This may seem a strange charge to level, if not against the cult of life or the cult of rights, then at least against utilitarians, who ostensibly take minimizing pain and maximizing pleasure as their over-riding ends or goods. As indicated above, however, utilitarianism does not identify pleasure and pain with bodily states; we may quite consistently pursue wholly disembodied, intellectual pleasures. True, some utilitarians might object here that all such pleasures, even those attending our enjoyment of art or music or mathematics, bear some bodily reference. The body that so enjoys, however, has been itself largely intellectualized, an object and creation of a moral ideal: a testament to the transition from mere animal impulse to self-actualizing agency. To be sure, such extensive re-fashioning of our enjoyments may prove salutary for securing a range of satisfactions otherwise unavailable to us. My point is more restricted: those intellectualized enjoyments may obtain not only apart from but in opposition to simpler, bodily ones. Such transformations may liberate us from animal impulses, elevating our capacities, even humanizing us in distinctive ways. At the same time, they come to define morally valuable pleasures and pain as those that attach to these elevated faculties. Here too, it's plausible both to require of self-actualizing agents that they endure bodily pain for a greater good, and that they disavow animal pleasures, especially insofar as they encourage identification with the body. Simpler pleasures, after all, may besot us and imperil our capacity to appreciate higher pleasures, inducing us to settle for lives of mere animals, mere pigs.

The utilitarian objection to living like a mere animal arises because we can act otherwise, and can pursue higher pleasures that develop distinctive human faculties of intellect, imagination, and delicacy of feeling. Granting even that these are distinctively human faculties, however, why are we morally enjoined to prefer them? One common proposal is not only because they are distinctly human pleasures, but because they are chosen in ways that simpler enjoyments are not. Simple pleasures and pains, after all, are subject to less choice than we would like, whereas for all three approaches, resistance to our animal nature is a moral mandate because that resistance secures our agency. Crushed under an onslaught of pleasures and pains, the human body proves morally suspect in its subjection to these experiences. For the cult of rights, such subjection in our agent capacity would truncate our autonomy; for utilitarians, such subjection would reduce us to animals; for the cult of life, while we must submit to nature's dictates, the value of that activity resides not in any bodily intentionality but in willed submission to a divinely authored natural order. On all three accounts, any such bodily intentionality embodies a morally valuable activity only insofar as that body is subordinated to and serves the will.

As such, not only does the body bear no moral worth in itself, it equally embodies no moral subjectivity or agency. For the cult of life, resistance to pleasure and embrace of pain are morally edifying. For the cult of rights, pleasure and pain are entirely what we make of them. Even for utilitarians, to make of pleasure a deliberate object of simple enjoyment, sans transformation by human will, intellect and imagination, is to debase our distinctive human capacities. On all of these accounts, if there are to be distinctive human pleasures, they would be human precisely because they are not enjoyed as ends in themselves, but only as serving the will in directing that enjoyment to greater goods or ends. Animalistic pleasures, after all, on all three accounts, lead nowhere: They are not only easily sated, and thus offer no spur to agent development, but are merely private whims. They are, that is, in themselves both private, and thus void of epistemic content, and subjective, shorn of moral content. Bounded within the irremediable privacy of our bodies, they neither convey anything truthful about how we inhabit the world, nor offer any norms of health or function or bodily integrity. As such, they neither disclose the world to us, nor author any distinctive moral normativity in their own right. To that extent, the next obvious question is – what good are they?

3.2 Life as we know it?

No greater evidence obtains for the widespread rejection of embodied human agency than the absence of references to love and sexuality in bioethics discussions. This may seem an unlikely premise, since so many current debates illustrate competing views of our reproductive practices. For the cult of life, all sexual activity is properly confined to marriage and must serve reproductive purposes, in prospect if not in fact. While some more liberal defenders of the cult of life affirm also a unitive function to sex, for example, in sustaining marital intimacy, that function remains forever subordinate to the first. Not only must all sexual activity hold open the prospect of reproduction, but any efforts to thwart that natural end are *verboten*. So over-riding is that primary function that sexual impotence precludes entering into a marital relation, and equally voids marital contracts previously consummated. That same principle alike precludes any recourse to artificial birth control measures. The central point underlying these proscriptions is that pleasure for the sake of pleasure is neither a natural good to be enjoyed for its own sake, nor an intrinsic good to be sought for its own sake. Indeed, on either of those counts pleasure per se would pose an intrinsic evil, an unnatural and thus disordered use of the human body. Nor is pleasure an instrumental good, as sexual activity may be indifferently pleasurable or not, or even painful, provided it serves its natural terminus: reproduction. To that end, unlimited sexual access is guaranteed to both partners through the marital contract, as we have no legitimate basis for willfully refusing openness to life. That last point underscores that, even for those who grant the prospect of unitive sexual activity. For example, in maintaining a marital bond between infertile partners, the human body per se authorizes no pursuit of pleasure in itself. Such bodies, rather, are subordinate to and serve the institution of marriage in its incubation of life. So vital is that service, that even sexual activity between infertile partners must be regarded as open in principle to the miraculous transmission of life.

For the cult of life, we must remain thus open to that transmission of life because that is a natural necessity into which we ought not to assert our wills. We cannot, they hold – against the cult of rights – make of our reproductive practices anything we wish.

Yet the human body as the cult of life conceives it is itself an instrument and a product of human will. Cult of life defenders insist, for example, that any non-reproductive sexual activity reduces both one's own and one's partner's body to mere means, to tools for pursuing pleasure. The evil in such activity resides in using another's body for one's own selfish ends. If the normative purpose of such activity is reproductive, however, each body is precisely that: a means to its own and the others' replacement. Cult of life defenders would object here that only sexual activity that aims at reproduction elides the unnatural and selfish assertion of will that reduces each partner to a means for the other. The trajectory here, they maintain, aims not at pleasure as a self-involved terminus, but at the provision of a new social bond, a family, and new life. Several points bear emphasis here. First, restricting sexual activity to marriage itself entails an assertion of will against nature, that is, against immediate bodily impulses. Once confined within such an institution, the insistence that marital bodies must be always sexually accessible is no less likely to reduce them to means. Indeed, on this view, forcing sexual activity upon an unwilling partner within marriage is morally superior to consensual sex outside of marriage. The bedrock of this position, after all, is the effort to exclude human will wholly from life transmission, and on that count, the willingness of partners to engage in reproductive activity is a codicil of the marriage contract, as a duty each owes the other

If that's the case, however, the reproductive and unitive functions of sexual activity may well work at cross purposes. Within marriage, this position precludes providing pleasure to a partner sans openness to reproduction. The most liberal of these approaches make some exceptions, for infertile or ailing or disabled spouses, for example, provided they retain belief in the possibility of a miraculous transmission of life. Given that last coda, however, any sexual activity is potentially reproductive. Against the cult of rights, the cult of life asserts that only sexual activity that admits the possibility of reproductive issue is naturally normative. Yet there is finally no natural constraint upon that activity, given the ever-present prospect of miraculous divine intervention. Nor, more strikingly, does any necessary link obtain between sexual activity and reproduction; quite the contrary, such activity is neither necessary nor sufficient to the transmission of life. It is unnecessary given the provenance of the miraculous, and insufficient given the insistence that the soul is divinely authored. On that last point, in effect, all human conceptions are immaculate, untouched by the vagaries of biological reproduction. As supernatural life courses indifferently through our contingent bodies, conversely, it neither degrades nor dignifies them; they are dignified, rather, wholly apart from such bodies.

Yet how, then, can we degrade ourselves or others, regardless of how we treat the bodies that enter into those practices? The cult of life thus seeks both to exclude human will from interference in super-natural life-transmission, an interference we cannot really perpetrate, and to assert the will's rightful supremacy in resisting natural sexual impulses.

No recourse to biological birth control, for example, can thwart miraculous intervention; our will is wholly extrinsic to the process. Conversely, to hold that we ought to resist some natural impulses inserts human will into our reproductive practices before they even begin. Moreover, if such enjoyments are, as the cult of life suggests, merely arbitrary, subjective, or selfish, they would be so in the amoral realm of natural bodies. Human bodies, after all, have on this position no distinctive goods in themselves, such that they could scarcely admit of any corresponding evils. Pleasure and pain could not qualify as such natural goods, this view suggests, because they attend bodily experiences that are inherently private, subjective, and incommunicable.

As such, they neither convey facts about the world or the interior lives of other persons, nor could they serve as normative guides. Were these assumptions true, we have no basis either for acknowledging the presence of particular others, or for evaluating how we may properly act with respect to them. The view that pleasure and pain are incommunicable, and are thus irremediably private, is at best tendentious. It may be true that we may not access another's body directly from within. Yet such epistemic certitude is not necessary to assay that someone is pleased or pained. Those experiences, after all, are themselves borne not only internally, but in facial expressions, body language and behaviors that convey largely non-verbal information, about one's insertion into the world. Here, the cult of life follows a huge swath of the Western philosophical tradition in espousing an unremitting skepticism toward the potential truth value of interior states, particularly those that are not represented propositionally. Not only can such states not be publicly assessed, these approaches insist, but they cannot be guaranteed to correspond to facts in the objective world that obtain independently of agents' judgments.

It is simply false, however, to dismiss such interior states as merely subjective because they obtain within another's body beyond our reach. Not only are such states communicable, as indicated above, but they occupy an objective world precisely because their apprehender does. When another person apprehends pleasure or pain that apprehension becomes part of the world that apprehender inhabits; thereby, it becomes a potential datum of others' experience. We may rightfully dismiss such experiences as irremediably private or subjective only if, in their inherence within the apprehender's body, they thereby enter into a transcendent or epiphenomenal universe of one, shorn of any attachment to the objective world that body inhabits, and to which that body remains subject. That last point exemplifies the extent to which we are made subjects precisely as that world impinges upon our bodies, as in pleasure or pain, that is, precisely as the world objectifies us. Pleasure and pain are not irremediably private, then, not only because they represent the impingement of objective data upon us, but because mutual apprehending of those data, as in shared pleasure or pain, magnifies those experiences, rendering them, for lack of a better term, social facts that alike come to inhabit an objective world. To this extent, I suggest, subjects bring each other into being, as subjects, by objectifying each others' interior states, such that apart from this shared activity we could speak neither of objectivity, nor of private, interior selves, but only of transcendent persons facing a wholly epiphenomenal world.

Not only do those interior states become objective data in the world, that is, but they are amplified by that mutuality of interior states, and thereby rendered more real. Any such suggestion may sound unintelligible to those for whom objective knowledge claims and ethical judgments are by definition impersonal, and attach to a world not of our making. Yet it is one thing to say that only impersonal knowledge reveals that objective world, and another to say that in knowing we add nothing of epistemic substance to that world. At its extreme, the former position implies that we know the world only as it obtains independently of us, as if we are not part of it. My point here, however, is not that we change the world by knowing it, but that that knowledge changes us. We do not meet pleasure or pain at a contemplative distance, for example, but as they inscribe themselves upon us. Yet however deeply they penetrate, they not only remain communicable, but are magnified when shared, because they disclose specific knowledge of another's interiority.

In the Middle Ages, celibate theologians, understandably bored, indulged in endless intellectual speculation concerning how many angels might dance on pin heads. A more worldly set might have puzzled over how a single experience shared can yield more enjoyment than two isolated experiences. Such Zeno-like paradoxes remain puzzling only if we believe, following the bulk of modern epistemology, that we are, as individuals, isolated and incommunicable, trapped in our bodies, unknowing and unknowable in our private, subjective states. This epistemic conceit, however, makes perfect nonsense of sexual intimacy, and voids it of any normative dimension. For the cult of life, for example, we degrade ourselves and our partners if we use their bodies to serve non-reproductive ends; yet the good of human reproduction is divinely authored. Given persons' inviolable dignity, however, we have no power to degrade them by using their bodies, since their dignity transcends their bodies: In using another's body, we simply do not thereby use their person. At the same time, even sexual activity confined to marriage and aimed at reproduction cannot dignify either partner. Human bodies per se are merely contingently related to reproduction: nothing we do to or with them induces the making of another person, which is a matter of divine provenance.

Moreover, we cannot take a marital partner's pleasure as a natural, intrinsic, or instrumental good – as all give way to the reproductive imperative, and as we cannot know, at any rate, what pleases them. To that extent, sexual intimacy, like human reproduction, is strictly speaking a contradiction in terms: we do not come to know another through the former, anymore than we bring another into being through the latter.

On that view, we can no more say that naturally normative sexual activity dignifies than that unnatural sexual activity degrades; the idea of any normative sexuality collapses upon itself. The problem, I suggest, is not only the insistence that pleasure and pain are not goods or evils, but that they are irremediably private. To be sure, however much persons may share the feelings, sensations, and beliefs, these cannot be rendered wholly transparent to others. So dense and impenetrable is that interior life taken to be, however, that both cults harbor intense suspicion toward that interiority. For the cult of life we act as persons only sans any essential reference to particular feelings or impulses. For the cult of rights, similarly, we act autonomously, act from ourselves, only sans such subjective sentiments.

At the same time, both cults are deeply inconsistent: the cult of rights asserts our unfettered autonomy, and then seeks to define the normative conditions under which we may exercise that autonomy, as if any empirical conditions could affect its use. The cult of life, similarly, asserts our transcendent dignity, and then seeks to define the normative conditions under which we may sustain that dignity, as if we have any power to imperil it. Those normative concerns arise, I suggest, only if we grant the primary premise both cults deny: that we are not only accessible or knowable in our particular persons, but that we are thereby partly constituted by those others, whether for good or for ill. By that first point, I mean that only as an object of intimate knowledge on the part of some specific others do we come into being as particular subjecst, both in ourselves and to them. At the same time, I mean to depict this ontological sociability quite literally, and so to maintain that only through such mutual constitution may we benefit or harm others in their persons. Only as internally related to others, that is, do we bring into being one or another mode of life for them, and only as such do we exemplify moral agency. Put differently, we are and must be simultaneously agents and patients. As moral patients, others quite literally constitute our bodies and personalities, in our conception and gestation and maturation; as moral agents, we constitute theirs, lending our genetic inheritances, our personalities, our labor. Only through such intimate intercourse are persons available to help or harm: not as disembodied souls or agents, but as embodied persons enmeshed in particularities.

Moreover, to depict our normativity as mutual embodiment implies strictly not only that our embodied experiences are real – insofar as our normative capacity is – but also that those experiences embody distinctive goods. Persons are subjects at all, I suggest, only because they are subject to bodily and social impingements, i.e. only because they are objectified both by a physical and a social world exterior to them. Through this mutual constitution, we can acquire and convey data concerning our own and others' interior states. Such data, however, are morally inert unless it's also true that, for example, pleasure and pain are goods or evils, such that they not only can but must be components of moral consideration. For the cult of life, such particular experiences are epiphenomenal, wholly inessential to persons as such. Thus that view leaves it as entirely unintelligible both how and why particular persons might warrant moral consideration in their particularity, and how we might dignify or degrade those persons if they are, finally, their inalienable worths alone, sans any particular elements. For the cult of rights, such experiences are equally and alike epiphenomenal, and alike inessential to persons, who are essentially not their particular choices, but their capacity to choose. Yet that autonomous capacity, like an immortal soul, is guaranteed by metaphysical fiat; thus this approach too leaves unintelligible what goods our choices might realize, beyond the bare capacity to choose, and what we're to defend, morally, apart from the inalienable autonomy we could scarcely surrender if we wished. If, that is, we are to defend persons in their particular persons, we must identify both what goods they realize, in themselves, and how we might imperil or enhance those goods. Neither cult can offer such a defense because the persons they seek to defend neither require nor even admit such defense; to the contrary, they bear no moral relation to each other at all.

We can bear such a relation, I suggest, only if our agency brings distinctive goods into being, such that we can either imperil or cultivate those goods. As transcendent souls or ends, we need no instrumental goods because we need do nothing to secure our absolute worths. We admit no natural goods because such worths are disembodied. Yet we can be moral agents at all, I suggest, only if we have some moral task, and we bear such tasks only if we are essentially embodied and mutually embodying. Only on those two counts can we affect others in their persons. from this it follows not only that persons are embodied as a condition of moral normativity, but also that that embodiment is a distinctive good. Both cults explicitly deny that prospect, insisting instead that human persons bear a distinctive moral worth only insofar as they transcend our mere animal nature. Instead of life as we know it, which traffics in pro-creating and dying, in pleasure and pain and grief, bioethicists of both cults traffic instead in immortal souls and autonomous agents, all finally invulnerable to the vicissitudes of illness, aging and dying, of bodily finitude. Both cults see in human living, in human animality, intractable degradation, and aim, at bottom, to drive the *bios*, the living, from bioethics, erecting in its place their respective assertions of our independence from a natural order.

3.3 What's love got to do with it?

To the extent that this sheer transcendence might attend our agency, however, it would make utter nonsense of the passivity that lends content to our moral lives. Self-professed defenders of life, for example, demand that the dying among us endure what they must to be who they are, dignified persons. While predicated on human dignity, this injunction is couched in love: of persons, of human life, even of God. Proponents of this view imply that only by thus enduring the dying process, whatever it brings, do we accept our finitude with due humility, foregoing the prideful assertions of will that would seek to shorten the process. In their bid for humility, however, such theorists insist that they alone know God's will, and have the facility to impose that will upon willing and unwilling alike, for their own good. They assert also that human life alone is of such import that, even when no longer wanted or valued in itself, it must be maintained, indeed, must be loved. Yet that requirement demands love not of living persons in their particulars, but of life; not of this particular person, but of a disembodied soul. Embodied persons, after all, are subject to the passage of time, of physical health, to distortions of personality, to failures of nerve and will. But what we are enjoined to love endures unperturbed through all such contingencies of living. On that count, not only any one soul but any one life is as good as any other, practically as well as morally. As such, we are enjoined to love all persons equally, to disavow animal attachments to particular persons in service to the selfless love of persons per se.

So conceived, however, what is it that we love, if we turn our attention wholly to an enduring soul? Nowhere is this query more confounding than in cases of romantic or familial love, which are, properly speaking, contradictions in terms. The cult of life prides itself both on its self-proclaimed love of life, particularly in defending its weakest human forms, and its systematic attention to the social significance of human sexuality and procreation. At the same time, the cult of life's unremitting hostility to embodied human life is most evident in this venue. For the cult of life, the human body's capacity to experience pleasure is at best a potential source of intrinsic evil, for instance, in non-marital sex. Moreover, physical revelation of the body in any but the most controlled social situations prompts shame in the one thus revealed, and incites lust or fascination in the viewer. At first glance these two experiences are inexplicable. We are not our bodies, but dignified souls; yet shame properly attends revelation of a transitory, fungible casing. Additionally, while properly speaking it is the will, not the body, that generates lust or fascination, this view nonetheless depicts non-marital sex as a sin or weakness of the flesh. In the latter case, moreover, the sin is taken to be an abuse or degradation of self and other not as bodies but as persons.

The moral basis for these injunctions is twofold. First, confining sexuality to marriage sustains the prime social institution for transmitting life. Second, concealing the body preserves the privacy of the marital relation, sustains modesty outside of that context, and thereby protects the dignity of persons. The most striking point here is the duality posited between animal lust and human love: seeking pleasure is animalistic and degrading, invariably reducing the other to a means to serve one's own selfish desires. The only way to curtail self- and other-abuse is via mutual use within marriage. Indeed, as indicated earlier, so eager is this position to forestall such potential abuse that it denies marital partners any basis for sexual refusal: they cannot use each other, that is, because the marital contract grants each unlimited claim upon the other's body. If we are not our bodies, however, it makes little sense to spend so much time protecting our selves – i.e. our souls – from the body's misadventures. Moreover, as disembodied substances, we are invisible to others, and clothed or not, our bodies remain extrinsic to us. Moreover, the accessibility of our bodies, in whole or in part, should equally prove metaphysically and morally indifferent. The idea that we can objectify or abuse ourselves, or that others can objectify or abuse us, whether in thought, word, or deed, makes no sense if our persons are inaccessible to them in their inalienable dignity. A human body cannot be degraded because it is not, properly speaking, dignified in the first place.

Quite the contrary, whatever value attains in bodily life draws its significance from a disembodied soul: it is not biological life, even in human form, that bears this value, but the invisible, intangible soul that persists though all bodily changes. How, then, does it matter at all morally if or how humans realize bodily pleasures and pains? The cult of life's tortured, deeply conflicted position here issues from the absolute contrast it draws between the love that attains between persons as persons, and the animal lust that sexual activity ostensibly serves. If the latter issues exclusively from selfish, subjective motives, and aims to serve only one's own pleasure, while the former alone exemplifies moral love for persons as persons, then the lone moral purchase human sexuality can evince is as a conduit – however inexplicably – to the dignified life that potentially passes through it. Conversely, love for one's partner as a person must resist lust, and indeed any partialities predicated on personality or bodily comportment or any other particularities. This ideal of love, however, purged of particularities, is not recognizably human. Moreover, to make of this experience an exercise of disembodied will and unfettered choice, and to presume that we thereby elevate the experience by distancing it from its passive and animal and particulate roots, embraces the conceit that our wills are wholly under our direction. For both cults, we are wholly beyond others' grasp, secure in our transcendence.

That inaccessibility reaches its apex in Sartre, for whom love is a doomed project, a clash of irremediable freedoms that are mutually transcendent, and mutually disembodied. Sartre famously locates in the human body our subjection to gravity, to others' objectifications, to the reduction of our possibilities of transcendence.[1] Against that abject embodiment, which he associates with being caught naked, seen, unwillingly rendered visible, he contrasts the grace of a dancer, who even unclothed reveals unfettered bodily movement, motions that conceal that body from any objectifying gaze, wrapping it in transcendence. That transcendence, however, does not reveal bodily but subjective intentionality: the subject does not animate but takes flight from the encumbering body. The objectifying gaze is deflected around the body by evoking attention to the dancer's project, her will and intention, such that the body fades into nothingness. Equally important, this flight is depersonalizing as well as disembodying. In its transcendence, it escapes from itself: its particularities of time and place. It is instead a triumph of the ever present transcendent prospect grace signifies: that whatever we are or were at that moment, we need not be. The objectifying gaze does precisely the opposite. It ensnares us in our body, in a person as conceived by the other, reducing our possibilities of escape. It makes us visible in and through those particulars ascribed to us by others, seizing from us our capacity for complete self-creation, and ceding that capacity to the other, who recreates us in his or her eyes. Worse, it permits, even enjoins each of us to see that other-created self, to become visible to our selves in and thorough alien eyes. The body thus revealed, whether as a source of lust or fear or revulsion or aesthetic enjoyment, is thus a product of others' power, the triumph of one will over another.

While for Sartre any intimacy threatens to reduce us to our bodies, for the cult of life that threat arises from our subjection to bodily pleasure. One common injunction of the cult of life, for example, is that all persons equally warrant love, and all human bodies are equally valuable. On this basis, we are enjoined to attend to the inner rather than outer qualities of persons. Beauty itself is morally suspect, and progressively voided of its physical and sensuous elements. These concerns take contemporary form in the cult of life's criticism of cosmetic surgery, with the latter's emphasis on appearance, and on the apparent packaging of persons. If we are not our bodies, that objection founders, since it wouldn't matter, morally, what we do to them. Conversely, if individual particularities are incidental to persons, then the selection of specific persons to favor is precisely arbitrary. If I'm enjoined to love all equally, in their persons, then one is as good as any other. I can offer no reasons, neither emotional nor physical, nor predicated on any other arbitrary preference, for one selection over another. Indeed, I can no more favor ostensibly internal qualities – of feeling, or affect, or moral sensibility, or personality, than I could physical ones, and on the same basis: I am required to love persons as persons. Accordingly, while for Sartre love is impossible, insofar as two freedoms cannot appear to each other in their mutual transcendence, for the cult of life, love must be morally suspect if it announces any preference for one person over another.

The central problem for both is that human love renders persons visible in their particulars, and thereby brings into being a relation not extrinsic but intrinsic to the partners. What Sartre's gaze introduces is not a single but a double vision: a self seen not only from without by different eyes, but from within by different eyes. The self thus seen, however, is not a previously fully formed self flushed into light by a harsh beam: rather, something new coalesces under that gaze. The person who thus emerges is unpredictable, and we live our bodies differently when we take new persons under our skin. Equally apt is this love's association with procreation, which evokes new persons inhabited by others' genes and voices and personalities and tastes and values. Only on this basis does the irremediable vulnerability of human love – to the vicissitudes of living – make sense; that is, it makes sense only insofar as that love attaches not to eternal, self-subsistent substances, but to living persons. Conversely, only this mutual accessibility of persons – to be brought to life by their intimates in their persons – make sense of our moral capacity to degrade or to dignify others, not as inviolate persons in the abstract, but as particular persons.

3.4 What good is life?

I stress that last point because love among persons as either cult conceives them is metaphysically vacuous and morally impotent. It has no moral power because it bears no substantive effect on transcendent souls or ends; at most, it reduces to a recognition of their worth as persons in the abstract. Moreover, that recognition itself lacks metaphysical or moral substance. Harbored amid agents' private interiority, it evinces at best a mute penumbra of feelings, associations and affects, all alike epiphenomenal. It marks no reality, not only because it attends each subject's incommunicable subjectivity, but also because its occurrence adds value neither to the world nor to others apprehended. Its irremediable privacy precludes the former; the inviolate dignity or autonomy of the other precludes the latter. Even if we respect or love some others, we do not thereby dignify them, any more than we might degrade them by withdrawing all respect. On this count, the cult of life proves life-denying because it elevates human dignity wholly beyond human impulses and desires and loves, setting in their place an intellectualized love for persons in the abstract. It locates human worth and value in transcendent heights wholly separate from living persons, and depicts persons as ultimately immune to the vicissitudes of finitude and embodiment. This view implies that we secure such moral worth only insofar as we disembody and depersonalize persons and our love for them.

If that were true, however, of what value would life prove in its biological or natural states, and what good would love be in its more familiar, more fragile human forms? If our biological living is merely a transitory state we pass through in our bid to reproduce persons, and is alike at most a contingent part of God's pro-creative process,

Then for example why regard sexual intimacy as metaphysically and morally integral to that process? If it adds nothing substantive to persons, in the genetic inheritance or bodily or psychic or affective comportments of the persons so produced, it is scarcely necessary to produce them in such fashion. Moreover, if it leaves persons thus untouched, it does not matter at all whether persons are produced in a naturally normative way at all. Indeed, insofar as we are charged morally with resisting animal impulses, and instead exhorted to love life and persons in the abstract, we could edify the reproductive process considerably by disembodying and depersonalizing it entirely, by detaching parents and partners from passionate animal attachments, and by urging instead the indifferent manufacture of bodies to which souls will be added at conception. Moreover, if that divine creativity is both untouched by human reproductive practices and leaves those practices untouched in turn, it can hardly be held to dignify them. The lone normative purpose of sexual intimacy, after all, is a mode of life transmission to which it is by nature and definition wholly extrinsic. Accordingly, such practices can only remain what they are apart from that function, namely degrading and dehumanizing activities void of moral merit.

As such, the cult of life should agree with the most extreme defenders of the cult of rights, who advocate a liberation biology that systematically disentangles human reproduction from biological animality. They also should embrace any means of manufacturing persons asexually as a great advance in defense of human dignity. If anything, the cult of life should seemingly embrace biotechnologies such as cloning and in vitro fertilization that require no such intimate, degrading and dehumanizing, interchanges. The cult of life, however opposes technologies that shift our reproductive activities from bedrooms to laboratories as unnatural and dehumanizing, the latter in rendering persons objects of human will.

Human will, however, can neither create nor dehumanize persons; persons are divinely authorized, and at most contingently human in any biological sense. Moreover, since the production of persons is supernatural, the material conditions of that production are in effect wholly immaterial, and are at best morally neutral. Moreover, insofar as natural human reproductive practices are inherently degrading and dehumanizing apart from the willed institution of marriage, they do not admit an inherent moral normativity; nor can any act of human will edify them morally. Since our bodies are wholly extrinsic to pro-creation, the lone prospect for morally legitimating sexual intimacy drops away.

At the same time, the natural normativity that the cult of life ascribes to some reproductive practices, and the corresponding proscription of other such practices, is itself a product of human will oriented toward a transcendent end. Normative sexual intimacy, on that view, not only requires a specific social institution, but is directed toward transcendent persons rather than natural bodies, toward reproduction rather than pleasure, toward the realization of a single transcendent end, another person, rather than at the cultivation of a social relation valued and valuable for its own sake. To the contrary, only insofar as such intimacy is a means to that transcendent end does it prove morally normative. As neither a necessary nor sufficient means to human reproduction, however, such sexual intimacy bears no such natural normativity. To that extent, the cult of life – no less than the cult of rights – renders our treatment of others' bodies morally neutral.

The natural fact of embodiment is incidental to sexual intimacy because it is not a fact at all – insofar as we deal in persons. On this basis, the cult of rights advocates unfettered will and choice in sexual activity, as it can be only what persons will it to be. While the cult of life rejects such unfettered choice as unnatural and degrading, however, it too depicts human love as a creature of moral will directed at disembodied persons. As such, its demand for monogamy and other ostensibly natural norms are wholly arbitrary.

Persons as persons, after all, are interchangeable. Nothing about specific bodies or personalities per se warrants respect, and any such valuations would instead be degrading precisely because persons are equally valuable as persons. Intimacy per se, physical or psychic, must prove morally suspect. Indeed, if life transmission is the lone legitimate impetus of such intimacy, the latter might be better served by polygamy than by marriage between pairs. Moreover, why enjoin human reproduction at all, if souls subsist apart from their embodiments? If we are not our bodies, but divine creations, the cult of life should be no less indifferent to the means of biological pro-creation than should the cult of rights, and on identical grounds, namely that we are inviolate persons. The cult of life, however, in opposing the cult of rights, affirms in proposed practice what it denies in theory: that the human body is essentially a product of human intimacy. Indeed, we are obliged to defend human life because it is vulnerable to our choices. Oddly, however, while intrinsic goods attach only to disembodied persons, intrinsic evil attaches to misuse not merely of the human will, but also of the human body.

In an impressive feat of metaphysical mayhem, this view maintains that while intrinsic goods attach to disembodied persons alone, intrinsic evils attach to what ought properly to be regarded as amoral bodies. As a matter of consistency alone, this account would suggest instead that such evils reside in the will that the body unwittingly serves. Yet even the will is morally epiphenomenal. It can neither enhance our moral worth when rightly oriented, nor diminish that worth when improperly oriented. Moreover, no use of the body, any more than of the will, can degrade or dignify; our absolute worth endures wholly untouched by our actions. Indeed, those actions are at most extrinsically and contingently ours, since they do not substantively qualify our persons. At the same time, however, the cult of life depicts the human body as occluded by shame, moral and metaphysical if revealed, even to an intimate partner, and as posing the ever-present threat of ensnaring its bearer in degrading pursuits of pleasure. Indeed, the body poses the double threat of reducing its bearer to an object of others and its own private and selfish enjoyments, and of inciting lust and fascination in any viewer. On this view, evil resides neither in the pleasure so pursued, nor in the will thus ensnared, but rather in the fact of embodiment. That evil resides, in other words, not in any particular bodily responses or evocations, but in our subjection to animal pleasure. The human body thus harbors that evil in itself, as over against our transcendent, disembodied dignity.

At the same time, this account joins the cult of rights in advancing persons' claims, as persons, to a right to personal privacy as against others' incursions. Indeed, both cults defend moral norms of personal privacy and bodily modesty as means of cordoning off persons' bodies, and thereby persons, from unfettered public consumption.

Those norms secure anything of moral worth, however, only if we are our bodies, and only if revealing human bodies thereby also discloses something of human persons. Both cults deny that prospect. Indeed, the cult of rights rejects in principle any reduction of human persons to bodies. As indicated earlier, for example, positions like Sartre's preclude any prospect that I may imperil another, in his autonomy, by objectifying him. To be sure, to be seen as Sartre describes the term, to be objectified amid another's gaze, requires that whether I wish to escape that sight or not, I cannot. It requires equally that I be ensnared not only in that others' sight, but thereby in my own, that I see and objectify myself not as I am, in my freedom, but as the object the other makes of me. That other's gaze, however, discloses nothing about me. I remain, in myself, invisible, irreducible to this gaze, a sheer transcendence. Whatever I make of myself, or others make of me, I remain an inalienable freedom. Conversely, that gaze could be a substantive threat to me, to my transcendence, only if it unveils something inescapable, only if it irrevocably ensnares my interiority. On Sartre's view, in fact, since this cannot happen, demands for privacy, for modesty, are unintelligible: as a freedom, I am invisible, intangible, wholly beyond others' reach. I am no more my body than I am any other contingent qualification.

On Sartre's account, not only can we not intrude upon others in their freedoms, however we conceive them, but their freedom remains entirely impenetrable to us. We learn nothing of them through sight or touch, which disclose nothing but our own conceptions of them. Even in sexual intimacy, our own conceptions alone echo back to us; our freedoms remain untouched. We are, after all, our autonomy, our capacity to choose, and in this are wholly unfettered by prior or projected choices. The cult of life objects here, of course, that sexual activity so conceived is wholly impersonal, reducing each partner not only to a means of the other's enjoyment, but a product of the other's will. Yet such reductions are no less metaphysically impossible for souls then they are for transcendent ends. On neither account do our bodies matter morally; their use neither degrades nor dignifies. We could assert moral prescriptions governing sexual intimacy, rather, only if such intimacy is possible among persons, i.e. only if it renders them visible in themselves, disclosing persons in mutually constitutive ways. Only insofar as persons thus embody and personalize each other, I suggest, do they thereby bear moral relations wherein they may dignify or degrade each other.

This point suggests first that proper object of human love is embodied human persons, valued not as instances of life or autonomy, but as living individuals, valued not despite but in and through their particularities. In affirming life and love in the abstract, the cult of life degrades living and loving in their human forms. Moreover, in valorizing disembodied life and depersonalized love, the cult of rights degrades not just human life in its bodily incarnation, but also any prospect for human and humanizing love among particular persons. Indeed, both cults reduce human to animal love, disembodying and depersonalizing it, and advancing instead ideals that attach to immortal souls or to transcendent ends. Insofar as persons are immune to others in their persons, that love remains untouched by time. This may well be a love appropriate to a God who is eternal and self-sufficient, who admits of no moral help or harm. Yet it admits thereby neither of pleasure or pain, of fear or joy, of gratitude or grief. It is what it is, as it is; extending necessarily into infinity it bears no kinship with human love, a love irrevocably scarred by our finitude. It is love not only intellectualized but rendered morally inert, attaching as it does to inviolate persons. Neither persons nor life per se can be objects of human love, I suggest, because the latter is shot through with contingencies, and bears no kinship with transcendent persons but only with those particular persons whose embodied finitude impresses some claim upon us. Those claims moreover, embody themselves only among specific intimate others whose mutual incarnations of body and personality become for me not only natural goods, enjoyed as ends in themselves, nor only instrumental, but also intrinsic goods, i.e. those whose ends and goods have become my own.

Both cults equally refuse any such efforts to root human valuations, whether natural, instrumental or intrinsic, in organic, embodied practices of living. Neither could in principle admit the prospect of natural goods, of bodily pleasures and pains avowed or disavowed in themselves. For the cult of life, mere bodily enjoyment without reference to transcendent goods marks in itself not good, but evil incarnate. Such pleasures and pains, despite these theorists' suggestions to the contrary, cannot qualify as instrumental goods. We encounter no such goods, as enduring pain or forestalling pleasure, even in service to human dignity, adds nothing to our moral worth. That worth, rather, being divinely ascribed to us, is not something we merit, but something we instantiate as persons. It transcends the vicissitudes of living, of illness and aging and pro-creating and dying, voiding them of metaphysical and moral substance. The absolute value of life so defended is thus not biological living in human form, but life per se, sans any essential reference to particulars of body or personality or affect. The vagaries of living thus neither affect nor effect us in our persons. The good of human life is metaphysically absolute and morally guaranteed against all incursions; the vagaries of embodied human living neither enhance nor diminish it. To the query "What good is living?", then, we must respond: "No good at all", as goodness transcends animal nature, eliding any organic or biological imprints. That conclusion may seem counter-intuitive, given the cult of life's longstanding allegiance to the metaphysical miasma known as natural law, and its ostensible commitment to love of human life. But the life this position professes to love consorts neither with embodied human persons, nor with embodied human love.

To the contrary, despite its hostility to the cult of rights, this position joins the former in a shared hostility to embodied human living. At the heart of their dispute is the role of human will in authorizing moral norms. While the cult of rights locates all norms in that will, the cult of life seeks instead to read them from natural processes. The latter, however, it wholly subordinates to transcendent souls. Humans alone prove moral, this view asserts, because we are emphatically not mere animals, but souls immortal. We can as such act in ways wholly contrary to biological imperatives, remaking our reproductive practices into the procreative transmission of transcendent life, and enduring our deaths with the understanding that we will quite literally outlast the body's deliverances. In these orientations the cult of life joins the cult of rights not only in eliding natural constraints, but also in affirming our moral agency in our capacity to act contrary to our ostensible animal nature. On neither account, in fact, do we have such a nature. For the cult of rights, too, what I've termed here natural goods would prove contradictions in terms. Subjection to pleasure or pain, in itself, would signify a constraint of our animal nature, and thereby, an affront to our autonomy. Nor could we characterize such goods as instrumental, unless we mean by that wholly arbitrary preferences selected by agents to serve other, equally chosen and arbitrary ends. Our lone good, after all, is our capacity for unconstrained choice, choice unfettered either by bodily impingements, or by the legacies of our prior selections. Since our moral task is, on this view, to make of ourselves precisely and only what we choose, we can be constrained by nothing extrinsic to ourselves if we are to be the persons they believe we are, in our autonomy. The cult of life, of course, opposes such out-sized autonomy as a denial of our nature as divinely created. Yet that dispute is finally vacuous, because persons conceived either as transcendent ends or immortal souls are metaphysically and functionally equivalent, and yield identical moral proscriptions, namely none at all, inviolable as they are in their personhood.

We are charged, then, with respecting autonomous ends or loving immortal souls in themselves, as instantiations of absolute moral value. We are charged, that is, with both disembodying and depersonalizing persons, insofar as we regard them morally. For the cult of life, for example, we are enjoined not to love persons in the specifics of their bodies or personalities, both because all persons, as persons, bear equal worth, and because moral love orients itself not to the contingent and transient, but to the absolute and the eternal. Indeed, love oriented toward the former bears its selfish animal origins, reducing those so loved to means to our own enjoyment, and degrading them, and us, in the process. To love persons in their dignity, conversely, we must do so apart from any reference to specifics of body or personality or affect. We must resist any such natural or animal influences because they are rooted in sensuous affects, and must locate judgments of beauty or grace or the like instead in the dignity of the loved person. Any reference to personal beauty, then, must attach to the person, and at that to enduring personal qualities that signify not the transient sensuous appeal of a particular body or personality, but the transcendent human dignity borne by persons per se. Against any natural or animal impulse to prefer some to others we are required to see all persons as equally beautiful, whatever their physical estates. We are charged with viewing all bodies, from the most twisted, deformed and dysfunctional to the most graceful, sculptured and functional as equally valuable. Indeed, it is instructive here that while cult of life defenders assert the wisdom of bodily or psychic repugnance to certain "unnatural" reproductive practices, they entirely reverse themselves here, denying that the body authors any norms in identifying or preferring particulars of sensuous appeal.

Instead, any natural preference for beauty or functionality or grace is dismissed as merely animal, and indeed immoral; not only does this position require us to regard all bodies as equally valuable, it alike demands that we regard deformities and dysfunctions as equally good, equally normative. Indeed, those terms are unintelligible because all bodies are equally good. In distancing our view of others from any bodily normativity, this position again joins the cult of rights in ascribing to those bodies norms derived not from nature, but from human will or imagination in the service of transcendent ends. To that extent, we may even be enjoined to regard all biological diseases and disabilities as embodiments of transcendent human dignity. Such is, for the cult of life, a demand on love, that it endure regardless of persons' biological fates. Here too, the cult of life echoes the cult of rights in rendering such love entirely an act of will and imagination. For the cult of rights, too, love escapes animal impulse: it is a creature of will, freely chosen and subject to perpetual revision. We make of those we love what we will, and could scarcely do otherwise, as they are inaccessible to us in themselves. While we fabricate them in our imaginations, however, we do not use them as means, not only because their freedom forever escapes us, but because that love discloses nothing of them to us. We are akin to monads, metaphysically inaccessible in our persons, and epiphenomenal in our bodies and personalities and affects.

These idealized conceptions of love, however, while the stuff of much romantic chatter – of a love eternal or a love sublime – are not the stuff of human life, of human living. While perhaps seemingly noble, their transcendent aspirations mark insistences themselves borne not of love, but of fear. In affirming human transcendence, they locate judgments of beauty among eternal verities secured against time's passage. Conversely, in affirming the sensuous appeal or beauty of a natural body, we acknowledge at once the inevitability of its passage. If we are objects and subjects of such judgments, we too, and those we love, would prove subject to such inevitable passage. For the cult of life, our lone proper, lone moral response to these effects of living is to deny them, to close our eyes, to will ourselves to see life in its transcendent dignity even amid the assaults of time, of illness, of dying. Defenders of this view claim that they are thereby exhibiting the wisdom to locate life's eternal beauty and worth even in its most biologically debased varieties. Yet the absolute worth or dignity they ascribe to life here is itself both wholly disembodied and void of sensuous pull: nothing attaches it to the embodied particulars of specific persons. Moreover, if it inspires any love of persons in their particulars, it does not do so insofar as it signals the enduring presence of a mysteriously intuited moral or metaphysical property, to be flushed out from interstices of flesh and bone. Rather, it would signify our intimate access to a personality to which we lend value. Any person, I suggest, bears no such fully formed properties awaiting revelation as his or her particulars of body and personality and affect are peeled away; that value instead coalesces in and through such revelation of those particulars in their particularities. Such, I will argue, is the metaphysical and moral value of human living, its procreation and bringing into being of particular persons in their novelty and specificity; such also is the metaphysical and moral import of human intimacy, its mutual evocation of embodied human agents.

4
Invasion of the Body Snatchers

4.1 We young immortals?

When Cicero noted that to philosophize was to learn to die, he likely had in mind less a biological process than the progressive detachment, the letting-go, of matters of trivial import to a life well-lived. Steeped in a fine stoic sense that death is part of a providential cosmic order, or a sturdy Epicurean conviction that death is nothing to us, most philosophers of his era counsel equanimity in the face of the inevitable. Even Aristotle, multi-tasker par excellence, for whom no time span would have sufficed to achieve all he wished, recognized the natural terminus of the human lifespan; our deaths mark the end point of our accomplishments, permitting a final evaluation of the worth of each of our lives.

For Epicureans, our biological extinction extinguishes us, such that we do not endure death precisely because we are forever absent to it. The limits of our capacity to sense bound our experience, rendering death insensible to us, and us to it. For Stoics, our deaths are no less ordained than our lives; their timing and manner assuming their own proper place in the cosmos. Against this cultural current, however, and standing in stark relief, were efforts such as Socrates' to depict what contemporary philosopher David Roochnik describes as "metaphorical immortality".[1] Confronting the fearsome prospect of dying, Roochnik suggests, Socrates may have sought mythological support to elide even the possibility of his personal demise. Even if Socrates' speculations were finally metaphorical, however, the idea of an enduring, even eternal soul has proved remarkably durable, culminating not only in the dualistic insistence that a non-physical component outlasts the biological body, but also in the assertion that that soul alone confers upon human beings, and human beings alone, a distinct dignity and moral worth.

So powerful is this idea that it jostles uneasily against our lived experience of grief and finitude. Defenders of the cult of life, in particular, insist both that human biological life be sustained as long as possible, and that biological death ushers us into an eternal life superior to our mundane earthly confines. These theorists hold on the one hand that the dying process reconciles us to our finitude and frailty, and on the other hand that the natural terminus of that process releases us to a greater life beyond our bodily estate. However desirable that eternal life may prove, they maintain, seeking to time or control the manner of our dying, seeking premature relief from the vicissitudes of that bodily estate, signal a "denial of soul," of the full existential weight of our mortality.[2] If we are to find any significance in terminal suffering, if we are to lend dignity to our deaths, we do so only by enduring that suffering. For that reason, the cult of life opposes any form of euthanasia, and most particularly, any species of assisted suicide. For theorists such as Gerald McKenny, for example, such practices are out-sized expressions of individual choice that aim, finally, to eliminate all markers of human finitude.

In contrast, he maintains both that some moral significance can arise only from suffering, and that the willingness to allow – even to demand – that persons suffer at the behest of more over-riding principles sustains a moral community through which persons may reconcile with their finitude. Indeed, he holds, some ills not only cannot but should not be medically eliminated, because we could not develop certain virtues without them. This point is echoed by Alasdair MacIntyre's account of the virtues of dependence.[3] We are, MacIntyre holds, subject to frailty and finitude from birth through death, and caring for dependents – children, ailing or aging adults, disabled persons – occupies much of our moral life. These activities require us to develop virtues such as charity, compassion, and empathy. Moreover, while such virtues may develop only among those who provide care, they invoke in turn virtues distinctive of dependent persons in their role as objects of such care or dependence.

While MacIntyre echoes McKenny in insisting that such dependencies cultivate virtues, neither account specifies how or why illness, disability and the like cultivate – as opposed to simply displaying or revealing, if not dissolving – an individual's character. This suggestion contravenes the common presumption that illness relieves individuals of many moral expectations and responsibilities. Persons acting under the influence of depression or physiological addiction, for example, are more often subject to medical treatment than to moral censure. Schizophrenics are more often medically than morally sanctioned, and such sanctions aim more at medical than at moral remediation. Illnesses and disabilities often suspend obligations of promise-keeping, decision-making and the like, whereas many untoward behaviors are excused on the basis of chemical imbalances. These accounts thereby negate the extraordinary range of ways in which biological constraints truncate, if not eliminate, human agency. Among the starkest examples are brain pathologies such as Alzheimer's, whose associated behaviors are medicated rather than remonstrated with. To be sure, much controversy surrounds our present fondness for substituting medical for moral remediation. But we're simply not likely to see schizophrenics as possessed by the devil any longer, or as exhibiting morally deranged characters. To the contrary, we recognize a vast range of constrained agencies, as, for example, among the very young and the very old, or those with extensive cognitive deficits. We regard such persons as requiring care precisely on these bases, because they cannot evince full blown human agency.

If they cannot enact such agency, however, how are their dependencies the breeding grounds for distinctive virtues? Nowhere is that contention harder to witness than in situations like advanced dementia, where the body – perhaps even the person – remains present, but any meaningful agency has been truncated by tangled brain plaques. On what basis may we assert the virtue of those who have no agent capacities, whose very self-awareness dissipates? We might locate virtue in some patients' on-going struggles to accommodate to disability and suffering and decay. But how can we attribute edifying struggles to those who have neither recollection, nor self-identification, nor perhaps even any recognition of what they've lost? Virtuous activity, insofar as it follows from our rational capacities, would seem to require some substantive sense of enduring human agency. But in cases like advanced dementia, to whom do we then attribute virtuous behavior, and on what basis? We might say, for example, that some virtues of dependence arise instead in learning to accept care, in accepting one's status as a moral patient. Such utterly unwitting submission to what we might term moral patience, however, evokes not virtue, but moral passivity, indeed, moral quietism, and that both among patients and care givers.

In our presence to those enduring the unfathomable, often intractable terrors of advanced dementia, or who are dying, cult of life defenders counsel us not to relieve but simply to share their burdens. Indeed, not only is medical intervention counter-indicated here, but our virtue resides in our refusal to eliminate that suffering. Cult of life defender Leon Kass, for example, demands of such patients that they maintain dignified and stoic attitudes when facing their own deaths.[4] Yet what of those who can make nothing of this suffering? That query is strictly apt, because those who do not espouse the cult of life's theodicy are no less enjoined to suffer and endure at its behest. And even if we grant this grand moral eschatology, can we morally demand of dying persons that they display heroic amid their own dissolution? Such accounts might well demand courage in patients who retain some semblance of mentality and agency. But what of Alzheimer's patients riddled with advanced heart disease or cancer? To demand that they, too, carry on valiantly, makes nonsense of courage and a parody of moral reasoning.

Moreover, with persons whose moral agency isn't yet fully compromised, but simply dissolving under the weight of natural necessity, these positions pose a greater burden. To their physical and psychic dissolution, we shall add the specter of moral judgment: Not only must they bear excruciating suffering, but must do so with courage and dignity, with mute acceptance and submission to the dictates of nature. Here the issue is less with the dying than with their duties and our expectations of them. On this basis, such accounts ignore even the most basic moral tenets, among which is the principle that ought implies can, or that we cannot obligate agents to do things for which they have no capacity. On all such accounts, we should not lower our moral standards for the dying as that would deny their dignity. Not only are we enjoined not to mitigate their suffering, we are authorized to increase their burdens, demanding of them that they face a staunch moral challenge – courage in the face of death – precisely as their agential capacities dwindle.

This conclusion should give cult of life defenders pause even if only because one of their chief laments, in excoriating any prospect of PAS, is our impatience with the dying and suffering, and our unwillingness to tolerate them in our midst. But their point is broader, because they resist equally the dying person's impatience with his or her afflictions. While they valorize patients' agency in enduring such afflictions, they excoriate that same agency when patients' fail to so endure them, or worse, seek premature release from them. In the case of dying patients who might seek premature release from their afflictions, these theorists insist that their judgments of their own lives' worths are morally irrelevant. They must be, because life's value is absolute, and inalienable, wholly apart from any individual's experiences or judgments or choices. But what then we do respect, in valorizing the dignity or sanctity of their lives? And what intrinsic value would a dying person find – or better, create – in enduring two weeks or two months of agonizing pain and delirium, when they could instead die in one hour after a lethal injection? Cult of life proponents would find that very question objectionable on two counts, first because they wish to exclude human will and choice from the dying process, and second because they assert that human life is an unalloyed good, such that we should sustain it even when we suffer enough to desire death.

We have no such right, Kass says, because that would oppose the inalienable right to life that is the moral foundation of all other rights. In support of this view, he approvingly cites Enlightenment philosophers such as John Locke and Immanuel Kant, who, he insists, deny agents both self-ownership and the liberty to destroy themselves. Unfortunately for Kass' argument, Locke makes precisely the contrary point. He notes quite deliberately that a moral agent has no liberty to destroy his life, except where a "nobler" matter than bare self preservation calls for it.[5] In this, Locke echoes the whole of the Western moral tradition in affirming that self-preservation contends with other goods for pre-eminence. We admire the courage of revolutionaries and explorers and martyrs because self-preservation is not an absolute good, because life as they find it is not good enough, because they aspire to worthier aims. We admire those who sacrifice themselves to serve their causes, their people, their ideals, their hopes. If we valorize moral courage, however, we must recognize its imminent threat to bare self-preservation.

This problem becomes even more prominent when Kass approvingly cites another Enlightenment philosopher, Immanuel Kant, as also denying us the right to kill ourselves. Kass grants that this citation may seem odd, since Kant regards the autonomy Kass excoriates as the foundation of our moral lives. Yet Kass reminds us that, for Kant, the human will is subordinate to a moral law that depicts persons as ends in themselves, and that precludes suicide, regardless of an agent's wishes, on the ground that such agents must respect the moral law they bear in their persons. Conveniently eliminated from this discussion, however, is Kant's related insistence that we cannot violate other equally compelling duties, even to preserve our lives. If we must lie, or steal, or break a promise to survive, we have no duty to preserve our lives, because not our lives but our persons embody the moral law. That moral law will continue nicely without me, and should I die in defense of some truth, or in service to a promise fatally kept, I have fulfilled my duty. Our over-riding moral imperative is not to preserve ourselves, but to uphold the moral law. Our unconditioned worth or dignity is contingent on nothing apart from our persons, and certainly not on our self-preservation as biological beings. Indeed, to be a person, to be a moral agent is, on Kant's account, to be an autonomous subject to and of the moral law – precisely in opposition to our animal nature and our desire for self-preservation.

4.2 The duty to live?

Cult of life defenders typically refer our dignity or sanctity finally to a quality or property divinely conferred upon us. If that soul is separable from the body, that body's dissolution poses neither an existential challenge nor a moral task. Moreover, those biological and psychic processes and how we live them attach not to our persons, but only to our contingent embodiment. As such, the moral worth of our persons would prove secure, inalienable, from the moment our souls are created, such that we could neither diminish nor increase that worth through our agency. What we observe, what we feel, the lived experience of these processes, is extrinsic and subordinate to the sanctity and dignity of human life. Indeed, these experiences are wisps of will, subjective ephemera. For the cult of life, whatever our own assessment of our quality of life, or its continued desirability, or lack thereof, we must nevertheless affirm its absolute moral value. That affirmation, however, is no more an intrinsic good than is its denial an intrinsic evil. For the cult of life, the willing affirmation of life's absolute, inalienable worth alone respects the dignity of persons. But that inalienable dignity obtains wholly apart from, and remains wholly unaffected by our agency. We neither create nor destroy, nor increase nor diminish our absolute worth through our actions. As untouchable souls, moreover, we elide the body's subjection to natural necessity. Yet in affirming that transcendent dignity and sanctity under any and all biological states, this position affirms not the value of human life in any natural or biological sense, but of persons. Our distinctive worth thus attends not our individual lives as embodied agents, but our generic status as enduring souls: souls contingently related to the vagaries of living, and to what the cult of life refers to – however incoherently – as the human condition.

Two metaphysical consequences follow here, both with severe moral import. First, this account renders the human body, finally, not a source of moral norms, but a morally neutral object. Second, this account excludes persons from nature's dominion. The hallmark of the cult of life is not recognition of our subjection to natural necessity, but the assertion that, as persons, we transcend that necessity, and thereby alone bear moral sanctity or dignity. Indeed, the very phrase human dignity properly signals an oxymoron, if we mean by "human" anything akin to a natural or biological kind. To that extent, the entirety of our lived experiences – of pro-creating, maturing, ailing, dying – are extrinsic to our persons, and as such, are void of moral significance. The very idea of a bioethic is oxymoronic, as our absolute worth neither attends nor is affected by the vagaries of biological living. Life per se, in its sanctity or dignity, is eternal, and bears no traces of biological constraint. Second, and more strikingly, insofar as natural necessity is wholly extrinsic to our moral lives, and provides no normative constraints on our wills, the cult of life's operative metaphysical assumptions are functionally equivalent to the cult of rights'. For the latter, too, natural necessity imposes no moral norms upon us, because our autonomy transcends nature. Persons prove autonomous agents precisely in their capacity to resist nature's impositions. On this account, the persons depicted by the cult of rights are no more intelligibly either subjects or objects of bio-ethical consideration than are their cult of life counterparts.

Like the cult of life, the cult of rights espouses a metaphysical dualism that leaves unintelligible how the biological vagaries of living or dying could affect us as persons. From its inception, this position's defenders, too, have depicted human worth or dignity as a moral property or quality that transcends nature. For Immanuel Kant, for example, that autonomy obtains not only apart from but in explicit opposition to human nature and in particular to the human body. We enact our autonomy by acting from moral duties, on the basis of rational imperatives void of any subjective, empirical motivations or bodily impositions. These duties command our will categorically: we ought to enact them even if they contravene our wishes, our preferences, or desires – indeed, any personal interests. So conceived, our autonomy not only escapes all impingements of animal impulse but enjoins us to act precisely contrary to such impulses. Indeed, for Kant our primary moral injunction is to make of ourselves what reason commands, i.e. autonomous ends which transcend our nature, which make us, in his terms, better than nature made us. To this extent, it would seem that while autonomous persons qualify as ends, the bodies which mysteriously shadow them would qualify as means only, objects of will vis-à-vis which our autonomy asserts itself. Kant himself often depicts our moral task as one of wresting our autonomy from the deterministic impingements of our animal nature. Neither pleasure nor pain nor happiness nor any other bodily or psychic affect qualifies as a properly moral motive, a properly moral imperative, Kant holds, precisely because such considerations subject the will to natural determinants, dissolving our autonomy. As such, natural bodies can neither authorize moral norms nor impose moral constraints on our wills. Quite the contrary, to admit such impositions would subject the will to what Kant terms heteronomy, its determination not by moral imperatives but by natural impulses. To claim, then, that we ought not to defile our bodies is on this view doubly mistaken: natural bodies in themselves bear no moral imperatives, and any claim to the contrary dissolves the will's transcendence. Absolute moral worth, that is, resides not in human life, but in human persons. As such, autonomous ends, like the cult of life's sanctified souls, elide the vicissitudes of living and dying. Cult of life defenders, of course, oppose suicide because it destroys any basis for the realization of moral values. But the absolute moral worth of a soul endures eternally. For his part, Kant echoes this view, maintaining that in killing ourselves we somehow contravene our status as ends. Here, Kant's objection censures persons who allow physical pain or psychic despair to determine their will. Thereby, he suggests, they reduce themselves to means, subjecting themselves to an alien, heteronymous imperative.

For the moral law he describes to preclude suicide, however, not only must we be capable of killing ourselves, in our persons, but we must also be able to deprive ourselves of our human dignity. Yet we can do no such thing. The moral law, no less than the sanctity of human life, wholly transcends our embodiment. In slaying a body, we can no more kill an autonomous person than we can an eternal soul. Conversely, in slaying that body, we leave untouched the moral worth of the person. We cannot render another person a means to our ends, even in destroying his body, because he remains unaffected by our actions. Similarly, we cannot render ourselves means to ourselves, because our moral worth obtains beyond our agency. We are, after all, ends in ourselves, inalienably, and retain that absolute, transcendent worth regardless of what others do to us, or what we do to ourselves. Indeed, I suggest, Kant can offer no coherent objection to suicide precisely because on his account, nothing of moral value is thereby lost or even imperiled. His primary moral injunction is that we act such that all autonomous agents could act likewise. Yet if all persons terminated their biological lives, the moral law would endure unfazed, as would the transcendent ends it authorizes. Of absolute moral worth are not our empirical selves, but those ends-in-themselves that elide all empirical determinants.

On neither cult's account is human life – in its embodiment – an object of deliberate moral maintenance; nor can it prove a subject authorizing moral norms for living and dying. Both positions, far from beginning with irreconcilable metaphysical premises about persons, unfurl instead from a common origin: human transcendence as the defining element of human worth or dignity. To this extent, however, while both accounts assert the worth or dignity of human life, neither specifies why human living – in its biological embodiment – bears any distinctive moral good, or why its dissolution marks any distinctive moral loss. For the cult of life, human life as created in God's image and imbued with a soul is intrinsically valuable. That intrinsic value endures beyond our deaths, however, such that our transient embodiment adds no intrinsic worth to it. Nor would that embodiment prove an instrumental good, as the soul once embodied can neither increase nor decrease its absolute worth through its actions. We might say instead that embodiment yields natural goods, such as subjective enjoyments and pleasures. Yet designating these experiences as natural goods is meaningless morally, as they add nothing to the intrinsic worth of persons.

While the cult of life takes enduring physical and psychic suffering as moral goods, then, it has no metaphysical basis for doing so. We can define no good for the body, because all conditions and qualities of living are equally good. As such, it makes no more sense to say that enduring pain yields moral value or disvalue than to say that pursuing pleasure, however attained, yields moral value or disvalue, even instrumentally. We cannot, that is, edify or degrade ourselves through our bodies. Nor can we identify health as a natural, instrumental, or intrinsic good any more than we can deem illness a natural, instrumental or intrinsic disvalue. Health cannot be an intrinsic good because our moral worth wholly transcends it; it cannot be an instrumental good because all bodily estates are equally good, and none contribute to our intrinsic worth; it cannot be a natural good because we are enjoined precisely not to favor some health status over another. An identical analysis, however, holds for illness, and on the same grounds. That result yields a more striking paradox: if suffering is an intrinsic good and pleasure an evil, then any efforts to eliminate suffering assert our wills illicitly. If health and normal bodily function are irrelevant to our moral prospects, and if all embodied states are equally good, then medicine per se is immoral if it takes normal functioning as its normative guide.

At the same time, however, the cult of life demands sustained treatment of PVS patients, for example, on the ground that all human life is intrinsically valuable. That intrinsic value, though, presupposes no biological state whatsoever: even being alive adds nothing to the worth of such persons, any more than being dead diminishes that worth.

Nor can such biological estates yield differential moral worth. If life per se is intrinsically valuable, that value either obtains or it does not, independently of these persons' experiences of it. Cult of life defenders insist that all lives retain their value wholly apart from any specific individual's response. But if life's value obtains independently of our experiences, and if persons retain their inalienable dignity independent of their actions, how can the dying persons responses negate or affirm that value? To hold life intrinsically valuable may imply that it enjoins certain responses on our part, such that failure to deliver such responses signifies moral failure. Even in that case, the unassailable value of life obtains regardless of the individual's responses. We can neither deprive persons of inalienable human dignity, nor trump the intrinsic value of life, precisely because it is life per se, not the living person, that is intrinsically valuable. Put differently, just as human dignity is unaffected by our actions, such that we can do nothing to alienate it from us, so too is the value of human life per se unreachable. Both terms render our worth metaphysically unassailable; thereby, they render it morally inert.

This systematic confusion leaves the cult of life in the same position that it excoriates the cult of rights for adopting. For the cult or rights, how we live and die are properly matters of choice not dictated by nature. The cult of life wishes to hold instead that our life processes embody a divinely created nature that authorizes ethical norms. That view ascribes to persons' dominion over nature as creatures made in God's image; yet it insists simultaneously that we contest the evils of the flesh with assertions of will, and resist assertions of the will – paradoxically – by willful subordination to nature's dictates. Despite the cult of life's identification with claims to natural law, it does not assert that whatever is natural is good. Quite the contrary, it demands incessant willed resistance to our natural impulses. Nor does it endorse living in accord with our animal nature, but requires that we assert our dominion over that nature, not only vis-à-vis other species but equally in our own moral lives. Indeed, in its formal elements, the cult of life joins the cult of rights in demanding that we resist central impulses of human nature.

For the cult or rights, reason must assert itself against our animal nature, against our emotional and biological impulses and constraints. To act with reasoned autonomy is to be liberated from such deliverances. On this account, while for the cult of life, illness and physical or psychic impairments mark no diminution in the value of human life, for the cult of rights those contingencies may bear whatever values we ascribe to them. More striking, not only bodily health or function or enjoyment but the entirety of biological living is deemed thereby contingent, inessential to our persons in their absolute value.

The life that the cult of life venerates is not merely indefinable in empirical terms, but is defined in contrast to those empirical trappings. The autonomy the cult of rights venerates is alike defined wholly in contrast to our embodiment. Certainly, both cults aim to under-write distinctive bioethics. Yet on neither account does the human body realize or author or embody distinctive goods. On neither account, moreover, is biological living – in itself – a distinctive good, intrinsically, instrumentally, or even naturally, that is, as a source of experiences valuable in themselves. To that extent, neither account can answer a simple query: what good is living – if it adds no distinctive worth or value to our human lives?

4.3 Death be not proud?

It shouldn't surprise us that neither cult contests the other's dualism, as they are united in a broader moral project: defending human dignity against any incursions of animality. This concert may seem unlikely, since one key battleground dividing the cults is whether human beings who do not display the first person self-awareness, interiority and agency – the functional markers of distinctive human capacity on both views – remain living persons. While the cult of life insists that human life, however marginal, e.g. as in PVS patients, remains fully dignified because it is human, the cult of right regards such dysfunctional lives as incapable of rational autonomy, and thus, as lacking the markers of distinctively human life, of a humanity that transcends biological animality. While these debates are thus often misleadingly couched in terms of the biological or even psychic quality of the life in question, that consideration is irrelevant to both positions. The cult of rights ascribes human worth to our rational autonomy alone; absent that, we are already dealing, effectively, with a living corpse. The cult of life extends human worth to any biologically human organism, yet does so not because the biologically human organism exemplifies any distinctive moral worth in itself, but because it acquires a penumbra of such worth through the infusion of a divinely authored soul. In both cases, morally valenced humanity is defined precisely in opposition to biological animality: we are valuable not because of but in spite of and in sustained opposition to our bodies. For the cult of life, we warrant moral consideration here because we are not animals; for the cult of rights, we warrant no such consideration, as mere bodies, because as such we are mere animals. Both agree: as embodied animals, we are morally worthless.

The cult of life ostensibly denies that latter point in insisting that all embodied states are equally valuable, that all biological states retain equivalent dignity because all equally signal the presence of persons. We cannot morally prefer, for example, biological health or pleasure over ill-health or pain; we must affirm rather that all such states bear equal moral worth. Any biological preference proves at most an animal impulse, and animal bodies yield no moral data. Moreover, to deem one form of biological life preferable to another instrumentally is to illicitly value one over the other: as we neither earn nor enhance our worth through our actions or capacities, no biological state can prove an instrumental good. We must, then, reject health conceived as organic functioning as itself an arbitrary preference: it is neither good in itself, as a natural enjoyment, nor good for the pursuit of any other intrinsic good. As such, the life of a PVS patient is precisely of equivalent worth to that of a fully functional person. As the quality of our biological lives is irrelevant to their worth, life per se is finally the lone object of moral maintenance. On these bases, the cult of life maintains, for example, that PVS persons can be otherwise healthy, and that it's morally obligatory both for them to accede to ordinary or natural means of life preservation, and for others to provide that preservation until the occasion of such persons' natural deaths. On these counts, the cult of life insists that nutrition and hydration always be provided, as they are neither "burdensome" to the patient nor "extra-ordinary" means of life preservation, but rather involve the provision of natural elements of survival.

On their own view, however, we could never illicitly burden persons by burdening their bodies: physical enjoyments add nothing of decisive moral worth to our lives, just as physical vicissitudes subtract nothing from that worth. As such, it is equally incoherent to say that natural bodies merit moral consideration. They may admit of natural enjoyments or goods, in processing food or water, or of natural ills if they do not undertake those processes, but neither is pain bad nor pleasure good in any moral sense. Moreover, no organic capacity of the body to sustain its health or even to perpetuate its minimal functioning is morally preferable to any other, again rendering it morally indifferent whether that functioning be cultivated or not. Moral consideration here attaches to the person wholly independent of any biological state.

But what then are we preserving? The cult of life insists that only by providing such natural needs do we respect the dignity of the person sustained. Persons morally conceived, however, have no natural needs; nor does their worth depend at all upon our moral ministrations. Rooted in a transcendent, eternal soul, not only the quality but the quantity of that biological life is irrelevant to its worth: we can neither diminish one's moral worth by diminishing the length his or her biological life, nor enhance that worth by extending biological life. More strikingly, insofar as even to afford nutrition and hydration reveals a preference for one biological state to another, i.e. the animate over the inanimate, the cult of life opposes its own over-riding injunction: if all biological constitutions are equally valuable, we have no basis even for preferring biological life over biological death. To that extent, even the natural instinct of self-preservation must be precisely that, an animal instinct only, offering no substantive normative guidance. Indeed, for the cult of life, not only must the provision of health, but even the maintenance of biological life, prove finally neither a natural, nor an instrumental, much less intrinsic moral good.

While the cult of life seeks to defend life in itself, then, it does so by abstracting that life from any biological basis, and thereby denies that the human body's natural needs or preferences per se are morally obliging. For as the biological quality of any human life is irrelevant to the moral worth of that life, on no basis are we obliged to provide for the former. Quite the contrary, not only enhancement, but therapeutic and even preventative health care would seem all alike *verboten*, as all would illicitly favor some biological states over others. Cult of life advocates might object that biological life is always morally superior to biological death. The human soul, however, harbors intrinsic moral worth because its life subsists independently of the human body. We have, then, no imperative to cultivate health or to sustain biological life. Rather, we are enjoined not to play God by preferring some states over others, and instead to allow nature to take its course. If all natural states are equally good, moreover, we have no basis, for example, for sustaining the biological lives of PVS patients; quite the contrary, to do so itself also plays God, immorally favoring some biological estate over another.

For the cult of life, we must regard the lives of PVS patients as, at bottom, as desirable and worthy as any others. This same injunction underwrites their objection, for example, to eugenics. Any such efforts to screen out disease or enhance human capacities not only illicitly intrude human will into the natural order, but degrade and dehumanize the persons so selected, rendering them mere objects of human design. Indeed, given the potential to genetically engineer their children, parents must instead affirm that one life is as good as any other.

Eugenic ends are wrong in themselves, regardless of intention or effect, because they deny that all lives are of equal moral worth, whatever their biological fate. This position, however, militates precisely and equally against sustaining the lives of PVS patients. In maintaining their biological functioning, we prefer one biological state to another. Moreover, in imposing such arbitrary preferences upon them, we render them no less objects of human will and of human design, creatures of human manufacture.

Accordingly, the claim that we degrade persons by failing to sustain their lives, in the PVS case, is no more intelligible than is the confounding insistence that we degrade persons by enhancing their health, and presumably their ability to live longer. To say that some medical interventions violate human dignity, we must hold that those interventions affect persons as persons, and that those persons bear some normatively human biological nature. If there is no normatively human biological health standard, however, we have no basis even for separating therapeutic medical measures from enhancing ones. To take a simple example, would hearing aids prove therapeutic or enhancing? To identify them as therapeutic, we would have to identify hearing not only as a statistical preponderance but as a natural norm, as a proper function of human ears, and deafness not as a statistical variation but as an objective dysfunction. The cult of life's account grants the statistical preponderance, but denies any normative preference for one over the other. Hearing aids would not, then, restore proper function, because ears admit of no proper function. Nor, however, would they prove enhancing, on the same basis. The very idea of proper function, as of health, must instead be dismissed, and all medical interventions would prove eugenics by other means.

The cult of life thereby maintains several inconsistent theses: that all biological functioning is equally good, that functioning biological life is intrinsically superior to death, that human life transcends biological function, and that human dignity wholly transcends human biology but lends dignity to body. While its tortured rejection of biological enhancement illustrates this problem, its results span the entire spectrum of beginning and end of life care. Defenders of the cult of life, for example, oppose not only genetic engineering, which they envision as assaulting human nature and truncating human dignity, but also more prosaic enhancements such as steroid use, which they regard as illicitly modifying the human condition. The claim that we have a biological nature that we should not modify, however, exemplifies the same eugenic effort this position ostensibly resists. If no measure of biological function or capacity is normatively human, or definitive of human worth, we can hardly take as a moral project the maintenance of any range of biological capacities, any more than we can imperil ourselves by changing contingent features of our embodiment. The claim that we have a human nature admits of no biological reference; that nature is defined *a priori*, and attached to a supernaturally authored property.

How, then, are biological enhancements from genetic engineering to steroid use even morally valenced, much less objectionable? For the cult of life, such interventions seek to exceed our natural limits. If human nature is a fixed essence, however, we cannot dehumanize ourselves. Conversely, if we can alter our natural capacities, and if all human capacities are equally good, then it does not matter how we modify our bodies, as our worths remain unaffected. Cult of life defenders press their point further, asserting that we both cannot and should not modify our essential nature. Rather, how we are biologically, at any point, should remain the case, sans any incursion of human will. But that injunction augurs against medicine in its entirety, as any effort to restore function or relieve pain prefers some biological states. More strikingly, because biological organisms mutate over time, any effort to keep them as they are, at any moment, would prove eugenic as well. Biological species, after all, are not fixed *a priori*.

Indeed, the cult of life, while excoriating human biological enhancement at every turn, underwrites its own eugenic: the injunction that we keep persons as they are. Cult of life proponents would reject the obvious rejoinder here, that such tasks are themselves patent assertions of human will. To the contrary, they would insist, what's human is natural and what's natural is human. But they insist equally that we are not our bodies, such that they offer no guidance in determining what qualifies as normative of human persons. Human bodies cannot offer such guidance not only because all are deemed equally good, but because they are equally good not in themselves, as biological organisms, but in their mysterious and contingent signification of dignified persons or transcendent souls. The latter need no particular mode of embodiment to exemplify their status as absolutely good; nor can any biological vagaries contest that status.

Indeed, that worth is wholly unaffected even by biological death, such that any moral difference posited between living and dead bodies is purely fictitious. Human bodies, that is, cannot be normative outgrowths of human souls, teleologically unfolded, unless we concur with an Aristotelian view wherein all developmental stages must be realized before full humanness and functional personhood are attained, and must be sustained lest humanness and personhood diminish. The cult of life denies that first point, insisting that human embryos exemplify human souls, and are already complete human persons. The human body is thus not a necessary but a contingent feature of personhood: the latter transcends the former, untouched, finally, by the vagaries of human living.

Defenders of the cult of life wish to assert a contrary thesis: that the human body is an organic or teleological unfolding of the human soul, and thereby attains dignity and moral status as a function of that divinely authored metaphysical substance. It is not, however, on their view a necessary function of the soul, internally constitutive of it, but an extrinsic property contingently attached to it. The soul is what is, completely, in its inception and prior to any human embodiment; moreover, it remains complete eternally, and is neither enhanced nor diminished by the vagaries of biological living. If no bodily status is sufficient or even necessary for full human personhood, we cannot say that specific bodily treatments are dehumanizing or degrading. Even in imperiling the markers of persons – individual subjectivity and agency – we imperil nothing of the soul's essence, either in ourselves or in others. Even the bedrock presumption of the cult of life's recourse to natural law, the imperative to self-preservation, dissolves on this account. Not only is no biological state normative, or necessary to sustain the life of the soul, but the life of the person wholly transcends the life of the body.

For the cult of life, we must reject any functionalist teleology like Aristotle's that roots the value of human life in our realized capacities, and thereby requires biological humans to qualify as persons. Only a teleology wherein persons are complete from their inception and forevermore, this cult insists, affirms the absolute value of human life. Yet so secure is that transcendent value that it requires nothing of us in our treatment of living persons. While this problem systematically undermines the cult of life's opposition to genetic and pharmacological enhancement, it is even more plain in their depiction of end-of-life care, and in particular in their opposition to physician assisted suicide (PAS).

Strangely, while cult of life proponents often lament biological enhancement as an effort to reconfigure the human body to the will's specifications, as an effort to turn a natural body into a machine bearing artificial powers, they advance no comparable objections to the indefinite life-extensions of, for example, PVS patients. Yet nowhere is the vanishing point between human and machine, between nature and technology, more patent. For the cult of life, we must perpetuate such lives by supplying the bodies' natural needs. We can deny that the means to sustaining these lives are patently artificial, however, only if we acknowledge simultaneously that the entire mode of life sustained here is artificial, a creature entirely of human will and artifice. The cult of life insists, in opposing genetic engineering, that human persons should not to be creations of human technology, mere objects of manufacture. Yet that is precisely what PVS patients are, hovering in a man-made netherworld that has no natural cognate or precedent.

The cult of life would object here that sustaining PVS patients signifies respect for the sanctity of human life and the dignity of human persons, so much so that we are obliged to keep such persons alive – even, if need be, against their previously indicated wishes. What then are we respecting? We are emphatically not allowing nature to take its course, but actively arresting the dying process. We thus are not respecting any natural normativity of the body. To the contrary, we are imposing our will in an out-sized effort to combat death. Oddly, while the cult of life opposes genetic and pharmacological enhancements as extending the will beyond natural human boundaries, it sees nothing untoward or artificial about extending biological life beyond the functional capacity of the body. Why resort to machines and artificial interventions to sustain a dysfunctional body but not to enhance a functional one? Strictly speaking, this question cannot be properly framed, as for the cult of life functional and dysfunctional are not moral designations; indeed, they are not even biologically intelligible ones. More to the point, it makes no more sense to do one than the other, because any distinction between the two is arbitrary. A body artificially sustained, a body artificially enhanced, a statistically normal body, and in fact a human corpse, all bear equivalent worth; all are equally good qua human bodies. I emphasize that point because while cult of life defenders often conflate the dignity of persons and the sanctity of human biological life, their own creationist metaphysics drives an unbridgeable wedge between them, leaving it as unintelligible, finally, how the human body could pose any normative constraint upon the human will.

The cult of life wishes to maintain that the body poses natural constraints upon the will. That same body, however, is entirely a construction of that will, a product of moral manufacture, of the insistence that persons are, finally, transcendent souls. The human body could restrain the will's activity only if it harbored some distinctive moral goods or norms that had an authoritative claim upon the will, e.g. that we should resist pain because it is painful, or seek pleasure for its own enjoyment.

Yet the cult of life denies this prospect. Against performance enhancing drugs like steroids, for example, they opine against the grave misuse of human bodies. But the idea of bodily misuse encompasses a normative objection only if the human body both admits of and entails proper modes of treatment as attaching to a normative biological constitution definitive of embodied human persons in themselves. It obtains only if persons are essentially embodied, and only if those bodies bear a distinct normativity, a distinctive agential capacity. Put more directly, the human body itself must prove not merely a patient of the will's evaluations, but a subject and a moral agent in its own right. To hold instead that human dignity transcends the human body voids the term "sanctity of human life" of any normative meaning, insofar as that life circumscribes any biological elements.

4.4 Was it good for you?

The dignity of human persons so conceived is de-humanizing precisely insofar as it alienates persons from their bodies, disembodying them. It is precisely not biological life that bears intrinsic value, such that the sanctity of human life means nothing as a moral norm. So conceived, human life admits of no natural moral norms, but only of the only will's deliverances, apart from which biological life is precisely worthless. That would seem a strange charge to pose against theorists who claim to advocate a culture of life, a culture whose operative bioethic values life absolutely. Yet the absolute value of human life as embodied in PVS patients sustained for years, decades even, if need be against their own previously stated preferences, poses a chilling specter. At the cult of life's inception, what we might term the original Black Death swept medieval Europe. A plague of epic, almost unimaginable proportions despoiled the population, cutting short millions of lives. This moment of history marks a footnote in the dreary confrontation between human life and natural necessity. It reminds us that for millennia, the looming specter of death was that it would come too soon, and we would be powerless to resist or delay it. The new Black Death takes an opposing trajectory: it poses the stark fear that it will come too late, that death will be kept at bay for indefinite stretches, well beyond our capacity to affirm life' continuing value to us. The cult of life, insisting incoherently both that we must sustain biological live as long as possible, and that we must not enhance that life's quality, exemplifies perhaps the chief danger of affirming life's transcendent value: that we sustain it for the sake of sustaining it, with no view to what that life might be good for, what distinctive worth a new life brings into being, and what is lost with that life's passing. The fear hinted at above, that we may die before we die, offers perhaps one clue, a hint referring to the creativity, to the generativity of human living, apart from which we might never pose a bioethic befitting living persons.

Indeed, for all its apparent veneration of human life as the over-riding moral good within bioethics, the cult of life is deeply hostile to human biological life as we know it, and most especially in matters of procreation. Despite its recourse to natural law, this cult posits a ceaseless battle of the human will against an animal nature that threatens ceaselessly to degrade us. Despite its recourse to the natural normativity of the human body as a moral guide, it asserts the wholesale transcendence of human life from any natural order. On these counts, it takes as its moral imperative not the demand that we live in accord with nature in any embodied sense, but that we transcend that nature as the over-riding measure of our moral worth. Accordingly, while the cult of life regards human reproductive practices as morally freighted, it cannot do so consistently given its creationist presuppositions. In denying that persons bring persons into being, therefore, the cult of life voids human pro-creation, like human living and human dying, of any metaphysical substance or moral normativity. While this cult makes extensive efforts to distinguish human from animal reproduction, that distinction is itself irrelevant because divinely authored souls bear at most contingent traces of their human embodiment.

At the same time, this account degrades the human body, denying it any distinctive metaphysical or moral normativity because it excludes it wholly from any creation of value. So conceived, human reproduction proves amoral and epiphenomenal, a locus not for the creation of novel value, but for the endless battle of the human will against human animality. For the cult of life, for example, animal sexual impulses are humanized only within marriage, and only as oriented toward pro-creation. Only that end, this position insists, redirects sexual impulses from selfish and mutually exploitative pursuits, such as pleasure, toward the natural issue of those impulses in their normative sociality, in their production of new life. To pursue pleasure for the sake of pleasure, recall please, is not to indulge an activity enjoyed in itself as a natural good, nor properly to pursue an activity enjoyable in itself, as an intrinsic good; nor can that pleasure prove an instrumental good, for example, in serving the "unitive" function of cultivating marital intimacy, apart from the pro-creative imperative. Even the latter, the cult of life insists, degrades both partners, reducing them to instruments of each other's will, against which only the natural normativity of human reproduction stands as a moral guarantor and bulwark. Our sexual practices, however, are no more affected by the transit of new life coursing through them than is the latter by the former. Supernatural creativity dignifies the persons that instantiate it, not the bodies that contingently attach to them. As such, those bodies neither bear substantive worth in themselves, nor bring such worth about.

We cannot, then, degrade or dignify persons in and through how we treat their bodies. For the cult of life, sexual pleasure requires moral authorization because it degrades persons unless properly oriented toward an intrinsically valued end. As a transitory and contingent matter, attaching to a transitory body, however, it can serve no such function even as an instrumental good. Not only does it pose no distinctive function in maintaining marital intimacy, as a good in itself, it alike poses no such role as an instrumental good in inducing procreation. For the cult of life, recall please, all unitive sexual activity, even between infertile partners, must admit the prospect of a miraculous transmission of new life. So conceived, however, as a contingent locus for the passage of divinely authored life, even playing tennis or gardening would qualify as potentially reproductive activities. The legitimating condition of any sexual activity, after all, is the mysterious arrival of new life, an arrival we can neither conjure nor thwart through our own agency regardless of what we do with our bodies. On this account, in fact, the body proves good for nothing in human pro-creation: not only does it add no metaphysical substance or moral worth to the production of persons, but its animal impulses conspire against the transcendence to which persons properly aspire.

The cult of life thus tries futilely to square an obdurate circle: sexual reproduction. In their vociferous objections to human cloning, for example, they maintain the natural normativity of sexual reproduction in the provision of novel, unique genotypes, while asserting that all persons so created are nonetheless transcendent souls, secure in the first-person awareness or interiority, privacy and agency that mark human persons. The latter conclusion follows directly from the creationist thesis, which, alas, negates the former.

If human persons can be produced through asexual means, then sexual reproduction is neither necessary nor sufficient, nor intrinsically related to the pro-creation of human persons, which occurs supernaturally. Yet if it is extrinsic to the production of persons, on what basis may human sexual activity prove normative? For the cult of life, segregating sexual activity from pro-creation invariably reduces the partners to mutual means. As the case of cloning illustrates however, there is on the cult of life's own position no inherent relation between human reproductive activities and the pro-creation of persons.

To this extent, all such activity makes of others' bodies objects of our use in the pursuit of pleasure, by which we inevitably degrade them. We do so, moreover, whether our own pleasure, or theirs, or both together constitute the object of our designs. Unitive sexual activities apart from their procreative prospects are in themselves illicit, after all, because they take such pleasure as their end, ensnaring us within our bodies, and inducing us to act like mere animals. Pleasure is, after all, not a natural good, but a bodily state to which we are properly indifferent. Nor can it be an instrumental good: as long as we pursue the pro-creative imperative, it matters not at all if we do so by inducing pleasure or pain or indifference in our partner; indeed, neither the actions nor intentions of either partner bear any moral substance here. So conceived, neither the biological body nor its use add metaphysical or moral substance to human pro-creation. Nor, conversely, may super-natural creation of persons add metaphysical or moral substance to human reproductive activities, which remain essentially identical as such to those of any other animal. Put simply, to these immaculate conceptions human sexual activity is wholly extrinsic. If such activities are not morally authorized through their ostensible procreative issue, however, upon what bases could they prove degrading or dehumanizing, or not?

For the cult of life, the respect owed to persons as persons extends a penumbra of dignity around their bodies. Yet that insistence is baseless insofar as the body unfolds not organically or teleologically, but only contingently from the soul. Yet even if we granted that metaphysically implausible thesis, how would we respect human bodies? The persons we're enjoined to respect, however, are by definition disembodied, transcending their bodies most vividly in their bid to eternal life. Moreover, because all lives bear equal worth, neither the particulars of their bodily estates, nor any elements of their personalities can be proper objects of our moral agency. Morally, that is, we can be enjoined neither to advance nor to diminish their health, or their pleasure, or their happiness, as either prospect is equally good; nor may we value persons differentially on the basis of bodies or personalities, as to do so would degrade such persons by making their worth to us arbitrarily predicated upon our preferences.

At the same time, that is, we degrade them equally if we take their pleasure as an object of our activity, or if we take pleasure in the particulars of their persons. For the cult of life, on either approach we attend not to persons as persons, but to persons as they meet our preferences. To take pleasure in another's personality or body, values that person insofar as he or she pleases us. Moreover, we improve matters morally here not at all by taking their pleasure as our end. Quite the contrary, to please them is to entangle them in contingent particulars. Inducing pleasure in them, for example, does not embody a natural good enjoyable for its own sake, but reduces them to their animal impulses. Worse, to take inducing such pleasure as my end degrades them because it renders them objects of my efforts, thereby ostensibly robbing them of their dignity. At the same time, however, that dignity is purportedly inalienable. Moreover, it does not attach to the person as embodied. How, then, do we imperil persons morally by inducing pleasure in them? For the cult of life, pleasure is neither a natural nor an intrinsic nor an instrumental good; at most, it proves an epiphenomenal accompaniment of some human activities. Yet it poses an ever present threat to persons' dignity, exemplifying thereby, presumably, a disvalue, and that not merely as an instrumental means in degrading persons, but as evil incarnate.

That conclusion is inescapable for the cult of life insofar as its lone moral guarantor is divine creativity. What's wrong with pleasure, such that we ought not to regard it as a good in itself? For the cult of life, to take or to induce pleasure in another dehumanizes them, degrading them both to their animal embodiment and to a means to our ends. While the cult of life voids pleasure of moral worth, however, it regards pain as instrumentally valuable, as morally edifying when endured, for example, to affirm the absolute value of life amid dying. On that latter count, the value of that willed affirmation resides in our capacity to resist animal impulses; conversely, the disvalue of pleasure resides in the indulgence of animal impulses. While that indulgence would seem to harbor a moral valence only insofar as it too was willed, however, the cult of life ascribes such indulgences to the body, deeming lust, for example, as much as sin of the eyes as of the will. To this extent, while the instrumental value of pain resides in its inducing us to transcend our embodiment, the disvalue of pleasure resides in its inducing us to affirm that embodiment. As such, again, the body offers no distinctive normativity: its own orientations toward pleasure and away from pain must be precisely reversed if we are to exemplify the dignity of persons. Since we must act precisely in willed opposition to the body's deliverances, however, any moral respect accorded to the body can only be directed to cultivate its transcendence.

That point, moreover, applies perfectly generally to all varieties of human intimacy. In taking another's pleasure or happiness as my end, I identify and try to bring about responses predicated on animal impulses, and solicited not on the basis of their persons, but merely of their contingent bodies or personalities. Strictly speaking, such efforts would seem to leave persons per se quite literally untouched. For the cult of life, however, to take such solicitation as my end not only arbitrarily favors some personal contingencies, but also drags the persons thus indulged into their own animality, degrading them. To say that I come to know them thereby is thus false. They are not accessible to me at all in and through their bodies or personalities because, as persons, they are not their bodies or personalities; they are, rather, their transcendent first-person interiority, privacy and agency, all securely cordoned off in their self-subsistent substances. Amid such interaction, I can discover at most contingent features of their embodiment and personality, features I ought not to value precisely insofar as I value them not as satisfactions for my own preferences, but as persons in themselves. To know them as persons, I need know only their metaphysical status as divinely authored souls; to respect them as persons, I need only turn my attention away from any contingent features, and toward their absolute worth in themselves. That phrase, "in themselves", moreover, is quite literally apt, as persons, instantiated through divine fiat, are wholly self-subsistent.

As such, human intimacy, like human procreation, proves an oxymoron. Insofar as persons can be intimate, they are so only through contingent features of their bodies and personalities, features not at all necessarily or organically related to their persons; self- subsistent substances, conversely, remain in accessible in their persons. To suggest, then, as the cult of life sometimes does, that unitive sexual activity bears moral worth as a means to maintaining marriage, proves false not only because no sexual activity may be morally legitimated by divine pro-creativity, but because human intimacy per se, whether interior to a marriage or not, itself bears neither metaphysical substance nor moral worth. We know nothing of persons, we discover nothing substantive about them, by knowing the transitory particulars of their contingent bodies and personalities. Moreover, we can locate no more worth in those particulars because persons are not their particulars. For the cult of life, we lose nothing of substantive value if we lose our health or function or even biological lives; we remain unaffected through all biological vagaries. Just as we neither come into nor go out of being, so too do these events not bring any substantive worth to us or to others. To say, then, that we should respect persons precludes any recourse to intimacy that attaches to particular bodies or personalities. To respect persons, rather, is to value them all equally, that is, to regard those particulars with equivalent metaphysical and moral indifference.

Absent this indifference, our impulses bewitch us. In asserting this out-sized power of animal impulse over the will, the cult of life thus follows the cult of rights in positing a species of metaphysical shame that attends us insofar as we are objectified by external forces. For cult of rights forbearers such as Sartre, we evince an ontological shame that culminates in the terror of being seen, which reduces us to an object in the other's sight, a creature of his will. This duality is most evident in our embodiment, which contrasts the passivity of the physical body against the agency of the subjective will whose activity wholly that transcends that body. On this account, the problem with being seen is that we're all but reduced to mere flesh. Shorn of our capacity for limitless self-creation, our responsiveness to being seen or being touched – to being acted upon – reveals the body's double threat: it ensnares us in inert pleasure, permitting the other to make of us whatever they will. For Sartre, we are only ever all but reduced to the flesh because we retain our inalienable freedom: the first-person interiority, subjectivity and agency that obtain remain forever beyond the other's reach. We are not our bodies, but our freedom, to the extent that we are anything. In this, his account seemingly poses an unbridgeable contrast to the cult of life's, which insists that we are precisely not self-creating, but created by God at our soul's inception. Despite that difference in metaphysical origins, however, the cult of life echoes Sartre's view of embodiment.

As with Sartre, the cult of life maintains that pleasure is undergone, is something done to us, is an alien imprimatur upon our will. While the human will is transparent and self-directed, the body is occluded, opaque, and receptive to external causes. So conceived, however, it can be at most a passive conduit of the will, not a source of normativity with claims upon that will. It bears, that is, no distinctive intentionality. Moreover, to suggest that the body warrants respect implies not only its normativity but also its subjectivity, its receptivity to moral harm if disrespected. Yet the cult of life negates both such prospects, as it depicts the body neither as essential to nor as constitutive of persons, and as in no way pro-creative. The body, thus expelled from the person, tracks animal impulses which are made moral – or not – at the will's behest. The will does not discover anything like a natural normativity within biological life, but is instead charged with subordinating nature writ wild. To that extent, natural law is an oxymoron, as nature evidences no normativity apart from what is willed invention of moral norms. The dignity of persons, conversely, wholly elides the vicissitudes of biological living. In this way, both cults prove deeply biophobic, dismissing not only the empirical conditions of living – as constitutive of human agency – but also denying any normativity to the body. If we are neither our bodies nor our personalities or any of our particulars, however, not only is nothing essential about how we live those particulars, but we have no basis – or need – for a bioethic to assay those practices.

5
Are We Good Enough?

The future of humanity is coming...to a bookstore or box office near you! It will bring violence, gore, death, destruction, mayhem, maybe a little sex, in other words, business as usual. By this portrayal, I describe here the post-humans envisioned by contemporary bioethicists. Haven't heard of these new creatures? They're long-lived, disease resistant, "better, stronger and faster" even than the bionic folk of television re-runs past and threaten – by definition – to end human life as we know it. Big deal? It is to cultists of both stripes, for whom no creation of fevered sci-fi imaginations is too extreme to eschew moral comment. As a discipline, bioethics is overrun with clones and cyborgs and chimera run amok. Fearsome as those creatures may be, they prove no match for the enhanced humans-cum-soulless-automata, who, defenders of the cult of life would have us believe, threaten to catapult us into a post-human future. Whatever their talents, after all, they would prove merely of human rather than of divine manufacture. Equally manufactured would prove any future persons designed to our specifications, whom the cult of rights would regard as products of our despotism. These future non-persons would mark an impressive feat: so advanced as to render us obsolete, and yet so degraded as to signal the destruction of human life as we know it.

5.1 Dehumanizing human dignity

The dominant concern among these critics is not safety or efficacy. Insofar as such efforts succeed, they fail, as they enhance human life only by degrading it, making future persons the objects of our designs. For the cult of rights, such acts impose our selections on future persons, truncating their autonomy. For cult of life defenders like Hans Jonas, we ought not to impose a determinate conception of our good upon future persons, as they must decide that for themselves. Future persons, however, are contradictions in terms; all persons exist contemporaneously in their personhood. As autonomous ends, such persons are persons sans any reference to their temporal locus. No "oughts" apply to their empirical nature, which their moral worth transcends, such that even extinguishing every embodied human being would leave the value of personhood untouched. To say that we ought not to change future persons, on the cult of rights' operative assumptions, is empirical nonsense, as it is beyond our powers – and moral nonsense besides, if, as critics like Jonas insist, persons by definition should not be the objects of willed moral action at all.

The cult of life takes an even harder tack in maintaining that we are already good enough, metaphysically, as designed by God, and morally, as the scope of our agency is normatively limited by our current powers, which we ought not to augment. However, this account, too, presupposes that human nature both is and isn't immutable. The cult of life, like the cult of rights, disavows genetic determinism, for example, so the human genotype cannot be the prime object of moral maintenance. Indeed, both cults grant, even if that genome is forever in flux as a natural condition of biological life, what's imperiled through genetic engineering is human nature, humanity, the human condition, as defined by our biological constraints and frailties. If those constraints are malleable, though, they are precisely not metaphysical givens, not boundary conditions upon the nature of humanity or the human condition. Conversely, a human nature endangered by biological interventions cannot be defined as transcending them.

This point warrants emphasis because both cults insist that persons should not be made, should not be objects of others' wills or designs – that the rights or the dignity of others preclude such despotism – that persons emphatically ought not to be the products of others' agency, of others' artifice. Yet both cults espouse dualisms that conceive persons – contrary to any biological nature – as autonomous wills or dignified souls – as creatures, that is, of human or divine will and artifice and design. Both cults resist the power and hubris they see in enhancement advocates, who would design future persons in their imagined images. Yet that charge applies equally to these critics, who fashion humanity into their favored cult-chimera. Chimera are, after all, ostensibly "artificial" life-forms made from materials from two species. Yet equally chimerical are the creatures of human moral imagination that both cults pose: eternal souls or dignified persons mysteriously haunting – yet wholly transcending – our biological heritage.

That very dualist hypothesis, of persons as essentially disembodied, essentially transcendent, makes persons no less objects of their creation, no less living artifacts. Indeed, when such critics of all stripes oppose genetic engineers as seeking mastery over human nature, they should note that their own efforts to control such technologies are no less willed assertions, are no less efforts to create future persons in their favored images, as divinely authored or as self-authored creatures. For both cults, for example, genetic engineering is dehumanizing, whether because it makes future persons objects of others' designs, or because it separates human reproduction from human biology. Yet both espouse ideals of human dignity that are themselves deeply dehumanizing. Both disembody dignity from any substantive attachment to the human form, enjoining instead a respect for persons inversely proportioned to any respect for the human body. On this point the cult of rights joins the cult of life in affirming the irrelevance of human bodily constitution for a person's worth: on both accounts, the value of health is derivative, assigned by human will wholly apart from any bodily intentionality.

For the cult of rights, we cannot know in advance what preferences future persons might have. We cannot know, for example, that given a choice between a world with and a world without polio, they would select the latter. Moreover, even if we did extrapolate such preferences to them, we still wouldn't be morally enjoined to act upon them. For the cult of rights, after all, we ought not to make future persons objects of our designs. As such, however, we are not simply proscribed from doing things with respect to them, i.e. proscribed from selecting for them. That injunction is much more general: since they ought not to be objects of our designs at all, we can no more say that we are morally obliged to select for them than that we are obliged not to select for them. We have no obligations – indeed no substantive moral relations to them at all – except insofar as they are identical to us, i.e. in the transcendent autonomy that remains beyond our reach. Precisely on that basis, it makes no moral difference whether parents select maximal health, refuse to select any particular health status, or select severely disabling diseases for their children. All are equally valid options because none affect the persons those children already are – whether as eternal souls or as transcendent ends.

For the cult of rights, autonomy transcends biology, rendering any particular embodiment a matter less even of moral choice than of moral indifference. The moral matter here is the exercise of autonomy, and as no exercise of the parents' autonomy can substantively restrict the child's, the specific contents of their choices – or even their willingness or refusal to choose – are alike matters of moral indifference. To object that they harm the resulting child morally by selecting one material form rather than another would on this view mistake a contingent fact about the child – its bodily comportment – for its worth, i.e. its autonomy. Moreover, to say that parents deprive a child of autonomy by selecting a disabling condition, e.g. severe brain malformation, presupposes that human autonomy requires some biological substrate for its exercise, a point this position rejects.

For the cult of life, similarly, persons transcend their biology. Nor does any child, qua person, result from the parents' actions or moral agency. On either account, to say, for example, that parents who could have prevented some biological disability but chose not to, thereby harming the resulting person, wholly mischaracterizes the point, as the parents' actions do not affect the child qua person at all. Parents and children bear no moral relation to each other as persons. Not only can parents not help or harm their children thereby, but they are in no intelligible way obliged to cultivate a particular biological constitution for the child. Nor could they be subject to moral censure. Ought implies can, after all, and to face a morally freighted choice here, parents would need either to identify a good to be independent of the child's preferences, or to identify an option that helped to constitute the child's good as a person. But health on both views is preference-dependent value, and in principle not assessable *a priori*, since it attaches to contingent embodiment, residing outside the domain of moral goods. Nor can we identify any goods for others. These injunctions thus prove self-refuting, as they oblige us to eschew making future persons objects of our design – while presupposing that that are not and cannot be such objects.

Indeed, while defenders of both cults insist that in advancing these positions they defend human dignity, there is nothing human about the dignity thus depicted, if we mean by "human" any biological reality. On both accounts, bioethics would be a contradiction in terms, as our moral worth transcends our animality, unfettered by human constraints.

That result is inevitable, because the concerns both cults advance aim to defend human dignity not simply from biotechnology but from biology per se; not from what we do, but from what we are. Both cults obsess so over questions of human identity, I suggest, not because they worry that that identity will be changed – as it could not be, if their operative assumptions are true – but that it will prove not as they wish to see it, in its grand transcendence, but as it is, in its essential embodiment, its essential transience, its vulnerability to the human agency that it both evokes and underwrites. The challenge here is not, as is often supposed, a clash between the scientific culture of biotech on the one hand and the humanistic or religious cultures that the cults of rights and life reflect on the other. It is rather that both cults finally deny that human persons really ail, suffer, die – which is to say that they really live, biologically speaking, and thus that the problems these biotechnologies address are substantively human problems.

To the contrary, both cults, in their very conceptions of human dignity, place the human body under direct, sustained attack. Both cults imply, for example, that a human world with preventable debility is better than one without: for the cult of rights, because we do not thereby impose our preferences upon future persons; for the cult of life, because whatever occurs naturally is good. Given the option of sparing future persons polio or Alzheimer's, then, we ought not to do that. Why? If persons are not their bodies, that injunction has no moral basis. Only if changing our bodies does change us does the question matter morally. If our bodily constitution affects our persons, we cannot avoid imposing a future upon others regardless of what we do. If we can prevent such diseases, but choose not to, it is strictly false to say that we are letting the future take its course, as that phrase embodies a neutrality and moral agnosticism no longer open to us. If we can prevent such diseases, but choose not to, the resulting future includes the fact of that choice unmade, of that possibility unrealized. It includes quite the opposite, in fact: a deliberate judgment on our part that a future with those diseases is better than one without. Yet our actual choices have been precisely contrary, as, for example in the case of polio. To say that the future was taking its own course before a vaccine became available is factually true. Once a vaccine did become available, however, to accept or reject its use equally became choices.

5.2 Disabling persons

The hoary moral phrases offered by each cult – the cult of life's "allowing nature to take its course", or its cult of rights equivalent, "allowing the future to determine itself" – too conveniently bury the operative imperatives of both cults. To refuse to prevent such conditions, when we have the power to do so, does not simply allow a future to unfold independently of our actions or inactions. The very terms (i.e. allowing nature or the future to take their courses) betray the agency rejected here, and no linguistic sleight of tongue absolves us from this. To allow either of these eventualities is to knowingly and deliberately disable future generations, insisting that they are better off with the debilities that have defined human existence up to now than they would be without them. These injunctions demand – on the basis either of an ostensible love of life, or of respect for human autonomy – that human beings remain, biologically, beasts of burden, staggering under the weight of relievable frailty. These approaches at the same time seek to disavow any responsibility for that perpetuation, rendering it instead as a proper veneration of human dignity. In the service of spiritual purification, the cult of life imposes upon future persons preventable suffering, willfully mortifying the body to serve a transcendent end. In the service of human dignity, it imposes upon future persons its own vision of what humanity ought to be – a vision rooted not in our biological nature, but in unremitting hostility to that nature; it imposes upon future persons, in service to a transcendent ideal of its own artifice and design, a vision of dignified human life defined wholly in opposition to life as we know it biologically; it imposes upon future persons, that is, an ideal creation of its own will – itself "playing God" under the guise of serving God.

By playing God, the cult of life itself means to describe an out-sized exercise of human will. Yet in wholly alienating human dignity from human embodiment, it not only deprives the body of any moral authority but thereby undercuts any natural constraints upon its own injunctions. While they infamously oppose "playing God," by which they mean setting terms of entry into the human community, they do just that in requiring that we impose upon future persons a forced frailty and medical malaise as a condition of their sharing in human nature and the human condition. It thereby commends its own variant of genetic and cultural cloning, requiring that we hand over to future persons biological and social constraints identical to those that we inherited. The future persons they seek thereby to defend from genetic engineers are, in their hands, no less products of hubris, of narcissism, of pride, of egoism, of the insistence that they be just like us as conditions of retaining their humanity and moral worth. Indeed, both cults bury the extent to which they engage in eugenics projects of their own, not by deliberately selecting one designed future, but by just as deliberately refusing to select, and by thereby deliberately imposing, current biological and social constraints upon future persons. That conclusion is inescapable, as biological vagaries are no longer the exclusive domain of God or nature or of some undetermined and unimaginable future, but admit of substantive choice that requires us to defend – where previously we did not – why, given alternatives, the current set of constraints is the best available to us and to our successors. The cult of rights, conversely, uses different language to advance the same premise.

They would oppose the above suggestion, for example, by insisting that the existence of biotechnologies does not enjoin us to use them in particular ways. The issue here, however, is not that we ought to use such technologies simply for the sake of using them; it is rather that in using them we may forestall demonstrable harm, whereas not using them opens future persons to those potentially preventable harms. The cult of rights here might join with not only the cult of life but the great bulk of Western moral theory in identifying acts of moral commission as more morally freighted, in themselves, than acts of omission. Yet the two here are equally deliberate and equally determinative of a particular future. In the case of polio vaccines and the like, for example, their use does not pose a future with polio as against an indeterminate future wherein nature passively pursues its own course. It poses a much more dramatic contrast, that between a future with polio and one without. On that count both cults, in demanding that we not make future persons objects of our design, thereby decisively choose the former option, affirming that a future which merely permits polio morally supersedes a future that deliberately engineers one without.

Both cults might object here, again, that in preferring the former option they are respectively affirming the value of human life or of human autonomy. But to hold that future persons ought to endure preventable disabling conditions in order to secure their dignity or autonomy espouses a bizarre moral agnosticism. In negating any positive responsibility we may have to those future persons, these accounts alike render unintelligible how we could have any negative obligations to them. On both counts, we have no positive obligations whatsoever, as persons are secure in their persons; yet an identical analysis holds for any negative obligations, on precisely the same basis. To say that we ought not to prevent such harms mutually entails that we ought not to pursue any goods on their behalf. As such, not only are we not enjoined to use such technologies, or even proscribed from using them, but we should not even develop them. All they can do, after all, is imperil – however inexplicably – transcendent human dignity or autonomy.

These injunctions exemplify a bizarre moral agnosticism because both cults unite in enjoining us to deliberately maintain scientific ignorance and technological incapacity. This deliberate maintenance of incapacity, moreover, unlike its epistemic counterpart, has immediate practical import. To withhold our belief because we lack evidence for a claim is one thing; to withhold our actions on the basis of our deliberately retarded scientific or technological capacities is quite another. In the former case, we merely acknowledge our factual incapacity; in the latter, we make of that incapacity an object of moral maintenance. Indeed, despite their self-proclaimed concern for future persons, both cults systematically and deliberately restrict the range of our potential obligations to them. If ought implies can, both void any oughts we might have with respect to future persons by deliberately diminishing the scope of what we can do, truncating any expansion of responsibility that might arise from such technological advances. Both cults, in fact, deliberately decouple technological expansion from any cognate expansion of our moral capacity and responsibility.

That point bears emphasis because on both approaches the dignity or autonomy of future persons not only restricts what we may do to or for them, but makes of our very self-induced powerlessness a measure of our moral probity. The cult of life, for example, deliberately makes matters of contingent historical fact, of past necessity, for example our inability to prevent or remedy certain diseases, into conditions of future virtue. They shift our default moral option from making a virtue of necessity – as in finding meaning in inevitable suffering – to making such necessity into a virtue for all time – in deliberately imposing that same suffering on future persons so that they can find the same meaning we did, even if it need not be a "necessity" for them any longer. Yet in reveling in "the nature of things" it induces an adolescent romanticism that occludes our responsibility for the conditions of human life. One such proponent Joel Garreau, for example, proposes a "Shakespeare test" as a means of recognizing future persons, who would prove human insofar as they identified with the common problems which have historically beset human beings.[1] As a measure of human identity, this standard might prove sensible if future persons both will and should face challenges identical to ours. Yet these theorists offer no defense, finally, for why we should impose upon future persons a future like ours, like the human past, complete with our frailties. At bottom, these views reduce to the insistence that these frailties are true and good and just simply because they're ours, because they've always been ours – and therefore always should be. On these counts, we might just as well update Garreau's suggestion somewhat and propose a Seinfeld test, qualifying future persons as human insofar as they prove as self-obsessed, neurotic, and navel-gazing as we. This current obsession with what it means to be human is after all a quintessentially adolescent indulgence, which presents the illusion of moral activity while sparing us any real ethical work in offering a better future for our successors.

It's equally an exercise in human hubris, a point lost on both cults, who present themselves as defending future persons from present person's out-sized pride. The cult of rights, for example, sees in its moral inactivity, in its refusal to judge among preferences, a signature of respect for future persons' autonomy. In opposing genetic enhancement, for example, they emphasize not the potential material risks or rewards of such interventions, but the *a priori* insistence that human life ought not to be an object of our design. The basis for that claim, however, is that persons are valuable in their inviolable capacity to choose, and wholly independently of any particular choices made. As such, our choices not only leave others unaffected but ourselves as well: We are all alike inviolable, not as the results of our own agency but because we are transcendent ends that we had no hand in creating. To imply, then, that future persons should be like us begs the critical point that that, on the cult of rights' operative assumptions, they will be whether they wish to or not, just like we are. We can no more modify them as persons than we can modify ourselves, secure as we all are in our self-determining capacity.

The choice both cults present, then, between keeping people essentially as they are, and catapulting ourselves into a post-human future, is patently fallacious. Both deny and presuppose the same premise: that sustaining human life is not a matter of moral inertia but of deliberate cultivation and maintenance. Moreover, both ignore that the most vividly post-human creatures that populate bioethics discussions are the transcendent specters both cults envision. For the cult of life, human persons are really eternal souls mysteriously haunting human bodies before securing their place in a post-human reality. For cult of rights, human persons are unaffected automata, brought into being through no human acts, and wholly transcending any merely human or merely animal determinants.

At the same time, while the cult of life defends the soul as harboring a self-aware moral capacity that separates humans from other animals, in matters of the gravest import, that agency is charged not with doing anything but with submitting to divine decree. For the cult of rights, conversely, while our autonomous capacity instantiates our transcendent moral worth, the specific decisions we thereby author are no more or less momentous than selecting paint colors or favorite sports; the autonomous person, after all, while self-determining, cannot be defined by any particular set of choices.

How, then, does anything we do with respect to these extrinsic processes of living pose the "implications for humanity" that both cults posit? On neither account is the human self a real agent, in the sense of bring distinctive value to world in his or her choices or actions. For the cult of life, absolute value attends the person by virtue of his soul; for the cult of rights, absolute value attends the person by virtue of her capacity for unfettered choice. Neither the particulars of body or personality or temporal locus, nor the specific content of one's choices, qualify persons as persons. As such, we are neither our transient bodily or psychic experiences – of pleasure or pain, emotions or affects – nor our choices or preferences – insofar as we are persons. To the contrary, as all of the latter embody at most arbitrary preferences, we instantiate goodness only in our persons, and we neither augment nor diminish it through our pursuits or through what we make of our empirical or transitory selves. We are our persons, that is, not out personalities or our characters, which alike leave our worth as persons untouched. As persons, conversely, we are neither really transformed by nor transformative of our experiences.

For both cults, inviolate persons are the lone loci of moral worth, the signature of first-person self-awareness and moral agency. Yet if persons are absolutely valuable, by metaphysical or divine fiat, we can neither enhance nor diminish that value through our actions. Nor, more strikingly, can anything we do to our bodies have any moral consequence. What, then, do we defend when aiming to secure human life or human autonomy, if we have, by nature, nothing to lose? For both cults, human persons are authoritative over their own experiences insofar as they exhibit self-aware agency. The dignity of the person, however, attaches neither to the privacy or interiority or subjectivity of a mind or psyche, nor to the particulars of a specific body, nor to the specific content of one's moral choices and character. It attaches rather to the transcendent status of personhood. As such, it is an not unduly intrusive demand of any particular person that he or she endure, in body or mind, pain that can be remedied, or any measure of psychic or physical ministrations, in service to human dignity or autonomy. On both of these accounts, neither the body nor the psychic subjectivity of the person per se has any normative claim either upon the person or upon other persons.

The cult of life, for example, enjoins dying persons to endure all manner of suffering to sustain the absolute value of human life, even if this particular mode of living garners no bodily or psychic satisfactions for the person or any others. Rather, dying persons, particularly those who might otherwise wish to die, ought to act precisely contrary to their preferences. At the same time, while the cult of life enjoins such persons not to shorten their lives, it does not require of them they prolong those lives as much as possible. The first prospect, they insist, intrudes human will into natural processes, whereas merely declining further life extension allows nature to take its course. Allowing nature to take its course, however, no more or less asserts human will than does its contrary. Moreover, not only are agents permitted to let nature take its course, they may even expedite that result so long as that expediency is an unintended by-product. Such persons may, for example, seek pain palliation even to the point of inducing death, so long as that death is not what the palliation intends. This infamous doctrine of "double effect" ostensibly absolves us of any agency in bringing dying about, rendering the death an unfortunate externality to the intended effect of relieving pain. This doctrine's own intentionality, however, is rarely called into question: ought we to valorize a moral principle that aims in its inception to relieve of us of any responsibility for the quite predictable effects of our actions? For the cult of life, so long as we do not intend death, our actions are licit.

Intentions, however, should on that view themselves bear no moral weight. Persons' mysterious instantiation of human life alone marks absolute value. We may no more diminish that value by what we intend, or what we do to our own or others' bodies, if for example, we kill those bodies, than we may augment that value. At the same time, even if we could somehow affect the value of human life through our agency, considerations of pain or suffering could in no way underwrite moral ends. Those experiences, precisely in their bodily and psychic interiority, are mere ephemera, metaphysically and morally. They do not at all qualify the goodness of life per se, which we must affirm wholly apart from any such experiences. On the cult of life's operative assumptions, of course, nothing we do affects our own or others' persons. Even if that were the case, however – and this contrary to their account – the intent to relieve pain could never prove a moral injunction. To endure pain, recall, is a moral imperative, an affirmation of the absolute value of human life. As such, even the intent to ally pain should prove morally suspect, as it prefers one biological state over another. The cult of life, of course, opposes the cult of rights precisely on the enactment of such preferences. Yet for the cult of rights a similar analysis holds: if we are to exercise our autonomy, it cannot be at the behest of physical or psychic affects like pain or suffering. Quite the contrary, dying persons may exercise their autonomy only to the extent that they bracket it off from such constraints.

For the cult of rights, that is, we may exercise our autonomy only insofar as we are self-determining, by which they mean free of any physical and psychic constraints; for the cult of life, we may exercise our agency only insofar as we affirm God's initial valuation of human life. The self-determining self thus remains forever empty, in itself, precisely insofar as it retains its autonomy; the eternally valuable self remains forever its absolute worth as divinely authored, precisely insofar as it remains itself. As such, on neither view does bodily or psychic dissolution imperil our first-person interiority or agential capacity; our dignity or autonomy endure untouched by the biological vagaries of living and dying.

At the same time, both cults advance their own conceptions of what has become a holy trinity in bioethics, the stirring defense of human privacy, dignity and modesty. This triad bears emphasis because it assumes enormous pride of place for both cults despite their insistence that persons are neither their bodies nor their psyches. If we are none of those things, unfortunately, no moral prescriptions follow about their treatment: instead, persons as persons alone authorize moral norms. Or, more accurately, both cults reserve to themselves moral authority over the ultimate disposition of such persons.

The cult of life infamously opposes anyone playing God, a role it arrogates to itself. The cult of rights likewise arrogates to itself the supervision of others' exercising their autonomy, on terms decided by – the cult of rights. Both thereby alienate individuals' decisions not only from those individuals, but from the lived embodiment amid which those individuals make such choices. In the case of physician assisted suicide (PAS), for example, the cult of life seeks to defend persons from their own choices, securing patients' dignity – even, if need be, against the latter's will. Cult of rights defenders, in contrast, permit individuals to make such choices; nevertheless they require that persons exercise that right only upon meeting criteria for autonomous choice defined by the cult of rights. Such individuals, for example, must be already terminally ill, in unremitting pain, and screened out for depression and the like. They may not, conversely, decide that their lives are no longer livable to them simply because, for example, they have degenerative neurological conditions, or are in the early throes of Alzheimer's, or suffer unremitting depression.

Accordingly, while for the cult of life we may not legitimately decide the value of our own lives to and for ourselves, for the cult of rights we make such decisions only if we do so rationally; in the former case, the cult of life, ostensibly at divine behest, is the first and final arbiter of the worth of our lives; in the former case, the cult of rights, ostensibly at reason's behest, is the first and final arbiter of our rationality. Both cults endeavor here to distinguish unlivable from merely undesirable lives: the cult of life by denying that the latter in any way entails the former, and the cult of life by segregating rationally defensible from irrational preferences. The cult of life thereby voids all such agent preferences of any normative weight, while the cult of rights ascribes such weight only to preferences that can be wholly segregated from physical or psychic distress. On the latter view, for example, unremitting pain per se is not a sufficient basis for a rational preference to end one's biological life, apart from a terminal diagnosis and screening out for any psychic maladies. Nor, on the former view, is it ever a basis for withdrawing the absolute value of one's own life. On both accounts, importantly, we act as moral agents only insofar as we act as transcendent persons whose agency is wholly un-occluded by our bodily or psychic states. Any personal preference to die as underwritten by the physical or psychic dissolution of an empirical self is thus demoralized, because those constraints deprive us of our agency. Whether by divine or logical decree, each cult locates moral authority not in embodied individuals, but in transcendent persons who do not, finally, ail or suffer or die. These accounts do more than de-humanize the human person undergoing these experiences, alienating them from the physical and psychic vagaries of living; they thereby wholly invalidate the reality and the value of that person's interior and embodied life – the reality to which they ostensibly pay homage in valorizing the privacy, modesty and dignity distinctive of human life.

They pose thereby a twin moral assault: in enjoining persons to endure what they might deem unendurable, both cults render unreal, epiphenomenal, and reduce to moral ephemera any bodily or psychic interiorities persons might bear, and replace that kind of living subjectivity and agency with a transcendent specter entirely authored by others. As such, despite their ostensible allegiance to the inalienable or inviolable dignity of human persons, both cults thereby wholly alienate that dignity from living persons, voiding them or any worth, in themselves, as themselves. That latter coda is critical here, as it underscores the extent to which neither cult offers an intelligible account of what its operative moral injunctions defend in their defense of persons. Disembodied persons require no modesty; unfettered wills require no privacy; transcendent persons require respect neither for their dignity nor their autonomy, which are invulnerable to time, to others, to the vagaries of living. So transcendent is this transcendence that it entirely escapes us, elides nature, elides not merely human life but the entirety of human physical and social and moral reality as we know it.

That point is illustrated vividly by Sartre, whose famous formula – that we are not what we are – throws the matter into high relief. For Sartre we are not what we are – as mere things are what they are – because we can always choose to be otherwise, such that it is false to say that we are anything whatsoever. Most pointedly, recall please, we are not our bodies, which present themselves as objects both to the other's gaze and to our own. Those bodies render us ostensibly visible to others, naked to their gaze. Yet we are not reducible to what they see. Rather, we retain our transcendence, escaping from their grasp; even if we try to see ourselves as they see us, try to reduce ourselves to objects, we do so only at our own behest, as a function of our own wills. For Sartre, we remain forever malleable because we can always choose to be other then we are at present. At the same time, however, Sartre describes with dismay the body's resistance to the will, along with its subjection to the gaze of the other, to gravity, to natural necessity, and indeed to everything of which the will is free. An analogous ambiguity attends the cult of life. On the one hand, defenders of this approach predicate norms of bodily modesty in particular on the premise that interactions of sight or touch among persons may prove uniquely intimate, rendering us accessible to each other in ways that may occasion distinctive moral harms. Persons, however, are invisible, and impervious to touch; their particulars of bodily and psychic life are not only epiphenomenal, but not even distinctively theirs.

At the same time, however, for the cult of life revelation of the body must be severely restricted, not only because it may incite illicit responses in others, but also because being looked upon as such alike degrades the person seen. Strangely, however, while reveling and seeing the human body are both widely proscribed on this view, as exemplifying moral harm to both parties, bodily modesty per se admits no such moral claim amid end-of-life care. In opposing physician assisted suicide, for example, the cult of life not only dismisses any physical pain as a moral consideration, but disregards any psychic distress that may attend being seen as one dies, as one dissolves before others' eyes. Against the familiar charge that much end of life care is not only futile but painful and humiliating, the cult of life maintains that such considerations signal our out-sized pride rather than the proper acceptance we should have for our dependence upon others in extremis. Not only should we accept unremitting pain and psychic distress in the face of impending death, we should equally endure with equanimity, possibly amid ever encroaching paralysis or dementia, whatever humiliations might accompany our being turned inside out before others' eyes, as a proper constraint upon our pride.

5.3 No additives, preservatives, or fillers?

On the cult of life's own operative assumptions, however, we admit no such incursions. For the cult of life, such forced intimacy and any shame that may attend it accompany our refusal to accept our finitude. Yet bodily finitude leaves us untouched, and our willingness or refusal to accept it should alike prove morally meaningless, as neither subjective state qualifies the worth of persons as such. Among the great ironies of contemporary bioethics, then, we must count the extent to which wholly supernatural conceptions of human dignity underwrite endless dispute over the natural normativity of human nature. The cult of life, for example, famously opposes unnatural interventions into human dying or reproductive practices as imperiling the transcendent dignity of human persons; yet those persons are by definition supernatural. Thus begins a series of irremediable metaphysical muddles: in vitro fertilization and cloning, while artificial, still yield divinely ensouled persons, secure in their receipt of this supernatural additive. Births assisted by fertility drugs, while unnatural, alike yield eternal souls, secure in their possession of this ultimate metaphysical preservative. Genetically altered humans, should they emerge, also bear the personhood that infuses them with human dignity, filling an unnaturally constructed body with inestimable moral worth.

The cult of rights, of course, resists such ascriptions of unnatural reproduction, denying that any natural or statistical norms are in their mere occurrence and regularity thereby rendered normative. We do not, they insist, imperil persons' dignity simply by reproducing them through technological means. The dignity so conceived, however, obtains because it is no less transcendent, no less supernatural, than that espoused by the cult of life. Indeed, on this account too, it proves a mysterious metaphysical additive, a preservative of inalienable human worth, a filler of human autonomy sans any reference to a particular agent. On both approaches, that is, human dignity is a metaphysical and moral given, a primitive datum or transcendent property of human persons, and not itself a product or achievement of human artifice or agency. A fixed, immutable property, however, not only requires no moral maintenance, but prescribes no natural norms; it neither requires any exercise of moral agency, nor proscribes any human practices. To admit of any moral norms, rather, human persons must embody a gap between what we are and what we might be – a gap that may be traversed by human effort and will.

If, after all, persons are simply and inalienably and absolutely valuable, we neither need do anything to bring that value into being, nor do we imperil it by anything we do in bringing persons into being – precisely because we do not bring persons into being at all; they are, rather, either divinely authored, or, essentially, *causa sui*. Were either position right, the specter of reducing others to means to our ends or products of our imagination would remain just that, a fanciful specter. More strikingly, neither as human persons nor even as particular persons are we in any intelligible sense subject to moral evaluation. For the cult of life, persons retain equal and absolute worth regardless of their actions; their agency does not at all qualify their worth as persons. For the cult of rights, persons retain their equal and absolute autonomy regardless of the specific contents of their choices or actions; their worth, too, resides not finally in what they do with that autonomy, but with the fact of its occurrence. On these accounts, critically, not only is one's own specific moral personality or character or embodiment of agential capacity extrinsic to one's worth as a person, but that capacity per se is metaphysically and morally inert. Its transcendent occurrence alone secures our status as absolutely valuable: it neither evokes moral maintenance in us, nor requires us to regard others in particular ways. We cannot alienate ourselves from our autonomy any more than we can from our souls. More vitally, if we cannot make of ourselves or others objects of moral assessment, then we have no basis for moral agency.

That point bears emphasis on three counts. First, the very prospect of recognizing moral norms presupposes that we may act in alternative ways: were our goodness simply ceded to us *a priori*, we could neither surrender nor augment it no matter what we did.

Were the natural simply good, and the good simply natural, for example, we would be what we ought, sans any effort on our part. Conversely, to say that we ought to live according to our human nature begs two critical questions. The very assertion of an ought presupposes the existence of counterfactuals: we can only say we ought to act in one way rather than another if we face several options. On that account, whatever is deemed morally normative of nature must be defended as such. Precisely on that count, however, the very effort to specify some such natural processes as uniquely normative is itself unnatural; that is, it is a product of human artifice and agency. Put simply, not only can we not infer conclusions about what is moral or immoral directly from what is natural or unnatural, but the effort to segregate natural from unnatural practices of living itself presupposes reference to moral assessments themselves not natural but normative.

For cult of life defenders, any natural norms are of course not merely natural but divinely authored, as the basis of their normativity. Yet if everything that occurs naturally is by nature good, we again need no moral norms. Nor have we any basis for separating artificial or unnatural interventions into human activities, as any willed activities would by definition qualify as artificial and unnatural. Indeed, even the most ostensibly natural practices, such as unfettered pro-creation within marriage, would prove unnatural and artificial, insofar as they would harbor human will and intent in the production of persons, which cannot itself be in any way a moral end. To say that all human marriages ought to be pro-creative, or even that sexual activity ought to be pro-creative, after all, not only illicitly prefers some species of biological life and function over others, but takes the production of persons as an intentional end in itself. Any such injunction, moreover, contrasts the premise that whatever occurs is good with the counter-factual assertion that some events – rather than others – ought to occur and are morally preferable.

Such injunctions, moreover, imply not only a metaphysical but a temporal gap between what is and what ought to be. If we simply are, as an *a priori* metaphysical fact what we ought to be, neither individual nor collective moral agency yields anything akin to moral progress or amelioration, or regression. Both cults worry that we might destroy human nature or dignity by rendering future persons the objects of our designs. Yet persons are timeless, and on neither account can they be identified as "future" in any sense. At the same time, both cults assert that we ought not to modify future persons, and that they ought to remain in their persons identical to us. If they remain identical to us as a matter of metaphysical fact anyway, however, the future is a matter of moral indifference to us. We can neither improve nor degrade it through our efforts, any more than we can improve or degrade ourselves, over the course of a lifetime, through our actions. To the contrary, I suggest, if moral agency is to prove anything more than epiphenomenal, not only must a gap obtain between what we are and what we ought to be, but we must be able to traverse that gap by remaking ourselves. We must, that is, regard ourselves as objects of our design, and re-design, as a condition of regarding ourselves as moral subjects or agents. In enacting our own agency, we must be able to objectify ourselves, to identify that some counterfactual ought to be brought into being, and to bring them into being through our own willed efforts. We must not only be able to designate such counterfactual as oughts, in other words, but render them realities, embodying them in our practices and in our persons insofar as they qualify as moral or practical or normative.

That point illustrates the third one hinted at above, that human moral agency per se is a product of human artifice, of the creative capacity to bring counterfactuals into being. The issue here is not merely that, lacking alternatives, we would need no norms; nor is it that, just as we must reject the naturalist fallacy – the insistence that whatever is natural is by definition good – we must equally reject what we might call the super- naturalist fallacy – the insistence that only properties of supernatural origin yield moral worth. Both cults identify human worth with such transcendent properties. More importantly, however, both cults arbitrarily ascribe that status to human persons, either by divine or natural fiat. As such, neither can describe any human conditions which would imperil or preserve that status. For the cult of life, God alone unilaterally confers that status upon persons, who can neither augment nor diminish it. For the cult of rights, that status emerges wholly mysteriously from nature or human nature. Persons on neither view play any role in the provision or cultivation or even the truncating of that status. Persons are not, on these accounts, moral subjects or objects at all; they are neither products of human agency nor ends in any intentional sense. For the cult of rights, we respect such persons, finally, not by recognizing their agency or first person identity or character, but by ignoring them, by refusing to make them objects of our moral judgments. For the cult of life, we respect such persons, finally, not by identifying their distinctive functions as persons, or their distinctive personalities, but by regarding them as all equally valuable apart from any reference to them in their particulars. To make of persons on either account objects of our moral judgments, after all, would either impose our own valuations upon their autonomy, or introduce differential value measures when we are required instead to regard all such persons as equally valuable.

The cult of rights might object here that respect for autonomous persons requires quite a different moral regard, namely respect for persons' capacity for autonomy, and that self-respect requires equally moral regard for the content of one's specific moral choices. If the ultimate worth of persons defended here is our capacity for autonomy, however, we have no moral basis for assessing our own or others' moral judgments or actions. The famous Kantian imperative that we choose as other rational agents would, and preclude treating those rational others as means, unravels not only because we cannot in principle treat others as means, but because we cannot objectify their moral agency at all. To treat them as mere means we would have to subordinate their preferences to ours. Yet on the cult of rights' own assumptions, even the severest force cannot impel persons to act against their wills. Even the hint that persons could be induced to act against their preferences denies the transcendent autonomy which underwrites the moral demand that we not manipulate them. Moreover, their preferences, as preferences, have no moral claim to respect, as they are empirical epiphenomena. How, then, may we reduce others – or ourselves – to mere means? Cult of rights defenders insist that we do so when we destroy our own autonomous capacity, as for example in subordinating our rational autonomy to transitory desires. If we do not create that capacity in and through our choices, however, we surely cannot destroy it in and through those choices either. Indeed, as a supernatural property, no such empirical desires or the like may properly imperil it. Nor can we impel others to act contrarily to their autonomy – which is, finally, the only way we might prove able to reduce them to means. Manipulating their desires or their bodies or their motives leaves their persons untouched; respecting the latter proscribes no such activities. Similarly, however much persons indulge their own motives or desires, they retain their inalienable worth and dignity and autonomy.

For both cults, in fact, the worth ascribed to persons wholly transcends the empirical particulars of their agency: their specific choices and values and actions. For the cult of rights, it is finally nonsensical to proscribe using others or ourselves as mere means, as the only means by which we could manipulate others or ourselves – our empirical preferences or desires – warrant neither moral respect nor moral protection. The proper object of our moral regard, rather, is the transcendent property of autonomy, not its instantiation in particular choices or personalities. For the cult of life, similarly, the worth of persons attaches not at all to their particulars, but rather to their status as ensouled persons. We properly respect such persons only by regarding them of equal moral worth, wholly apart from their actions, intentions or valuations. As such, they can in no way be objects of our moral activity. Not only are persons products of divine rather than human pro-creation, but their status as such is inalienable regardless of what persons do to themselves or what is done to them. Since our lone basis for respect for such persons attaches to a supernatural property invulnerable to human agency, that property per se evokes no particular norms. At the same time, we should not then regard other persons as objects of moral consideration, precisely because they wholly transcend human agency. The issue here is not that we ought not to intervene in their life prospects – as the cult of life suggests, ironically, in proscribing genetic enhancement – but that we cannot do so because we lack the agential capacity, the power, to do so. Accordingly, any suggestion that we can imperil persons should, on both cults' accounts, signify the sheer hubris they both excoriate, as it implies the incursion of human agency into transcendent human nature.

For its part, the cult of life differentiates itself from the cult of rights in its ostensible rejection of such hubris and in the restraints it imposes on human agency. Yet on neither account is embodied human agency, finally, an element of transcendent human nature. As such, on neither account may we ascribe substantive moral responsibility to embodied human persons, because in lacking moral objects, they offer no bases for identifying moral subjects. For the cult of rights, our autonomy is inalienable, such that we can neither imperil our own or other persons'. For the cult of life, our dignity is inalienable, such that we can neither enhance nor diminish it. We can neither make ourselves more or less autonomous, nor more or less dignified, because these are absolute properties we bear supernaturally, not products of our activities or practices. As bearers of absolute moral worth, moreover, we cannot endeavor to improve either our own moral characters or the moral prospects or capacities of persons per se. As such, any and all of the artifices by which we pursue our empirical preferences and ends must prove amoral, as they leave us untouched, neither improving nor diminishing our persons. To say, for example, that we should or should not genetically engineer future persons is unintelligible, not only because "future persons" is a contradiction in terms, but also because we have no moral relation to other persons as persons. Our agency attaches at most to their empirical features, which merit no moral concern.

Indeed, while both cults identify human agency as a definitive element of human beings, they equally deny that agency any substantive moral task. In securing inalienable human dignity or autonomy, they render it invulnerable to human agency, and render human agency morally impotent. We are products, then, not of ourselves but of God or of transcendent nature, and are means to ends that are in neither case our own. In precluding our being objects of human agency or will – for good or for ill – we are equally precluded from being moral subjects, moral agents, and creators of moral value. For the cult of rights, our worth attends our autonomy, and is unaffected by the choices that autonomy comes to embody. For the cult of life, our worth attends our transcendent dignity, and is unaffected by the particulars of our persons. Nothing we do or create – or become in the process – adds to or diminishes our moral value. To say then that persons can be objects of others' wills or their own makes no more sense, metaphysically or morally, than to say that persons are subjects of such wills, insofar as that subjectivity – lined by particular choices and valuations – proves epiphenomenal. On both accounts, those ends or goods bear no moral worth precisely because they are brought into being in and through human agency, which, lacking any distinctive moral task, yields contingent, transitory preferences.

Persons are, after all, no more their characters than they are their bodies or any other empirical traits. Were those accounts true, however, they would unravel not only any real continuity of individual personality and character over time, but also any mutual objectifications whereby we might redirect our actions in light of our own and others' ends. To be a subject, I suggest, is to self-objectify; yet that subjectivity is rooted in mutual interactions, in being objectified by others and in objectifying them in turn. Amid these social processes, others instill in us languages, values, ideas, concepts, and symbols that allow us to objectify ourselves, to see ourselves as others do, and to reconsider our own activities in light of their responses. I propose calling languages and symbols and the like technologies because they serve analogous functions to such tools: they permit large-scale social coordination. At the same time, these tools are no less natural, no less ours, and no more or less artifices, than is the biological capacity for speech formation. I stress this point because both cults, in their opposition to genetic enhancement and analogous biotechnologies, contest not merely their artificial nature, but the extent to which they ostensibly threaten to render persons objects of human technology and human artifice and human design. Personhood, however, is itself a product not of nature but of human agency; indeed, it is among our most enduring artifices.

5.4 We can rebuild him ... ?

We find in nature, after all, no great chasm between human biological nature and human tool use. Even if we did, neither cult takes as it prime object of moral defense human biological nature. To the contrary, both define human worth in opposition to that nature. For both cults, biotechnologies such as genetic engineering pose the specter that we will come to identify ourselves ever more closely with our technologies, becoming their products. Yet that concern denies and affirms the same dubious premise: that we are essentially isolable from our tools and technologies. Were that the case, such technologies would prove morally neutral. Against that prospect, both cults assert that they objectify and permit substantive changes of persons by persons. So too, however, on that account, would technologies like languages and social mores and political systems. For both cults, biotechnologies somehow pose prospects for changing ostensibly transcendent persons in ways these other tools do not. At the same time, their accounts of persons embed human artifices as a condition of their supplying any moral warrants, or even of addressing some ostensibly much simpler questions, such as where persons come from in the first place.

In this vein, no contemporary issue in bioethics generates more heat – and less light – than the prospect of human cloning. On this as on so many other matters, cultists of both varieties stand united. In defense of human dignity, the cult of life objects that any cloning of persons is unnatural and thus immoral, as it manufactures persons in a novel, technologically mediated way. In defense of human autonomy, the cult of rights objects that cloning deprives individuals of their right to an open future. This point was made by cult of rights representative Hans Jonas, who maintains that these technologies usurp so much control over nature that they render us not their producers but their products. Yet both accounts founder when specifying either how reproductive cloning violates natural norms, or how it flouts human dignity. The cult of life, for example, affirms accepting the normativity of nature's course, and the wholly passive role of persons in the transmission of life, and precludes recourse to any artificial means of preventing such life transmission. It does not, however, proscribe artificial means of life maintenance or even extension, such as vaccines and antibiotics. To that extent, if cloned embryos are unnatural and thus *verboten* simply because they are technologically mediated, vaccines and the like would seem to prove equally *verboten* on precisely the same measure.

For the cult of life, however, such means of life extension are not merely licit but morally mandatory. To be sure, defenders of this position insist that, in PVS cases for example, artificial nutrition and hydration are morally mandatory because they supply natural needs. However natural these needs are, however, they are supplied through patently artificial means. Life and death, proponents of the cult of life maintain, are wholly dispensed by God, such that we should not intervene in their natural provenance. Sustaining the life of a PVS patient, however, does precisely that, and neither more nor less than would ending that life. For the cult of life, interventions such as tube feeding and ventilation, however technologically mediated, supply the body with natural and thus obligatory needs, whereas cloning synthesizes natural components into an artificial product of human manufacture, a clone. As maintained earlier, however, the entire mode of life of a PVS patient is artificial, whereas the mode of living induced by cloning or IVF or the like would prove strikingly natural, empirically. Embryos, however produced, unfold biologically like any others. Nor does the cult of life assert that cloned persons would prove soulless automata; to the contrary, their moral objections attach to the process of cloning, not its result. As persons, clones, like persons produced through any other means, bear souls created by God *de novo*. They remain, as persons, wholly unaffected by the means of their natural inception.

At the same time, while cloning or IVF might prove artificial as technologically mediated processes, deliberate twinning or delayed fertilizing have natural cognates and natural precedents. To say that cloning creates a technologically manufactured and novel mode of life is much less apt than to say that PVS signals a technologically mediated and wholly novel mode of life. To say that we violate nature's or God's intention in human cloning, but not in PVS, is patently inconsistent, as both bend natural processes to human intentions. Moreover, to hold that cloning or IVF artificially create life, whereas PVS does not, begs the critical question. In cases where all biological functions are taken over by technological means, after all, we may well espy a vanishing point between natural and artificial life. Insofar as such lives are maintained not only technologically but at our moral behest, they are products of human artifice and not of nature in any intelligible sense. Indeed, to hold that PVS states sustain natural human life, whereas cloning confounds natural life, not only renders incoherent any conception of natural norms but illustrates precisely what the cult of life otherwise denies: that we cannot draw a strict demarcation between our biological nature and the artifices and technologies – both physical and moral – which constitute it.

In the case of PVS, for example, the cult of life does not simply make new artifices mandatory; rather, those new norms are predicated on a wholly novel view of the natural human lifespan, which may now include years or even decades in PVS states. This point bears emphasis for the following reason. Before such technological artifices for sustaining

PVS lives were invented, those lives did not exist. Absent the power to sustain such lives, we plainly had no obligation to do so. Now, however, the cult of life insists that such newly natural means to life extension are morally obligatory. Even if we grant that such means, however artificially manufactured or supplied, are natural, however, the broader point remains that an expansion or our technological power has thereby expanded the range of our moral responsibilities. While drawing that conclusion for sustaining end-of-life care, however, the cult of life draws precisely the opposite conclusion for the provision of beginning-of-life care, as in cases like cloning and genetic engineering. In the latter cases, even if we could extend natural life, say by genetically engineering persons to be more resistant to specific diseases, we ought not to, as that would prove an unnatural intrusion into God's or nature's provenance. We are, that is, morally obliged to extend the natural lives of PVS patients, even if by entirely artificially induced means, while we are equally precluded from extending the natural lives of cloned or genetically engineered persons, even if by means less patently artificial than those used to sustain PVS patients. Why the systematic asymmetry between beginning and end of life care? For the cult of life, only God creates and only God may reclaim human lives. But if that principle entails human passivity in reproductive practices, it ought equally to entail human passivity in our dying practices. On this premise, the very prospect of sustaining PVS lives, like that of cloning, should prove equally immoral, on exactly the same grounds.

Indeed, one often cited dispute between both cults is the extent to which persons exercise agential power over the disposition of human life. The cult of life, for its part, rejects the cult of rights' often alleged hubris, its assertions of pro-creative liberty, and of the dominion of individual agents over the course of their own lives. This disagreement may seem to contrast very distinct conceptions of human power over human living and dying. Yet the cult of rights, no less than the cult of life, takes as its primary moral task not the expansion but the diminution of such power, and with it, the diminution of any human moral responsibility for the empirical prospects of future persons. This may seem a peculiar charge given the cult of rights' ostensible emphasis on individual autonomy. Yet just as the human dignity that the cult of life valorizes is so transcendent that it requires no moral protection, so too is the autonomy that the cult of rights valorizes so transcendent that it requires no moral protection. In both cases, the ultimate value of human persons is inviolable. Both cults thus pose the same paradox: they take as a primary moral challenge to bioethics the power that present persons may exert over future persons, yet depict persons as powerless to affect one another, and morally blameless regardless of what they do with respect to others.

For the cult of rights, for example, reproductive liberty might seem to secure for parents a right to clone themselves. We need not, after all, on this view regard one and only one means of conception as naturally normative, nor reject cloning simply insofar as it is technologically mediated. At the same time, many cult of rights defenders object, while naturally occurring twins may grow into unique individuals with their own talents and tastes and propensities, clones will lack, the *inalienable* right to an open future, unselected and undecided by their parents. Genetically, however, clones and twins are functionally equivalent. We hardly say of identical twins that their natural occurrence counts as an affliction, that their distinctive worth has been imperiled by their lack of genetic uniqueness. Nevertheless, such critics insist, parents who design or even clone their children will aim to have an undue influence upon them as the mature. All parents, however, impose a genotype upon their children. Whether chosen or left to natural lottery, it is simply false that any child selects its range genetic potentials. Such is biological reproduction that it cedes the genetic potentials of one generation to the progenitors of the next. Similarly, parents have extraordinary discretion to make choices for their children: their religion and values, their education and future prospects. Not only do they inherit their genetic and social potentials from their parents, children are also invariably subject to the possibility that their parents will view them as status symbols, as objects to satisfy their own whims, rather than as individuals. Genetic selection of potentials may be another venue to impose those whims, but not one that differs in degree or kind from the imposition of social expectations, habits, or the like.

Moreover, on the cult of rights' own operative assumptions, neither genetic nor social impositions by parents may affect, much less effect, persons in their persons. For the cult of rights, our autonomous capacity springs forth *de novo*, as a creature of individual will. Just as the cult of life depicts persons as unfolding teleologically, sans any substantive reference to any empirical conditions under which that unfolding might occur, for the cult of rights, too, the emergence of individual autonomy is neither biologically nor socially nor temporally mediated. On neither account do persons come into being in and through human relations extended over time, nor through biological maturation, nor through a substantive personal identity that endures over time. Such persons, rather, bear personal relations neither to their bodies, nor to their personalities, nor to their characters, nor to their social relations.

Persons, that is, are on neither account brought into being by persons; rather, they emerge supernaturally. As such, not only are the conditions of their biological inception extrinsic to their persons, so too is the entirety of their biological and social disposition. To object, then, that persons ought not to be objects of other persons' intentions or moral projects presupposes what both accounts otherwise deny: that we can be affected, and indeed effected in our persons through others' actions.

That presumption illustrates the metaphysical and moral bankruptcy of both characterizations of human dignity and autonomy. Both accounts, after all, in placing others persons wholly beyond our reach, negate their moral reality precisely by rendering them invulnerable to our actions. If, that is, everything that we can affect – their bodies, their personalities, their social presence – is inessential to their persons, then their real, enduring value transcends their bodies, their personalities, their characters. If, moreover, we do not bring persons into being through our pro-creative practices, if we do not affect and indeed effect persons in and through those practices, then the latter bear no moral freight. Bioethicists of both cults wish to subject such practices to sustained moral scrutiny; yet if they neither dignify nor degrade human persons, neither enhance nor retard human autonomy, then they admit no moral trajectory. Such practices become moral, rather, only insofar as persons are objects of others procreative acts, and in fact prove to be living artifacts of their progenitors. I propose the term "living artifacts" quite deliberately, to capture two inescapable features of human procreation amid life as we know it: first, that no matter what we do within our pro-creative practices, whether through our actions or inactions, we cannot help but affect persons in their personalities, bodies and characters; and second, insofar as persons are their bodies, personalities and characters, they are likewise inescapably both the objects, and thereby alone, the subjects of such practices.

If, that is, those pro-creative practices bear any moral power, they do so only insofar as they bring persons into being, that is, only insofar as they render persons the objects of deliberate human activity and agency. As passive conduits, whether of gametes or souls or unfettered freedoms, present persons bear no moral responsibility to future persons, positively or negatively. To insist, moreover, that present persons ought not to subject future persons to technological modifications presumes that biotechnologies are artifices in ways that moral injunctions are not. Alas, to maintain that we are already good enough, that we ought not to modify human nature, no less imposes the preferences of the present upon future persons. Nor is that any less playing God, any less designing future persons to a deliberately selected specification, the deliberate maintenance of human nature as it is. Nor may we maintain that we are merely letting nature take its course when we deliberately elect not to use or to develop particular biotechnologies. The willful refusal of power, after all, enjoins the willful refusal of responsibilities that we might, but choose not to, accept. To admit that is one thing. To present it simultaneously as a natural or normative inevitability, and a measure of our moral probity or moral wisdom, is quite another. This point bears emphasis because both cults reject any view of human persons as living artifacts, as the handiwork of human agency. Yet only so conceived, only insofar as persons are accessible in their persons and are really their bodies and personalities and characters, may we have anything akin to a bioethic befitting human persons not in their supernatural adventures, but amid human life as we know it.

6
Engineering Bioethics

The previous chapter posed a double-sided query: Are we good enough? That might be asking whether we are already good enough as is, metaphysically as well as morally, in our persons. But it might also raise the issue of whether we're good enough to use emerging and proposed biotechnologies responsibly, as, for example, to dignify rather than to degrade human persons. At the same time, both cults presume the basic premise of the first formulation, and thus preclude any prospect of the second. This point gives the lie to the first great fallacy of contemporary bioethics, the sham intimation that it engages in anything like what philosophers have historically deemed practical rationality. It is, rather, neither practical nor rational. Quite the contrary, in setting the very terms "practical" and "rational" in opposition to each other, it cements its position as a practice of power.

6.1 Biofallacies

I do not mean, as many contemporary theorists might, that bioethics does not admit practical rationality because it yields no rational consensus. This meta-ethical point has drawn extensive attention given its emphasis in Alasdair MacIntyre's *After Virtue*.[1] In his path-breaking work, MacIntyre diagnoses contemporary moral disputes as rationally incommensurable. Starting from incompatible moral assumptions, he argues, these competing positions admit of no rational resolution. In MacIntyre's widely influential model, the occurrence of such irresolvable controversies itself signals the presence of incompatible assumptions. The current controversies between the cults of life and rights, on everything from birth control to PAS to abortion, would seem to exemplify his model. Those debates, however, start with functionally equivalent metaphysical assumptions about persons, and from these beginnings they draw competing conclusions. And among the most striking elements of these controversies is not the level of disagreement, but rather of agreement, that they garner on matters ranging from cloning to genetic engineering. In such cases, both cults agree: future persons ought not to be the objects of present persons' designs. Moreover, while these cults may draw competing conclusions on stem cell research or abortion, those disagreements would not arise if either cult reasoned consistently from the assumptions they share about the nature of persons.

Despite the cult of life's obsessive opposition to stem cell research, for example, destroying embryos leaves their personhood untouched; despite the cult of rights' support for such research, none of its practical results, however ameliorative, could really affect persons. Persons as they describe them, after all, are not biological at all: they neither age, nor ail, nor die, nor pro-create, as persons. In their serene transcendence, divorced from all biological or social impingements, souls and autonomous ends or agents, as the cult of rights and the cult of life respectively conceive them, are functionally equivalent. They arise from equally mysterious metaphysical sources, and under-write moral claims equally contrary to the transcendence they ostensibly secure. Neither cult, for example, offers its skeptics a metaphysically intelligible and morally efficacious account of when human life begins that warrants rational assent. Yet such consensus is not forthcoming not because these cults begin from rival premises, but because neither makes human biological life an object of its enquiry. At the same time, both posit a wide range of fruitless controversies predicated on their alleged disagreement over whether human life begins at conception, or quickening, or birth, or upon attainment of one's driver's license.

That these controversies have proven so intractable is often taken as evidence that serious issues are at stake, that both sides aspire to truth and that one will win out, with the other finding itself "rationally vanquished" in MacIntyre's martial language. Others see a clash between scientific and theological views of human nature, a clash insoluble insofar as such views admit different evidentiary approaches. Contemporary bioethics, however, exhibits no such textures. For the cult of life, not only is scientific ignorance insufficient to exclude anyone from making authoritative pronouncements about cloning and stem cell research and the like, but serious attention is still owed to the antique moral claim that we ought not to seek certain knowledge. Unsurprisingly, given these epistemic standards, this cult advances its signature claims, such as its infamous insistence that human life begins at conception, despite the biological fact that conception is a process rather than an event, and in flat opposition to its own insistence that life is unilaterally, and supernaturally, created by God *de novo*, sans any relation to natural biological processes.

No more scrupulous, the cult of rights renders unintelligible how autonomous persons create themselves, while advocating all manner of moral guidelines to protect the exercise of an autonomy that, metaphysically, admits of no empirical constraints whatsoever. This cult leaves largely unexamined the metaphysical assumptions its own norms contravene, and the broader question of whether those implausible assumptions are in fact necessary to sustain the human agency we observe. If it can be constrained, much less imperiled by such contingencies, after all, it cannot be as unfettered as they propose. If that's the case, what must follow about that basic assumption? It would seem that whatever conclusion we draw here, we must reject the original assumption of a wholly unfettered autonomy, as inconsistent with our experience of human agency and with the norms they commend to sustain it. Yet proponents of the cult of rights prefer instead to defend an unfettered autonomy we do not witness, if need be, by ever more narrowly proscribing the conditions under which persons may be said to act autonomously.

As such, there's nothing distinctively philosophical about bioethics insofar as it does not even aspire to truth. Quite the contrary, on both approaches articles of faith go uncontested, baseless assumptions go unexamined, and gross ignorance of biological and psychological facts is mutually counseled, lest we be forced to admit that the self-conceptions with which we entered these debates might require modification. In place of any aspiration to truth – which animates practical rationality traditionally understood – we witness the newest Frankenstein to populate the current bioethics scene: the President's Council on Bioethics. The very idea of doing ethics – or anything else – by committee should give us pause. It signals first and foremost, I suggest, the surrender not only of any aspiration to truth, but even to minimal consensus. In its stead, it endeavors to give maximum representation to a cacophony of competing voices all appealing to distinct normative sources: nature, various gods, ancestors, prophets and seers, great men, laws of mysterious origin. This composition underscores the extent to which both cults engineer bioethics in a fundamentally irrational way, fabricating their moral authority whole cloth from metaphysical assumptions that negate such authority. More strikingly, these efforts to engineer moral authority yield what we might term a Tragedy of the Moral Commons.[2] While Hardin's well worn phrase concerns an abandoned commons, however, I wish to reverse his analysis and to consider the implications of rendering public, and subject to common assay and governance, matters that are properly private.

What bioethicists of both cults do, I suggest, is precisely that: they seek in their fabrications of moral authority to render the inner life and private workings of living human persons – in their ailing, aging, procreating and dying – objects of public moral scrutiny and redirection at either cult's behest. They engineer bioethics, that is, not by extending private moral concerns into legitimately public practices, but by extending fabricated public concerns into legitimately private practices. On both cults' premises, the entire panoply of bioethics issues – from genetic engineering to stem cell research to euthanasia to cosmetic enhancement – should be matters of indifference to us. Yet both rush headlong in the opposite direction, insisting that any or all of the above imperil our persons. They imperil "us," moreover, even if others do them, but not we ourselves. If "we" allow genetic enhancement, we're told, we are directly implicated in degrading future persons. If "we" allow PAS, we are directly implicated in negating the transcendent moral worth of those who undergo it. Yet how did "we" acquire such out-sized power over transcendent others, that we can alienate their inalienable dignity, or imperil their unfettered autonomy? Partly, I suggest, because philosophical bioethics has doubly foundered: first by failing to contest metaphysical dualism, and the destructive moral ideals that dualism promulgates; and second by authorizing an unprecedented moral assault on personal privacy under the auspices of human dignity and autonomy.

In support of that first charge, I submit as evidence the strikingly high degree of irrationalism tolerated in bioethics, as exemplified by what I'll describe here as Franken-Fallacies. This dirty dozen of logical errors is so widely accepted in bioethics debates that their presence often goes unnoted. First, and among the most prominent, is what we might term the Intentional Fallacy, an analogue to the naturalist fallacy. The naturalist fallacy, recall please, notes that we cannot infer what should be directly from what is. Admitting that such inferences are fallacious precludes our drawing moral conclusions from non-moral, or natural facts. Many bioethicists reject claims that commit the naturalist fallacy. Yet they remain amenable to the insistence, sans any evidence, that nature has an inherent plan, and that in interfering with that plan we contest nature's wisdom. This view underwrites the injunction that we should let nature take its course. It also underlies the insistence that human nature per se poses a "special factor" such that human nature, alone within the natural order, bears an absolute moral worth.

That insistence illustrates a second flavor of the Intentional Fallacy, the assertion of that absolute worth as predicated on baseless assumptions about human nature. It is false biologically, for example, that human nature is immutable. If our worth is predicated on a mutable genetic makeup, we are forever in danger of losing it. Rather than respond to this challenge, however, defenders of these claims more often contest the science, redoubling their efforts to read intentional design into natural processes, or denying that evolutionary theory or molecular genetics teach us anything about ourselves. Indeed, some theorists extend that point further, insisting upon a moral right to deny evolutionary theory, or to allow people to make up their own minds. Science, however, is not a matter about which we may believe whatever we please, if we mean by the term any endeavor to understand biological life as it is, rather than as we wish it might be. To hold that we have a right to believe what we wish on the basis of faith is one thing. But to claim moral authority over others' right to believe, or to act, on the premise of maintaining one's own faith, marks these positions off as embedding Intentional Fallacies, and as efforts to maintain particular faiths either without or in direct conflict with any available evidence.

While the Intentional Fallacy is meant to complement the naturalistic fallacy, the latter, too, makes its presence felt in bioethics, under what I'll term here the Blind Man's Bluff Fallacy. This fallacy asserts that preventable illnesses or disabilities, like blindness should not be prevented, because they are enjoined by God or nature and are goods in themselves. Bioethicists who advance such views are quick to identify efforts to prevent such disabilities as gateways to a Brave New World, wherein persons are only admitted into the regnant social community if they meet exacting quality control standards. The basis of this objection, however – the insistence that some health or functional state that is or that seems to be bad or undesirable really is good or desirable – bears striking similarities to the Double Speak so chillingly depicted in George Orwell's dystopian novel *1984*. The social engineers that Orwell describes twist their society's language beyond recognition, inverting the meanings of common words. Such thought-policing is alive and well in bioethics, and is advanced, for example, by those who ally any efforts to forestall preventable disabilities with Nazi-style eugenics. Such language is eminently salutary, replacing the need to evaluate such proposals with the demand that we affirm that all persons, and thus all biological estates, are equally good. That no account of personhood advanced by either cult supports any inference from the worth of persons to the worth of any biological estates is conveniently overlooked. Put directly: human dignity, as they conceive it, cannot dignify blindness.

Such positions, moreover, evoke a third logical lapse that we might call the Aspirational Fallacy. A species of equivocation, this pattern of ill-reasoning mistakes human dignity, as an ideal to which our institutions and practices might aspire, for a real metaphysical fact embedded in every person. In making of human dignity a quasi-Platonic Form rather than a practical activity or a moral ideal, this fallacy voids it of any moral power or task. Conceived as a transcendent and inalienable property of persons and as attaching to them either as a product of divine or of human self-creation *de novo*, it negates any role that human persons, as moral agents, might have in the provision or maintenance of that property, i.e. in the degrading or the dignifying of others in their persons.

Indeed, one paradox of the Aspirational Fallacy is the moral inertia it adduces. If human persons are absolutely and inalienable valuable, as a matter of metaphysical fact, the entire premise of moral activity – that there is a gap between what we are and what we should be, and that we are enjoined to close that gap through our agency – dissipates, as we can neither enhance nor detract from our absolute value through our agency. This fallacy mistakes the moral task that an ideal of human dignity might propose – that we dignify rather than degrade persons through our actions – for an already realized metaphysical and moral fact, undercutting any basis for substantive human agency.

The moral inertia that this fallacy induces joins forces with a cognate epistemic failing that we might call the Seinfeld Fallacy. This pattern of exuberant ill-reasoning, strikingly, attends equally cult of life defenders, such as Leon Kass and Bill McKibben[3] and cult of rights sympathizers like Joel Garreau.[4] On their accounts, bioethics seems less a branch of practical enquiry than a literary exercise or an endeavor in theological apologetics, its end in either case being that most venerable humanistic pursuit: navel-gazing. For Kass and McKibben, biological finitude defines the human condition, and relieving it threatens to change what it means to be human. They leave unexplained, of course, how essential elements of our nature or condition could be changed, as for them our essences are immutable. If we can change those features, conversely, then the human condition is not simply a matter of natural or metaphysical necessity. Rather, it begs the critical question: if we can modify this condition, we cannot simply assert that the human condition, as it is and has been, is thereby normative for us, such that we should actively maintain it. Yet that unreasoning recourse is pursued equally by Garreau, who proposes, as a means of defining the human condition, a Shakespeare Test, wherein any challenge posed to human beings within the orbit of Shakespeare's corpus qualifies as a defining element of the human condition.

Most striking about these approaches, I suggest – and the reason that I propose a slightly different designation – is their shared, navel-gazing, self-aggrandizing assertion that the finitudes and frailties we currently face are not only good in themselves, but ought to be deliberately maintained, lest we imperil the humanity of future persons, who may then end up being significantly different from us. All three theorists cited above, in fact, exemplify this worry: that our successors, should they face different life conditions, will prove unrecognizable to us, and we to them. The plain premise underlying these concerns – that the human future ought to be like the human present and the human past – is never stated explicitly. Nor could it be, given these theorists' cognate assertions that we should not to make future persons the objects of our designs. The flagrant inconsistency of these assertions – and the determined refusal to acknowledge how efforts to make future persons exactly like us exemplifies the eugenic hubris they otherwise excoriate – illustrates what I wish here to designate the Seinfeld Fallacy – to wit, the assertion, sans evidence or reason or argument, that not only we are good enough as is, but we should also stay that way *ab eterno*.

That both cults so inflate our own moral and metaphysical significance is patently ironic; in their more self-aware moments, perpetrators of the Seinfeld Fallacy might see it for the expression of out-sized hubris it embodies. Yet that fallacy works its greatest logical mischief only when coupled with its obverse: the Brave New World Fallacy. This genus of illogic, a variant of appeals to popular wisdom, evokes vivid dystopian imagery: clones run amok, spare parts organ harvesting, alien-human hybrids, and all manner of Franken-creations. Simply whispering this term in conjunction with any biotechnology spares speaker and hearer alike any need to assay the costs and benefits of the proposed intervention. It thus serves well those critics who regard any prospect of the human future being unlike the human past or present with unremitting hostility. Any effort to modify that future, they assert, degrades, dehumanizes, or usurps future person's dignity, dragging them into a Brave New World neither at their behest nor of their making.

Opposing the onslaught of Brave New Worlds requires battling not only against recalcitrant logic, but equally against science, against which defenders of both cults wield what we might term the Galileo Gambit. This variant of special pleading, beloved of humanists, renders persons – not only metaphysical exceptions to biological constraints, but unique bearers of a transcendent nature beyond science's ken. Galileo's crime, recall please, was severe: he denied that the human universe was the center of the natural universe, and was proven right, challenging a cherished self-conception built largely on faith and wishful thinking. That such human conceits die hard is undeniable; he was formally pardoned, grudgingly, only after half a millennium; many bioethicists refuse to forgive him even to this day. Rather than learning from our history (one purported rationale for our humanistic studies), we seem determined to repeat it, to sustain our belief that we are metaphysically special even if we do so only by deliberately sustaining our ignorance of ourselves. This prospect is illustrated in many bioethicists' responses to the prospect of genetic prediction, which might herald more effective ameliorative measures: this has been met stoutly with the charge that persons have a right to ignorance of their future, a right rooted, apparently, in the insistence that we ought not to pursue certain questions, and ought not to attain certain kinds of knowledge.

That insistence might augur the graver fear that we will come to regard such genetic predictions as imprimaturs of persons' fates. Yet that fear itself heralds what I'll call here the Head in the Sand or the Inertial fallacy, which presumes either that we bear no responsibility for deliberate ignorance, or that we do so only insofar as sustaining such ignorance is a measure of our virtue. The Head in the Sand fallacy authorizes moral claims contrary to observable evidence and hostile to evidentiary support. Thereby, it licenses, for example, the redoubtable court of public opinion, or worse, that most patent of logical abominations – the President's Council on Bioethics – to assay biotechnologies like genetic engineering – while granting extraordinary latitude not to scientific but to theological considerations.

At the same time, this fallacy morally legitimates not just ignorance, but even deliberate ignorance, and so evokes the Inertial Fallacy, whereby bioethicists of both cults foreswear any responsibility for goods forestalled or harms permitted under the auspices of deliberate ignorance and deliberate refusals to act. Attending this result, in turn, we might espy the Fallacy of Principled Inaction. We may, for example, find representatives of both cults insisting that we should not engineer out genes for specific diseases, even if that option presents itself. This assertion has a strong adolescent appeal, not only in sustaining our transcendent self-conception but also in allowing us to pick and choose our moral responsibilities, such that, for example, responsible parents might provide insulin to a diabetic child, but not genetically engineer that child to prevent the disease in the first place. The first intervention, such positions imply, is therapeutic, the second is enhancing, If both interventions secure health, however, they may both just as readily be deemed therapeutic as enhancing; conversely, if failing to provide insulin yields harm, so too would failing to prevent the disease given the possibility of doing so.

For bioethicists of both cults, of course, the key point here is that parents should not have options with respect to their children's genetic constitution. Both cults then cling futilely to efforts to distinguish between therapeutic and enhancing medical interventions, illustrating thereby what we might term the Frankenstein Fallacy – the bioethicists' variant of the venerable slippery slope. In their traditional form, slippery slope arguments predict disaster in a series of premises, none of which are supported. Many bioethicists perpetrate such arguments in prophesizing Brave New Dystopias. Despite their ominous warnings, however, their insistence that genetic engineering to prevent disease differs in principle from injecting vaccines to prevent disease remains just that, an insistence. That point belies equally the claims advanced through the New Kid on the Block Fallacy, under whose banner bioethicists of both cults commend exceptional moral conservatism, on the ground that emerging biotechnologies pose unprecedented challenges to humanity.

Vaccines are one thing, they insist, but germ-line genetic engineering? Things are gravely different now, the cults shriek in unison. Really? They always are. Just as every generation rediscovers sex, every bioethicist discovers a new moral challenge. And just as every generation laments the prospects of its successors, these radically new problems nest less in the biotechnologies themselves than in the fear of novelty they evoke, and in the timeless human belief that change is degeneration. Yet that change is an endemic feature of human life, and a moral crisis only if we insist – against the entire weight of history – that we're the ones who got it right, that life as it is now is as good as it gets, and that "different" is, by definition, a moral degeneration. This point harkens back to the ancient fallacy of Appeal to Tradition, which might more aptly here be deemed The Future is Now Fallacy. This pattern of unreasoning completes the circle started by any appeal to tradition: just as the former asserts that whatever is ought to be, now and in the future, because it is now, the latter implies, conversely, that whatever is not yet ought not to be because it is not yet. But these injunctions make nonsense of human agency. This dissolution of human agency is illustrated equally vividly by the Yuck Factor Fallacy, a particularly tortured variant of specious scholasticism perpetrated most notably by Leon Kass' assertion of "the wisdom of repugnance."[5] In an essay of the same title, Kass claims that the visceral, emotive opposition cloning often rouses embodies a latent moral judgment indicating the wrongness of the act. Ascribing wisdom to such a visceral response, however, is ironic insofar as many such responses arise in complete ignorance of how cloning works, biologically, or how ubiquitously it attends natural life. Moreover, while Kass commends this repugnance when it attaches to cloning, he would excoriate the same response if it attached to grave bodily disability or to the decay that attends ailing and dying. Indeed, he enjoins us to reject cloning due to the wisdom of our repugnance for it, but to embrace bodily frailty and decay despite our equal or even greater repugnance. Far from being a reliable moral tutor, the Yuk Factor that he commends ranges arbitrarily across whatever practice Kass opposes or favors. To that extent, we might rechristen the Wisdom of Repugnance the self-proclaimed Wisdom of Kass.

That tenor – the insistence that whatever one personally dislikes is morally illicit – underwrites the last of the dirty dozen, the Playing God Fallacy. This fallacy highlights many endemic disputes between secular and theological bioethicists. Yet that emphasis is misleading, as the key logical fallacy this proclamation embodies is the insistence that acts of commission decide the future in ways that acts of omission do not, and that, analogously, we are morally culpable for acts of commission but not for acts of omission. As a matter metaphysical fact, however, the future is equally a summation of what we do and what we omit. That point is illustrated handily by a familiar economic device known as an opportunity cost: for any unit of money or time invested, we must consider not only the yield produced, but also what opportunities we passed over. I stress this point because those who accuse genetic engineers, for example, of Playing God, hint that by modifying genetic prospects, they thereby degrade persons, whereas by doing nothing, they leave persons unaffected, and are blameless for our inaction. Yet this is doubly false. Either acts of commission and omission both affect persons, or neither does. We can scarcely assign responsibility for one without the other. Proponents of this fallacy, now legion among bioethicists, assert as their moral touchstone that venerable medical bromide:

first do no harm. Yet they presume that the only way we may do harm is if we act, as if acts of omission, by definition, cannot yield grievous moral harms all their own

6.2 The indignity of human dignity

In his influential essay on "The Ethics of Belief", William Clifford maintains that it is always wrong to hold beliefs without adequate evidence.[6] While he emphasizes the negative consequences of insufficiently supported beliefs, he also underscores the moral challenge posed by willful, deliberate ignorance. I mean by that not privately held beliefs casually accepted, but publicly asserted beliefs deliberately sustained contrary to available evidence and imposed upon others apart from their wishes. I stress that contrast because both cults predicate their claims to public moral authority over matters bioethical upon distinctive conceptions of personhood. On both accounts, what makes us persons is precisely not what we are in our particulars of body, or mind, or social relations. For the cult of life, the transcendent soul has a teleological trajectory and moral terminus, apart from which any opacity is deemed a metaphysical malformation and a moral failure warranting intervention for the person's own good. For the cult of rights, similarly, the autonomous will has a transcendental capacity for self-legislating; anything that occludes that self-determination imperils the will's autonomy, and warrants intervention for the imperiled person's own good.

On these accounts, both cults void bodily or psychic life or social intimacy of metaphysical or moral substance, rendering them evanescent epiphenomena that mysteriously shroud persons. So conceived, both cults should maintain that persons, bearing inalienable dignity, are already insuperably secure in their absolute worth, and that the contingencies of their bodies, psyches and social relations are matters of metaphysical and moral indifference. Far from drawing such conclusions, however, both cults move in the opposite direction, espousing paternalisms that license them to inspect, evaluate and redirect persons' wills or souls – the embodied psychic and social ephemera otherwise dismissed as epiphenomenal – insofar as they imperil the ostensibly inalienable dignity or autonomy that persons bear. In authorizing such paternalisms, however, and so in reserving to themselves the task of identifying what is good for persons, sans reference to the particular human beings in question, they fabricate a species of moral authority that extirpates the bodily and psychic interiority and privacy apart from which human moral agency – like human autonomy or human dignity – is unintelligible.

While this paternalist challenge is endemic to bioethics, nowhere is it more evident than in the very public battles over the right to die, advance directives, and physician assisted suicide (PAS). On these matters, cultists of both camps deliberately and determinedly seek to render public an astonishingly private act, perhaps the one truly private act of our lives. I can imagine nothing that is more distinctively mine than my life and my labor, a point long advocated by slavery's most ardent opponents, who insisted that one's life and labor not by entirely placed in the service to others' ends and projects. Yet today I am surrounded by bioethicists who insist that my death is not mine but a social act subject to moral norms, an event bearing such grave moral import that they will defend my capacity to complete it properly – even, if need be, against my own misguided agency. Cult of life defenders predicate that protection on their belief that my death is a moral project, a reenactment of a grand moral theodicy within which I am at most a passive vessel. For cult of right defenders, while my death may be mine, and I may even have a right to die, that death must finally be on their terms, as adjudicated by ethics committees, legal safeguards, and professional dispensations.

Despite the apparent contrast between these approaches, both make of my death and dying a matter of rights and duties, an object of others' moral demands, and thereby place it under the dominion of those others. Even those theorists who maintain that I have a right to choose the means of my death require substantive constraints upon my exercise of that right, and accord ultimate authority to others in deciding both the value of my life and its proper moral conduct. For the cult of life, my life is always absolutely valuable wholly apart from its value to anyone in particular – including me – so much so that it must be protected even against my own agency. This result is palpably evident in the hostility shown even to the idea of self-determination amid the dying process. In his essay "Self-determination run Amok," for example, cult of life defender Daniel Callahan laments the growing resistance to medical paternalism that he sees as heralded by the right-to-die movement.[7] As he notes in a related essay, two claims support that movement: an assertion of patient autonomy, and a more traditional injunction to relieve suffering.[8] Yet medicine's role, he maintains, is to relieve the physical and psychological distress attending illness, but not the "existential" suffering that attends dying. To the contrary, our moral task here is to discern when we must accept the suffering of another and when others must accept it for themselves. Indeed, he characterizes suicide per se as an evasion of dying person's moral obligation to bear the existential distress of dying in a way that models for his or her neighbors how to live under adverse circumstances.

Here, Callahan joins a chorus of theologically motivated bioethicists who insist that our only proper response to such suffering is not "escape" but "courage". Not only do they reject the claim that such suffering might prove meaningless, they insist instead that it reenacts a grand moral theodicy – and if this not good in itself, it is good as a means to moral purification. Two points warrant emphasis here. First, these positions wholly dissever the value of particular lives from particular individual's wills. Callahan, for example, denies that the subjective, mutable preferences of particular persons – expressions of physical or psychic pain or social distress – license individuals to decide the value of their lives for themselves. Rather, he insists, such lives always retain their absolute worth wholly apart from the individual's judgment. While he wholly invalidates such persons' valuations of their own lives, he at the same time predicates the value of that suffering precisely upon that individual's taking it up as a willed moral task. Thereby, he wholly subordinates that person's preferences to a public moral task.

That task, moreover, need not be recognized or even espoused by the individual, but may be imposed upon the dying person, for his or her own good. The dignity to be had in suffering and dying accrues from how it is managed by the individual, and the entire process is subject to moral assay. In particular, the person cannot seek to truncate or ameliorate his or her dying, as doing so, however inexplicably, undercuts the inalienable dignity of transcendent human life. Dying and ailing, however, are hardly generic processes. As Sherwin Nuland describes in *How we Die*, no two deaths are identical, any more than any two lives are. Some persons may well be in a position to pursue the noble, courageous deaths the cult of life demands of all of us. But many will not. Will we then regard those who fail at this task, or who slip into senility or paralysis or intractable, interminable pain or suffering, or who shrink from their passing, or who never had the psychological faculties to complete this process, as moral failures? For the theorists noted above, any efforts to elide such suffering evade our moral responsibilities to others. Even *in extremis*, we are charged with being examples of how to endure suffering and to die well. Even *in extremis* we are morally culpable, and are subject to moral critique.

Yet to advance that case, we must know, *a priori*, that all such suffering can and ought to be borne by individuals despite, and even contrary to, their subjective, private, mutable preferences. We must assert, that is, that they serve some good that wholly transcends the good of individual as identified for themselves, and can thereby be legitimately imposed upon them for their own good. Exactly how dubious that premise is, is illustrated by Callahan's claim that a proper moral task, for physicians or bioethicists, is to discern what suffering others should bear, and what distress they should accept as obligatory. Bearing such suffering is not a private act, he insists, but a public referendum on the value of human life sustained even amid suffering. If all lives bear absolute worth, however, it is nonsense to suggest either that that value is at the same time subject to such ostensibly public referenda, or that it is somehow imperiled if individuals act as if it were not, since its values transcends those actions. Conversely, it would be equally dubious to suggest that enduring such suffering somehow reaffirms or augments what is already an absolute good. Neither presumption makes sense, of course, because persons as the cult of life conceives them do not suffer, and nor do they embody substantive agency.

Even if we did bear such agency, moreover, there are strict limits to how much good we could make of such suffering if that task is beyond our capabilities, as it may well be for those with advanced dementia, for example. Do we then view those deaths as meaningless, as undignified, as inhuman, because they were not borne properly? The antique moral injunction that ought implies can, that we cannot be morally obliged to do the impossible, applies strikingly here. It is equally dubious that persons are morally edified by watching intractable suffering, and by not ameliorating it – in others – as a measure of their own moral worth. Cult of life defenders like McKenny even grant this point, acknowledging that it may seem cruel to preclude relieving ostensibly relievable suffering, and arbitrary, apart from the theodicy he embraces. Nevertheless, he insists, being present to those who suffer, particularly to those who suffer seemingly pointlessly, is integral to the "reconciling community" wherein the living display their virtue thereby, and within which the dying may locate the ultimate spiritual meaning of their dying.[9]

That arbitrariness remains precisely the point, however, because the cult of life demands that even those who reject their operative theodicy suffer and die under its auspices. In making such persons the unwilling or the unwitting objects of their moral assay, and in using that suffering as a means to our own moral edification, cult of life defenders bear a striking similarity not to virtuous dispensers of care or moral guidance, but to sadists. That analogy may seem extreme. Cult of life defenders would object that they do not demand that dying persons endure such suffering for their own pleasure or good, but for the good of the dying themselves, in retaining their dignity. If that dignity, however, no longer has any purchase on the individual's own valuations of his or her own life, then what are we defending for them? The absolute value of any life endures regardless of what they or we do. Nor can the object of moral concern be the specific individual, whose embodied judgments have been voided in service to a higher good.

Indeed, given their view of human life's absolute value, cult of life defenders would deem as hubris any self-determination in the valuation of one's own life. But if we affirm that persons are valuable as individual agents – as we must, if persons are to prove morally culpable – then the height of moral hubris is not self-determination, but rather the insistence that we can and should unilaterally decide for others the value of their own lives to them. That moral hubris reserves to itself the authority to deem others lives' and sufferings meaningful on terms imposed upon them. Cult of life defenders would bristle at the hint that they impose anything upon persons. They defend, they proclaim, ultimate truth and the dignity of human life. As indicated previously, however, absolute values, wholly disembodied and transcendent, neither need nor even permit any such defense. Moreover, that charge is strictly apt because such critics rail against individuals controlling their own deaths, while reserving that control for themselves. Indeed, insofar as they assert the authority to speak for God, they pose an infinitely greater act of hubris than those who endeavor to speak simply for themselves.

Such objections have long agitated the cult of rights' support for the right-to-die movement, not only in resisting an imposed theology, but in opposing the dominion that some thereby illicitly exercise over others' lives. The more liberal among such theorists assert a right to die as rooted in individual privacy and autonomy, in the capacity to be self-legislating that underwrites moral agency. For such critics, that right affirms not the negative end of minimizing suffering, but a positive right to dominion over one's own life, as against interference from others. While many such positions aim to defend each individual's right to confer ultimate value upon their own lives, however, in the context of physician assisted suicide (PAS) in particular, these positions most often place the ultimate power to make such decisions in a series of professionals, who are charged with evaluating the potential agent capacity of ostensibly autonomous persons. For the cult of rights, at the same time, our value resides in our unfettered and disembodied autonomy, the capacity upon which our right to dominion over our own lives is predicated. As such, no embodied vagaries, such as physical pain or psychological depression, may affect that autonomy. Yet most proponents of PAS go to extraordinary lengths to protect that transcendent autonomy, lest empirical constraints imperil persons' ability to exercise their agency. Accordingly, under the most widely known proposals, such as the Oregon Law, persons seeking PAS must meet externally defined conditions, such as being terminally ill and in intolerable pain, and must be repeatedly screened for psychological "fitness".[10]

To determine the value of continuing one's own life, then, one must consult with others, and meet conditions those others would deem rational bases for ending one's life. As such, while, for example, encroaching paralysis and impending dementia would not pose sufficient reasons to petition for assistance in dying, exhibiting a terminal condition accompanied by intractable pain would. Proponents of these more restrictive guidelines most often cite concerns about preventing persons from being pressured to act against their wishes. Yet this very paternalism is precisely what is called into question by the admission that persons are the final authorities in the dispensation of their own lives. Why does a terminal condition accompanied by intractable pain qualify as sufficient to warrant PAS, while encroaching paralysis and dementia – which may be more distressing – do not?

Strictly speaking, if persons are disembodied autonomous ends then none of these constraints are worse than any other, as none attach to persons per se. If, however, as the paternalism noted above implies, persons' autonomy is constrained by bodily or psychological or social affects, then how can we decide for everyone which sets of affects should be actionable and which shouldn't? The conditions the Oregon law set, for example, imply that the physical pain accompanying a terminal condition involves more suffering, and is less bearable, than a long, slow descent into paralysis and dementia. Yet we would seem to make no more individual decisions, then, about what makes our own lives valuable to us, and what would most truncate that value. Moreover, even if we presented this matter to the court of public opinion, the decisions of some majority would not thereby invalidate those of a minority in deciding which conditions would be more or less bearable, as all would be predicated on the same bases: individuals' valuations of their own lives.

Indeed, if for the cult of rights, the value of human life resides in our capacity to value, to make autonomous decisions, it would seem that we'd have to affirm the right of persons to make that determination, whatever its content, as individuals. Even that point, however, rings in the language of rights, and with it the implication that we have some legitimate interest in and claim on individual's decisions on this matter. Defenders of a right to self-determination, for example, nonetheless circulate endless codifications of the circumstances under which human life might be deemed more or less valuable to persons, or suicide rational, or permissible, or even obligatory. All beg the critical question of the extent to which dying belongs to our own individual authorship, sans any moral assay.

Implicit in all such discussions, after all, is the demand that any such suicide be justified: that it be rationally chosen or reasonable to some imagined others. Equally implicit is the cognate presumption that in suicide, we somehow implicate others in their persons. Yet the issue here is emphatically not the value of human life per se, which we may well wish to perpetuate, but of *this* life and what it has become in the present to itself. Howsoever we die, it is simply false that that process can devalue everything that came before it, as if in refusing more of our own lives we are thereby despoiling human life in its entirety.

6.3 Is dying a moral project?

At the same time – and here's the practical problem – to demand of persons that they have obligations to human life and to others, or even to themselves and to the moment of their last breath, intrudes public deliberation into what can only be, finally, irremediably private assessments. For the cult of life, any countenances of PAS, even those posed as mercy killing or as respect for individual autonomy, conjure remnants of Nazi medicine. They forget that whatever ends the Nazis pursued, mercy wasn't among them. More strikingly, they forget that Nazi doctors worked precisely not in the service of individuals but at the behest of state coercion in the name of a higher good, precisely the rationales the cult of life embraces in service to its own ends. While cult of life defenders would bristle at the analogy, both monopolize moral authority over the worth of persons' lives, such that those who disagree may be subordinated to a greater good. This great animator of moral mischief – the imposition of a greater good upon others, for their own good – has a long and disgraceful history, which the cult of life advances. Yet its siren song seems equally lost on those who would resist an imposed theodicy in favor of their own favored brand of paternalism, under the guise of human autonomy or human rights.

For both cults, the central issue remains not the existential meaning of death and dying but its moral import. The cult of life, rendering human life an absolute good, imposes it upon willing and unwilling persons alike, in complete disregard of the living individuals themselves. The cult of rights resists such impositions, but with the critical qualifier that the good of an individual's life be adjudicated by a range of professionals. On this basis, we face a patently modern absurdity: bioethics by committee. That gross absurdity reaches it height in the toxic stew that is the President's Bioethics Council, wherein competing voices contest among themselves with appeals to God or nature, to psychologists or sociologists or economists, to seers and sages, to philosophers and theologians, to physicians or poets, to historians and scientists, all seeking to forge a "consensus" on the meaning of human life and the proprieties of dying. Compounding this moralism run mad is the insistence, among bioethicists, that we need ever more public discourse on issues like PAS. From this cacophony of voices, they seek to fabricate some new species of moral authority. They might be better served by recalling instead an ancient metaphysical premise: from nothing, nothing comes. More pointedly, such efforts get the analysis precisely backwards. The issue here is not whether we could get a rational consensus on what might constitute a good death, but rather whether we should seek such consensus at all, as a means of exercising moral authority over how individuals die.

To seek such authority presupposes that dying is a moral project, wherein we are fully and irremediably answerable to others even on the occasion of our death. For both cults, however, persons do not die. Nor do their subjective preferences or judgments color the inalienable worth of human dignity or autonomy. Human agents could scarcely thwart divine providence; nor could they imperil inviolable human dignity through a mere assertion of a transient will. Conversely, the dying process leaves autonomous agents untouched. For the cult of life, my body and psyche and social relations drop away to reveal an immortal soul; for the cult of rights, my autonomy, unfettered by any biological contingencies, just mysteriously dissipates. At the same time, however, both ascribe moral content to the dying process. For the cult of life, the existential distress that attends dying is a means of moral and spiritual purification, a prospect from which we should not seek premature escape. For the cult of rights, the bodily and psychic dissolution that attends dying may imperil our autonomy, such that we require supervision, lest we fail to die autonomously. Given both cults' operative assumptions, of course, dying well or dying autonomously are equally nonsensical, and on precisely the same basis: we are not our transient psychic and physical states at all, but rather transcendent persons.

The existential distress both cults address, then, imperils only this subjectivity, as it signifies withdrawal from bodily and psychic and social life. To insist that we find generic moral significance in this process is nonsensical, because that valuation would still attach entirely to the transcendent nature of persons per se, and not at all to the particulars of this particular person. As such, how could this one singular death matter morally at all? The cult of life, far from defending the interiority of the dying process, aims to defend the worth of transcendent human dignity from that subjectivity; the cult of life, far from defending that subjectivity, aims to defend our transcendent autonomy from any subjective impingements. Indeed, the dying process should then prove amoral, as what passes away is not transcendent value at all, but mere epiphenomena. The moral project of dying, so conceived, would attend individuals only incidentally, and only insofar as their subjective valuations accorded with the inalienable worth of persons – a worth those valuations would leave untouched.

Yet it is precisely this privacy or interiority which both cults, in their defenses of human dignity, most directly imperil. These accounts turn any metaphysically intelligible or morally efficacious conception of human dignity inside out, because they seek human transcendence in a disembodied property, rather than in the irreducible personal privacy and bodily and psychic interiority that attends the vagaries of human living. In this, they relentlessly degrade human persons in their efforts to secure human transcendence. This may seem an extreme charge, since bioethicists of all stripes obsess over the unintended consequences of emerging biotechnologies and medical practices, demanding that the latter do no harm. While they impose that grave moral injunction on such practices and tools, however, they are heedless of the harm they do, to the quality of our living and dying, in and through their defense of ill-conceived moral ideals and the practices they legitimate.

Among the most striking examples of this propensity is both cults' effort to cling to a metaphysical dualism that liberates human worth or dignity or autonomy from the impingements of illness, aging, dying, and grieving. Thereby, they relocate human life to a transcendent realm ostensibly more real than that which we inhabit in and through our bodies, our psyches, and our social relations. For philosophical bioethicists, this re-engineering of human life has venerable roots tracing back to Plato's philosopher-kings, whose knowledge of the Ideal Form of human life offered them a unique moral authority. Alas, philosopher-kings are hard to come by, and the Forms continue to prove elusive, even millennia later. Current bioethicists, however, undeterred by history and experience, continue in such efforts to re-assign our moral authority over our own individual lives, in their intimacy and individuality, to more qualified arbiters. Indeed, the qualified arbiters have spawned an entire industry for themselves, dedicated to informing us about the value of our lives, to us, and how we should tend that value, at their behest.

In reserving such out-sized authority to themselves, however, and in seizing it from those who bear its practical consequences, both cults do exactly what they oppose on moral grounds: they reduce such persons not only to objects of the cults' designs, but also to means to their own ends. Both accounts base the value of human life on a transcendent feature shared by all and asserted to hold sway *a priori*, over all particular valuations. As such, both cults void individual bodily intimacy, psychic interiority, or personal privacy of any metaphysical purchase. In stripping from individual valuations any such purchase, they overlay their own purported moral authority upon them. Thereby, they void those particulars – of bodily comportment and valuation, of psychic interiority and inter-subjective intimacy, of personal privacy – of any moral worth. Unsurprisingly, then, they deem the deaths of individuals inconsequential. If either cult is correct, the entirety of the human life cycle leaves persons unaffected, and how we live, or how we die, should prove matters of moral indifference.

6.4 The sanctity of power

This confusion culminates in the President's Council on Bioethics, which appears to be at the height of its *powers* (emphasis added) when groping for eternal verities amid flights of theological or existential fancy. To date, this council has yielded agreement on precisely one premise – the sanctity or dignity of human life. But where does that dignity come from, and what does it require of us? It would help if the qualified arbiters could agree on where we find it. Does it haunt the agonized dying processes the cult of life valorizes, like a rarefied Platonic Form. Or does it reside in our efforts to elide such a death, as the cult of rights commends? No definitive answer is forthcoming. Human dignity, instead, turns out to be more akin to pornography or obscenity: the qualified arbiters know it when they see it. Except, alas, that we cannot see it; it inhabits not the visible world available to our senses, but the intelligible world accessible only to intuition. Indeed, the same vision of human dignity is supposedly available to all of us, as it remains unaffected by its residence in particular bodies or minds.

Both its metaphysical reality and the moral truths it underwrites, then, as Plato famously maintained, should be available to every rational apprehender, as a condition of their moral authority.

For his part, Plato remained consistent with the practical implications of his metaphysical dualism. While he accorded ultimate moral authority for the good of individual souls' to his philosopher-kings – who alone had full knowledge of the Forms – he took an entirely dim view of medicine and its concern for the body. For Plato, medicine was an inferior craft because it treated the body. Physical disease, moreover, typically signified a disordered soul, and finally warranted moral rather then medicinal ministrations. Like Plato, contemporary bioethicists of both cults ascribe human worth or dignity or sanctity to a transcendent soul or property or capacity. Unlike Plato, and wholly inconsistently, they simultaneously seek to read – from these transcendent heights – moral guidance in the care of the transient, and worthless, body. They ascribe the moral worth of the body entirely to these transcendent forms, and from the latter aim to prescribe how we should live our bodies. It might go without saying here that Plato's teacher, Socrates, took his own life, and insofar as he regarded himself as a physician of the soul – the only proper sort – he might be deemed the most famous perpetrator of PAS to date.

But that point cannot go without saying precisely because for the entirety of the moral tradition he inaugurated, the human body is not only epiphenomenal but in no way authoritative in the dispensation of the soul. Bodily health and comportment were, on his view, at most external signs of virtue. They were neither instrumental to the good of the soul, nor intrinsically good in their own right. The metaphysical dualism that Plato affirms reserves moral authority to the philosopher-kings in identifying the eternal verities to which our souls must conform, for our own good. But the body is beyond their ken because it does not participate, except as a mere shadow, in the transcendent reality to which our souls properly belong. As such, matters of bodily comportment are matters of relative metaphysical and moral indifference. We can know nothing about the body, after all, as it proves a mere specter or shadow of the true objects of knowledge. Nor can the body prove a source of knowledge; to the contrary, it occludes our apprehension of the real, transcendent forms. Nor can the body be either a source of moral knowledge or an object of moral regard, as it dissolves into unformed matter. At the same time, Plato ascribes moral authority to the philosopher-kings only insofar as they grasp the truth of human life and acquire the wisdom to direct it. Only because they grasp this truth, he insists, can they exercise moral authority sans the corruptions of power.

Most contemporary philosophers are skeptical about our prospects of locating the knowledge Plato depicts or identifying the philosopher-kings capable of arbitrating it. Contemporary bioethicists have no such qualms. Current debates may be rationally incommensurable, they might grant, but that challenge can be addressed by more debate, more committees, and more position papers. For such bioethicists, our public policies, like Plato's Forms, embody our conception of the worth of human life. For such bioethicists, unlike for Plato, those policies range unintelligibly over empirical epiphenomena at most contingently related to human dignity or autonomy. On both cults' own accounts, after all, we should regard bodily dispensations as occurring outside any moral realm. At most, they should prove appearances in Plato's sense, and on the same grounds. The empirical stuff of life – our impulse, tastes, preferences, pleasures and pains, hopes and fears, all of the valuations particular to us as individuals, proves epiphenomenal, as do any of the affects or effects of our agency as embodied persons. So what basis remains for a bioethic? For Plato, the answer was straightforward: none.

Indeed, current bioethics debates, as embodied in the President's Council on Bioethics, would be wholly unintelligible to him. The council prides itself on representing competing voices: physicians, theologians, scientists, philosophers, seers and sages, all vie to defend their own conceptions of human dignity and the policies and practices appropriate to that dignity. In this, it takes what is epiphenomenal, deliverances of the senses, of feeling and preference, of individual judgment and valuation – and from this volatile stew of subjectivism, it futilely seeks to distill universal truth. It seeks to decant practical wisdom from our pooled ignorance concerning the "meaning and worth" of human life. I term this pooled ignorance not because it reaches no consensus, but because the issue for Plato is never consensus about meaning, but apprehension of moral truth. Even if the Council reached unanimous agreement on what human dignity is, after all, that consensus alone would not prove the agreement's truth. That's accomplished, rather, by apprehending the Form, which transcends all individual viewpoints by definition. For Plato, democratic fabrications of moral authority – sans the requisite truth of the matter – signal not truth but tyranny, not practical wisdom but raw power, seized by force or fraud.

Such sanctioning of tyranny is precisely what bioethicists do when they indulge in transcendent flights of fancy which are imposed upon others as eternal verities, and which thereby strip individuals of substantive moral authority over their own living and dying.

Indeed, I suggest, among the primary tasks of philosophical bioethics should be a sustained effort to undo the moral damage done, to bioethics, by metaphysical dualism. Central to that damage is the insistence that persons are not their bodies, but something greater, such that whatever pleasures or pains our bodies bear offer neither epistemic knowledge – about the reality of human living – nor guidance for assessing moral norms. In this insistence, such views propose not sustained attention to the physical and psychic realities of living, ailing and dying, but grand moral narratives – of finitude and redemption, of the triumph of the human will over nature – wherein we transcend our mere embodiment. We should not be surprised then, that in the vast and burgeoning bulk of bioethics work, we may find innumerable references to human dignity and autonomy, and astonishingly few to pain and grief and loss. Nor should it surprise us that we meet with an endless stream of case studies, the differences among them blurring into the undying march of humanity into the transcendent heights, sans any substantive reference to the particular losses encountered along the way. Such theodicies, both secular and theological, make perfect sense, if we lose nothing, really, in ailing and dying. The enduring subtexts of such stories, however, are authored not by transcendent specters and their would-be defenders but by more familiar authors: Mother Nature, and her ever faithful consort, Father Time.

Neither nature nor time plays any role in such case studies, since the former have no grasp on transcendent beings. Like all other potentially individuating realities, they too reduce to the transient epiphenomena of embodiment negated by both cults. And that would seem a fitting conclusion, as it is ultimately not human intervention, but nature and time, from which both cults wish to secure us. The great threat to both cults from practices like PAS, after all, is not that such practices somehow negate a transcendent value – as if that were possible – but that they so graphically affirm the intransigence of human embodiment and human finitude. Defenders of PAS, or as they more often describe it, physician assisted dying, suggest rightly that this is not properly a species of suicide at all, insofar as it is the dying body that initiates the process. It is the dying body that seizes hold of the dying person, wresting away the value or worth of continued living to that person at that time. To accede to that impingement, both cults suggest, is life-denying, as it negates the transcendent worth of that life under any circumstances. Yet these cults are themselves life-denying in two pernicious ways. First, they negate the authority of the living body, wholly subordinating it in service to a transcendent end that, in itself, denies among the most basic features of biological living, organic mortality. This point is especially salient for the cult of life, which insists that we accept our finitude, while demanding simultaneously that we resist it with every dying breath.

Second, both cults render the dying person a moral patient, relocating his or her moral agency outside the intimacy and interiority of his or her dying process. In distilling the moral authority of persons from that of embodied human individuals, these accounts negate the metaphysical and moral substance of living or and dying in any empirical guise. Unsurprisingly then, they opposes practices that might enhance living or ease dying as themselves life denying, and against which they aim to defend human life in its most idealized conceptions. Both cults, despite their moral pretensions, are rear guard actions to defend us not from emerging biotechnologies, but from the changes such technologies may adduce in our self-conceptions, among them, our real subjection to nature and to time. Yet they ignore the extra-ordinarily high and ever-increasing price we pay for our supposed pricelessness. If human dignity has any metaphysical purchase on embodied human living, and any substantive moral content, it does so only insofar as it attaches to the irreducible bodily interiority and personal privacy of persons. At the same time, any conception of human dignity that hands one person's moral authority – over their own life – to another, degrades and abrogates that dignity precisely because it voids the agent capacity – that lends any distinctively moral worth to human living.

In insisting that all lives are livable, for example, both cults truncate the bodily intimacy and psychic interiority that attend human living and lend it its distinctive valuations. Both cults would object that our empirical quality of living has nothing to do with the dignity of human life. Yet a human life that so transcends the vagaries of living affords us precisely no norms for how we ought to attend the vagaries of dying. At the same time, if those subjective valuations bear any moral substance or worth, they admit of no rational commensurability, precisely because they are particular to individuals. On that count, no one can decide for another which quality of life proves tolerable. The key issue here, then, is not that our assessments of quality of life are incommensurable, but that any demand for such commensurability drags properly private assessments into public arenas. Indeed, I suggest, debates like that over PAS are illicitly engineered by bioethicists, in a bid to fabricate moral authority where only power resides. Why do we need bioethics councils and committees? To decide what we ought to do, insist both cults. Yet not only are there no generic public obligations to be found here, there is equally and more vitally no "we" here – in anything but a bare additive sense.

That conclusion may seem peculiar insofar as bioethicists of all stripes have over the past half century engineered a campaign of mass paternalism of epic proportions. These are not new in history, of course: crusaders, missionaries, witch burners and the like have always been with us. The crusaders had the good of heretics in mind, and even Nazis the good of the master race. Whose good do contemporary bioethicists serve? Mine, they insist, and yours, and well, everyone who doesn't know better, who doesn't know how to properly value human dignity. While they vitally wish to defend my life, however, and even if need be from my own misguided agency, they do so by voiding the intimacy and interiority and agency that make it mine to value, i.e. by doing for me something that only I can do. Perhaps they wish to spare me the trouble of so valuing my life. But they are thereby aspiring to spare me of the labor of living as a moral agent. In referring that valuation process to others, they out-source the moral work of living. In so re-engineering my life, they maintain that they have both a legitimate interest in and legitimate authority over my life's work, and that I have comparable license to exercise such authority over others. We witness, for example, endless public debate over others' dying moments, as in well publicized right- to- die cases. Such "cases" are posed as public controversies, as if anyone but those most intimately involved have a legitimate interest in, must less authority over, such activities. These controversies, fueled by bioethicists on all sides, perpetrate a pernicious moral voyeurism.

At the same time, these bioethicists *cum* agent provocateurs suggest that we as a society must come to some consensus. But how does an act as private as dying become a public trial and referendum and spectacle? It does so because whatever the rallying cries of human dignity or autonomy or the sanctity of human life defend, it is emphatically not the bodily intimacy and psychic interiority that attend our lives in their particulars. Such irreducible privacy has few partisans among bioethicists. It cannot, because it poses an irreducible barrier to the legitimate authority that one moral agent might exercise over another. It opposes, that is, the rank fabrication of moral authority by which both cults reserve to themselves the capacity to render ultimate dispensations upon how others live and die. Yet it is precisely this personal privacy, I suggest, which underwrites any morally efficacious conception of human dignity or autonomy or agency. It is alike this privacy which both cults endanger, in their purported defenses of human dignity, and which must be secured, if human dignity is to prove anything more than an empty slogan.

7
Who Do Bioethicists Think They Are?

The previous chapter exemplifies a basic paradox enacted by both cults: they oppose efforts of to engineer persons through biological innovations. Yet they combat those efforts, and the biotechnologies which underwrite them, by themselves re-engineering persons through social means. From their physically, psychically and socially embodied origins, both cults aim to recreate persons in their own images, making them over into the transcendent specters they spin from their moral imaginations. At the same time, they depict human persons not as essentially constituted by their specific bodies or minds or personalities or social relations, but as essentially identified with transcendent properties. These timeless properties, however, cannot essentially qualify human persons who procreate, and age, and ail, and die. Nor can they, secure in their transcendence, dignify particular human persons in their human particulars. To the contrary, only human practices – aimed at personalizing specific persons – can secure that end. Only on that basis, moreover, may we value human life for what it is, as irremediably embodied amid the contingencies of nature and of time.

7.1 The object of my affection?

Both cults, in insisting that a substantive chasm obtains between human persons and biotechnologies, ignore two critical points. Future persons cannot help but be the objects of present persons' choices, whether through acts of commission or omission; conversely, present persons cannot help but be the subjects of such technologies, selecting through their action – or inaction – which persons will come into being, and which will not. Both cults would object here that such suggestions uncritically espouse a technological imperative, a presumption that we should use enhancements simply because they are available. Against a supposed technological imperative, they impose what we might term an inertial imperative: the suggestion that if we simply decline to use or to develop such technologies, we are then not making a moral choice and not selecting a future. Yet even as individuals we can readily recognize our futures for what they are: the sum totals of what we do, and what we do not do.

The human futures that both cults ostensibly aim to defend in fact exhibit a precisely analogous texture, as a collective summation of human action and inaction. Both cults see the matter otherwise, however, contrasting persons as they are now with the supposed post-human persons we will create in the future, as deliberate objects of our designs.

Future persons, they insist instead, should be left to their own devices, either to unfold teleologically, as sprung *de novo* from God's will, or to create themselves from the unfettered power of their wills. Such creatures, however, would themselves prove more radically post-human than anything the most rabid futurists or technophiles envision.[1] For the latter, human persons remain irremediably subject to the empirical constraints that souls and autonomous ends wholly transcend. Indeed, both cults render such constraints entirely immaterial. For the cult of life, we should value all lives equally, and reject any interventions that prefer some health states over others. On this view, we can lend no normative content to the term health, and no moral content to the practice of medicine, precisely because all lives are equally valuable. For the cult of rights, we cannot measure the quality of life except as arbitrarily willed by autonomous individuals. Not only should we not make such choices for others, they insist, we should not seek the capacity to have such choices, as that would impose our preferences upon future persons. On both accounts, then, we simply cannot say that a future world without polio or Alzheimer's would be better then a world with these diseases, as we cannot and should not decide for future persons what their genetic potentials should include.

That's nonsense on a grand scale, particularly if the cult of life's avowed creationism is true, since human will could scarcely thwart divine agency. Cult of right defenders make analogous charges, maintaining that parents cannot know what their future children will want, and that selecting a child's genotype is too determinative of that child's identity. Yet, how children acquire their genotypes has no effect on their self-creating capacity if they are autonomous ends.

Moreover, both cults, while opposing parents' selections of health preferences or even traits like eye color as too determinative of their children's futures, license parents' extensive rights to make substantive choices for their children's futures, in selecting their religions, their values, and their educational prospects. Both cults thereby presume that genetic inheritances are more determinative of personal identity than social inheritances, despite their shared insistence that persons transcend biological constraints. Yet as these debates themselves illustrate, social inheritances are no less obdurate than are genetic inheritances. Both cults' conceptions of human dignity, for example, aim at constructing persons of a specific type.

For the cult of life, that end is to sustain persons with all manner of disabilities, preventable or not, as an affirmation of human dignity as wholly unqualified by biological constraints. For the cult of rights, that end is to secure the autonomy of future persons from the imposition of present persons' arbitrary preferences, including those that would prevent future disabilities. Thereby, they alike reject any association between health and the good of human life, and any link between the empirical quality of human living and its transcendent good. To the question what good human life is, any answer must refer to a non-empirical source. While our bodies may experience pleasure and pain, these can neither be natural goods(as entertained by our animal nature), nor be transmuted into instrumental goods by the will (since we need do nothing contingent to secure our transcendent worth), nor be valued as intrinsic goods (as that would tie us irremediably to an animal nature). The human body thus tells us nothing normative about how we ought to live.

If either cult believed these premises, bioethics would be much simpler. Each cult could go contentedly on its way, and leave those who seek human enhancement to their own devices, to do as they wished precisely because nothing they do will matter. Yet both cults do the opposite, alike insisting on the one hand that persons should not to be objects of human design, and on the other that persons should remain as they envision them. The basic problem is plain. Both cults suggest that we may somehow harm persons by genetically engineering them, yet deny that human persons are made through human activities. Both reject the latter point as an assertion of base human despotism and hubris. Yet however future persons receive their genotypes – by nature, by God, by human selection, by mail order – it cedes them a genetic inheritance over which they had no choice, and over which their progenitors did. To say that we should not prevent avoidable maladies does not assert that we are powerless against the inevitable, but that we are unwilling to forestall certain ills, diseases, or debilities, in favor of ostensibly greater goods, like human dignity. The recourse to moral injunctions is instructive here, as their great power – and temptation – lies in their ability to depersonalize decisions, to accord them to God or nature or reason or norms of medical practice or the weight of tradition – that is, to reassign them to any source but ourselves.

Both cults, in insisting that we should not choose particular futures, and should not even seek the capacity, for example, to create a future without Alzheimer's, assert in fine adolescent fashion that we can pick and choose among our responsibilities. We may or must treat the disease, they intone, but not by preventing persons-with-Alzheimer's from existing in the first place. That any such qualification of persons is nonsensical on their own account escapes proponents of the cult of life. Conversely, whether we choose for future persons or not, we no less impose our preferences upon them. At the same time, to ascribe such selections to God or nature not only negates human agency but any conception of human embodiment as essentially qualifying persons, and so as authorizing some selections over others. These ascriptions, too, have the dual benefit of relieving us of moral responsibility for future persons and sustaining both cults' vaunted self-conceptions. Yet they thereby not only dehumanize human dignity, but also alienate authority over human biological life to transcendent ends for which they then claim no responsibility. Both cults, rather, ascribe responsibility for those values to extrinsic authoritative sources, while reserving to themselves the power to impose those values upon others for their own good.

What both cults perpetrate, then, is what they claim to oppose: outsized efforts to remake persons in their own image. That effort, in turn, dehumanizes and depersonalizes persons, rendering them wholly creatures of both cults' moral imaginations. In securing their personhood, that is, both cults make persons into transcendent moral objects, sans any substantive agency of their own. Thereby, persons are shorn of their bodily, psychic or social concomitants, none of which warrant substantive moral consideration. To object to either cult, for example, that future persons should not be made to suffer needless debilities or diseases evokes the immediate counter that they are first and last persons, sans any reference to their bodily estate. That their bodies suffer may well be granted. Yet that consideration remains forever subordinate to their status as souls or ends. Not only is their bodily suffering voided of moral weight, so too is the distress of their parents. Children so conceived, as persons, are subject not first to the private, preferential love of their parents, but to their public status as persons, as bearers of rights or responsibilities. For the cult of life, such children and their parents should endure their travails in service to a greater good. For the cult of rights, such children bear rights as persons. Accordingly, the disposition of such children's lives is not a private parental matter, but a matter of public assay; it is not a matter of private grief but of public debate.

On these accounts, both the bodily interiority of the children ostensibly defended, and the psychic subjectivity and personal privacy and agency of their parents, are systematically negated. More strikingly, persons are enjoined to discount, morally, both bodily suffering and psychic grief, and to substitute for them the public assertions that all lives are equally good, and equally warrant personal parental love and social investment, such that even if we could prevent such travails, we should not. Yet these moral demands require a depersonalized and dehumanized species of love, a love untouched by grief or loss, and itself dehumanizing and depersonalizing. For all the piety those twin charges evoke, neither cult lends any substance to them: What could it mean, really, to dehumanize an immortal soul or an autonomous end? For the cult of life, love properly conceived extends equally to all, lest it signal animal preferences; for the cult of rights, it is wholly a creature of will, such that it properly says nothing about its object but only about the preferences of its subject. On both accounts, partial love attaches to transient epiphenomena, and so proves not only uninformative about its objects, but morally also base, precisely because it does not attach to persons as persons.

It's unsurprising, then, that bioethicists, who ostensibly traffic in life and death and sex and birth and finitude and grief, speak so rarely and so unintelligibly of love. That's the case not only because they deny its epistemic merit, but also because they deny the reality of its objects. Cult of life defenders demand that we love all human life in the abstract; cult of rights defenders insist that, finally, we love only ourselves, or perhaps better, our autonomy. In neither case are particular persons in their specificity proper objects of love. For the cult of life, that result is salutary because making particular persons objects of love subjects them to our use, degrading them. For the cult of rights, that result is salutary because it retains each subject's freedom. On both views, moral love, as accorded to immortal souls or ends, is subject neither to time nor to biological vagaries. Yet just as each account elevates the worth of human persons by voiding them of any contingent human elements, so too does each account dehumanize love. For the cult of life, moral love must prove impersonal, lest we use others for our own purposes. For the cult of rights, we must preclude not only using others as means, but also any subjection to sentiment that imperils the will's autonomy. On both accounts, partial love poses a stark moral challenge, threatening to ensnare us in animal enjoyments, in selfishness and egoism. Conversely, morally licit love must prove selfless, on both sides of the equation, at least insofar as we are dignified or autonomous persons.

To love or respect someone as either cult demands, however, requires us to remove that person from their body, their psyche, their specific social relations to us, and also to value their absolute worth sans any prospect of suffering or grief, whether on their part or ours. As mutually invulnerable persons, we must also maintain that the life they feel is not life as we know it, such that if, for example, they withdraw any valuation of their own life, we must demand that they instead regard their life as we know it, substituting our interiority and agency for theirs. It licenses us, that is, to enjoin them to disregard the deliverances of their own subjectivity, hollowing those out and putting others' judgments in their place. While we may respect or love or preserve the absolute worth of that human life, then, we do so by devaluing the preferences, feelings, and personality animating that life, negating their validity. To say that we thereby depersonalize or dehumanize such lives would be, for both cults, false, as persons are not their particulars. On that premise, both cults systematically drain away the lived interiority of the persons they defend, not only by substituting others' valuations for their own, but first by negating the metaphysical and epistemic reality of each individual's interior life. Pleasure and pain, fear and sorrow, are all deemed epiphenomena.

Yet only using such particulars can we describe the grief that attends dying or ailing, the regret that we can no longer be what once were, the recognition that what we once valued is dissolving before our eyes. That grief asserts as irreplaceable precisely the incidentals – of bodily presence, personality, and subjectivity – that both cults disregard because they signal irreducible particularity. That both cults wholly disregard the metaphysical and moral weight of such particularity is illustrated vividly in their treatment of PAS. Here, both cults assert a presumption in favor of sustaining human life, the cult of life proscribing PAS in principle, the cult of rights authorizing it only by securing external judgments upon the livability of a specific life to the particular person charged with living that life. Yet such proscriptions add to the dying person's bodily dissolution a second assault. Indeed, so concerned are both cults with the preservation of human dignity and autonomy that they perhaps conceive murder too narrowly, identifying it wholly with the dispensation of the body. For the cult of life, "we" must love our lives; yet that love must attach not to out particular lives, but to the dignity of life per se, to which our individual valuations must give way. For the cult of rights, our respect for persons enjoins us to ensure that they make autonomous decisions, even if as adjudicated by others and contrary to their own wills. That such demands thereby entail a pernicious brand of suicide of their own design escapes both cults, as does any recognition that imposing such demands on others is murder by other means.

That conclusion may seem extreme. But there are few more apt descriptions for moral injunctions that demand of ostensible agents the wholesale substitution of others' valuations for their own. Both cults wholly objectify others, hollowing out their interiority and rendering it morally inert, such that the agency of individuals as individuals is replaced with a kind of agency authorized entirely by others and by reference to transcendent metaphysical properties. They protect others from suicide then, it would seem, by finishing them off themselves. Conversely, love or respect as moral charges presuppose the opposite trajectory – that persons are both objects and subjects of each other. Philosophers have, of course, long debated what makes up our personal identity, positing features like souls, memories, bodily or behavioral patterns, minds, characters, and even self-authoring fictions. These accounts, however, invariably prove incomplete. On the one hand, they presuppose that such identity is reducible to a singular property or set of properties, and that our self is somehow simply located within our bodies, and not at all located in others. At the same time, even those philosophers whose accounts of personal identity most vigorously assert our independence both of biological and social constraints– philosophers such as e.g. Sartre – recognize the power of observation, of what he termed the gaze, to qualify how we objectify others, and are invariably objectified in turn.

The great paradox Sartre depicts is that our self-consciousness, while stirred to life amid becoming someone to another, comes into being as precisely not what it is, as a thing rather than as a collection of infinite possibilities. At the same time, while that other aims thereby to objectify me, he can never succeed because I am nothing he conceives me to be, and in fact, am nothing in particular at all. Sartre's account implies both that such objectifications are inherently falsifying (such that they tell us nothing about the other) and that they are inherently violent(in that being anything in particular imperils our prospects for absolute transcendence). That such objectifications are forever incomplete, however, insofar as I can modify them, signifies not their falsity but their contingency: just because I am some set of qualifiers now need not preclude my capacity to modify them. Conversely, while others may objectify me and create me in ways not of my choosing, I constitute them in turn. As such it is strictly false to say that I am located simply in me, or that those others are located simply in themselves. Moreover, on this account, persons are neither wholly transparent nor wholly opaque to each other.

For both cults, persons are not only wholly transparent to each other but also identical in their absolute worth. Pleasures and pains, trapped within the lining of the body, remain mute and incommunicable; admitting no public referees, they have no claim to deliver knowledge about that body's experience. Griefs and sorrows and joys and loves, secreted within psychic interiority, tell us nothing about the objective world we apprehend, nor are they available to others. As such, I can know precisely nothing of another's interiority, and that very opacity invalidates any epistemic, metaphysical or moral claim that others' interior lives might have upon me, precisely because they have been rendered epiphenomenal, transient, ephemeral - unreal. The self-perpetuating logic of these presumptions unfolds unabated: pleasures and pains, sorrows and joys, preferences and wishes, partialities and needs and sentiments, all prove at best illicit ties to our animal nature, and at worst, occlude our prospect of valuing persons as persons. Insofar as such opacities remain private, they have neither epistemic nor metaphysical purchase on others. Moreover, insofar as I am really not those particulars at all, but a transcendent end or soul, they are precisely worthless, morally. I can neither know what others wish, nor aid or thwart them in their pursuits. Nor can I devalue them in their persons, precisely because their transcendent persons are secured *a priori*.

As they are identical to me, after all being mutually independent and secure in their inviolate transcendence, my indifference or hostility to their preferences or needs or wishes leaves them untouched. Nor can I enrich or enliven their interior lives by my attention or assistance. Neither interiority, moreover, adds anything of novel value to the world, as persons are all persons; nor is that interiority either an object or a subject of human creativity or agency, but remains forever as it was at its inception, invulnerable to harm. Yet how then can such persons be killed, or grieved, or mourned? How can they ail and die and procreate and share a world in common? And how can anything they do matter –morally– if it affects nothing beyond their own interiority? Such agency is possible only if persons are mutually affected; if that private interiority bears metaphysical and moral import. At the same time, I suggest, mutual affectability requires a metaphysical intimacy wherein, to the extent that we transcend our particularities, we do so not as disembodied ends or souls, but within our mutual location in others, and them in us, i.e. insofar as we take up residence in each other as mutually constituting. What brings persons to life, as particular persons, is not their human commonality, but this mutual evoking of interiority which underlies moral agency. Such mutual regard is morally freighted, in other words, only insofar as that mutual accessibility seeds alike a mutual vulnerability, and with it the power to dignify or degrade others in their persons, to cultivate or to thwart the individuality – the interiority, subjectivity and privacy – of persons, apart from which human dignity and human autonomy have no meaning and no worth.

7.2 Getting too personal again?

From birth control to in-vitro fertilization (IVF) to embryo selection to abortion to the treatment of anencephalic infants, the cult of life wages an aggressive campaign to subject the entirety of our procreative practices to public authority. Against these incursions, the cult of rights mounts a rearguard defense of personal privacy, a legal construct subject to prevailing political winds. The ensuing battle over our prospective procreative liberty would seem to pit the two cults irremediably at odds. Yet they are not disputing, as is often supposed, the boundaries of that privacy. For the cult of life, no such privacy right exists; for the cult of rights, it is predicated on persons' ability to act autonomously. For the cult of life, no such privacy exists because persons must leave to God the beginnings of human life. For the cult of rights, such privacy exists only because persons can act autonomously of all bodily, psychic and social constraints. While the cult of life extends human dignity, unintelligibly, to every vestige of human life, the cult of life extends the moral status of persons as ends, unintelligibly, to rational agents. On these accounts, they disagree over how widely our moral concern extends. The cult of life, for example, insists that embryos and anencephalic infants are complete persons, whereas the cult of rights denies that premise, insofar as such beings lack a rational, autonomous capacity. So conceived, these disputes would indeed seem rationally incommensurable, as they contest a primitive moral premise: who counts as a person?

Even settling that question, however, offers no guidance in our procreative practices, if the latter author bodies rather than persons. These disputes over privacy rights arise from the identification of persons not with their bodies, or psyches, or their social relations, but as souls or ends. On both accounts, our value resides wholly and entirely in our commonality to others. Unsurprisingly, even the privacy defended by the cult of rights bears no essential reference to persons' bodies, or psychic interiority, or social relations – which embody nothing warranting substantive metaphysical import or moral worth. Privacy so conceived is, rather, wholly impersonal, attaching not to individuals per se but to instances of a type, autonomous ends. As such, just as the cult of life defends the worth not of individuals in their particulars, but of human life in its sanctity, so too do cult of rights proponents defend not the worth of individuals in their particulars, but of autonomy in the abstract. These ideals - of the dignity or sanctity or autonomy of human life - do not serve the good of human living. To the contrary, particular human lives are forcibly impressed into their service.

The cult of life, for example, demands of persons that we love all human life equally, such that hastening or even allowing the deaths of anencephalic infants degrades the sanctity of human life in itself. This insistence brooks no discussion, much less compromise with critics who affirm the rights of parents to make such decisions for their children. Still, the right asserted here is not of parents as parents, but of persons as persons, as self-determining agents. Against a defense of life for the sake of life is posited a defense of autonomy for the sake of autonomy. We might again follow MacIntyre here in depicting this dispute as rationally incommensurable, as advancing two competing premises only one of which may ultimately secure rational consensus. Even if we grant the dubious prospect that social consensus per se is rational, the broader question remains whether this is properly a matter of public discourse. For MacIntyre, such debates are interminable only because they issues from rival premises, and thereby devolve into assertions of private interests and preferences. Secure consensus on such premises, conversely, and such disputes can be rationally resolved. This analysis, however, presumes that such issues are properly matters of public discourse, and that persons are, in their agency, wholly transparent.

So construed, persons, as individuals would have no right to privacy in the exercise of their agency. For the cult of life, we have no such right in principle. Yet for the cult of rights, too, rational autonomy precludes reference to interests and preferences. The moral object of such privacy rights is not individuals in their specifics, but autonomy per se.

Moreover, such privacy rights license all manner of incursions into bodily interiority and psychic subjectivity and social relations, to ensure not that persons are making decisions for themselves, but that persons are enacting the necessary conditions for exercising their autonomy. Cult of right defenders would insist that the two are identical. We act as autonomous persons, after all, only if we are free of bodily and psychic and social impingements. As such, for example, we may have a right to PAS. But this can be the case only if we are unconstrained by bodily or psychological or social impingements, as certified by physicians and psychologists and social workers and the panoply of expert strangers designated to confirm that we are acting as ourselves. I may have a right to IVF, or to embryo selection, but only if I do so for the right reasons, as determined by public authorities. This emphasis on preserving the conditions of autonomy precludes any moral privacy, as rooted in the bodily interiority and psychic subjectivity and social relations of particular agents, as over against the moral authority ascribed to others. To the contrary, it drags the entire domain of our ostensibly private valuations into the arena of public assay.

Defenders of the cult of rights might object that they aim to secure agents' privacy in the language of public rights. Yet the language of rights itself has been co-opted by the cult of life, which asserts the unalloyed right to life of embryos, of PAS seekers, and even of anencephalic infants whose parents might prefer for them an easier death. Such rights are patently nonsensical, since on their account persons neither come into being nor pass away at human behest. Nevertheless, this cult asserts the slogan that all persons have a right to life, a slogan whose sheer rhetorical force conjures ostensible moral responsibilities. Persons who engage in sexual activities, we're told gravely, must bear the consequences of those actions, including unwanted or severely disabled children. Not only must those children be brought to life, they must be loved equally as all others, as predicated on their absolute worth and dignity. This insistence, however, is itself morally disordered, to use familiar cult of life language, in three critical ways. First, it entirely disregards any consideration of the child's good, as over against the person's transcendent worth or value. That worth, as judged from without, may prove entirely worthless from within a severely malformed body. Still, they insist, that body bears the sanctity of human life, and secures its right to sustenance on that basis.

The defense of human life enjoined here attaches not to this particular organism, nor even to its humanity as a biological reality, but only to an instantiation of human dignity. So conceived, that being reduces to a moral object, a construction of our moral imagination that must be secured lest it imperil our worth and the worth of humanity per se. As an immortal soul, however, it needs no such ministrations; nor would easing its biological death imperil its dignity. To insist that that its biological life be sustained not for its good but for ours and for the good of all humanity, and as a measure of our virtue, not only reduces that specific life to a means to ends extrinsic and perhaps even contrary to its own ends, but borders on a bizarre species of idolatry, of human egoism writ large. Cult of life defenders would insist instead that such injunctions signal generosity and love of human life in all forms. Yet the power they ascribe us, to dignify or to degrade, opposes their theology. Persons are complete at their divine inception, sans any necessary biological development. Conversely, depriving persons of such a contingent existence could scarcely imperil them.

To assert instead a right to biological life, and to impress cognate responsibilities upon parents to secure this right for their children, affirms a completely contrary point. It implies a dependence through which parents both affect and effect their children. It implies, moreover, that this dependence attaches them not merely as persons to persons, but as particulars in their particularities. Even if a right to life of persons is established, for example, and even if we assert that embryos are persons, neither premise obligates a particular person to bring a specific embryo to term. If a person's right to life is predicated on its status as a transcendent soul, it can scarcely claim any moral interest in securing an empirical life, any more than it can claim moral harm if such a life is denied. At the same time, if frozen embryos embody an absolute right to biological life, persons per se would have some obligation to bring them to term. Not only, that is, must we forestall abortion, but we must enjoin the forcible implantation of such extra-corporeal embryos, even in unwilling persons, who must alike subordinate their private preferences to the public good. This conclusion may seem extreme, but the ascription of an absolute right to life to extra-corporeal embryos entails precisely this new species of immaculate conception. It cannot matter, after all, if the persons thus impregnated consent: they are enjoined, rather, to welcome and to value any human life.

The valuations thus demanded, however, are not finally public but private, and may only be rendered through the bodily interiority and psychic subjectivity impressed into service to the absolute value of human life. So conceived, that interiority and subjectivity would prove a fungible means to others' ends. As such, however, the apparent dependence of persons upon each other, as exemplified in gestation, birth and child-rearing, in bodily and psychic and social investments that can only be rendered amid private relations, is simply that, i.e. apparent. In asserting such absolute rights, the cult of life aims to encapsulate the love of human life that they maintain should underwrite all procreative practices. They thus seek to defend the insistence that all children are to be equally welcomed and sustained by their parents.

The sheer power of any child's dependence should give us pause here, however, and that on two counts. First, as indicated above, a generic right to life cannot entail responsibilities among particular persons, particularly insofar as their worth is predicated not at all on their contingent particulars, but only upon their inviolable status as persons. Second, and conversely, if we hold instead that those particulars – of body, mind and social relations – do bear moral worth, we must equally grant that to impress those particulars into unwilling service to a transcendent end not only exercises extraordinary dominion over individuals' bodily and psychic and social lives, but itself degrades precisely what it ostensibly secures from degradation: persons in their persons.

If our moral task is to secure transcendent souls or ends amid our procreative activities, after all, we succeed no matter what we do, as such beings are inviolate. If, however, our moral task is not simply to transmit transcendent kernels (as one might pass inadvertently swallowed watermelon seeds), but rather to dignify the persons procreated thereby, then we must maintain both that we not only effect such persons in their persons (by bringing them into being), and that those procreative practices affect them in their persons (dignifying or degrading them). If persons have a moral right to biological life, after all, something about that life must both warrant moral regard and protection, and so be vulnerable to moral harm, that is to human agency. At the same time, to assert such a moral right, the cult of life would have to defend also the premise that some particular individuals have distinctive moral claims upon other particulars individuals within procreative practices. Biological living, unlike personhood, attaches irremediably to specific embodiments, and entails for its creation specific bodily, psychic, and social relations. To invoke love as a procreative moral force, I suggest, presupposes that human persons are not mutually transcendent souls but mutually constituting particulars who bring each other into being through such valuations.

For the cult of life, human love cannot prove procreative, their claims to the contrary notwithstanding, because it brings nothing into being under its own auspices but endlessly and contingently decants kernels of absolute worth. So conceived, human procreation implies neither distinctive modes of embodiment nor of psychic or social life, as persons are unaffected, both metaphysically and morally, by the contingencies attending this succession of souls. For human love to prove procreative rather than simply replicative, and moral rather than simply sentimental, it must be alike volitional, intentional, and personal, a love which cannot be obligated because it must be freely offered, and must include the capacity for refusal. The cult of life would reject any such suggestion as failing to love all persons. This position maintains rightly that willingness to affirm a child in his or her individuality is the operative moral principle of parenthood. Yet in demanding that love as a duty, it negates its practice as a volitional, intentional project. To affirm individuals in their particulars, after all, is precisely not to value all lives equally, but to assert the value of this one in particular. It is not to value persons in their transcendence of all particulars – of body and psyche and social attachment – but to value them as embodied in and through those particulars. It is to bring to life persons as distinct persons, as irreducibly new centers of bodily interiority, psychic subjectivity, and personal agency. It is, to put it directly, to engage in person making.

Such persons, moreover, are not extrinsically related, as self-subsistent ends or souls. Rather, they inhabit one another through shared genes, shared languages and cultures and traditions, shared preferences and tendencies, through the shared valuations amid which they constitute one another as particular parents and children. Both cults would deny this mutual constitution, insisting that persons are not, and ought not to be, other persons' creations. If we are not "man made," we of course secure our transcendence not only of other persons but of biology per se, and abandon any need for medicine or biotechnology – or bioethics. We also make utter nonsense not only of our biological and social nature, but of our self-identify and agential prospects. Both cults espouse much philosophical nonsense on this point, locating our first-person interiority, subjectivity and agency only in what we share in common, as souls or ends, and clearing away as epiphenomenal clutter the pleasures and pains and memories and feelings and thoughts and hopes and baseball statistics that constitute our empirical lives. Yet in so seeking ourselves, our self-identities, in these inviolable substances, we are, alas, doubly lost. First, the real paradox of a person's ostensible self-identity is not that it endures through time and apart from all such contingencies, but that it is that individual's at all, at least not exclusively. To the contrary, the need – metaphysically and morally – to sustain personal privacy, and the injunction to cultivate it as a moral end, stirs to life because we are not self-subsistent, but are in part comprised of others' genes and habits and personalities and are irremediably the products of others' valuations. Amid such mutual constitutions, personal privacy is not an inviolable property attending our dignity or autonomy. It is, rather, an object of deliberate cultivation insofar as persons mutually evoke the bodily interiority, psychic subjectivity, and personal agency that constitute it.

7.3 My right to your life?

I stress this point because the privacy ostensibly at issue in disputes over procreative liberty exists for neither cult as a moral reality. Cult of rights defenders might object that they posit a right to such privacy precisely to defend agents' private preferences, as in cases like PAS. Those preferences, however, are not sources of moral agency or authority but are morally authorized only insofar as they are autonomously formulated, as the cult of rights proscribes. Those preferences bear no moral authority when they attach irremediably to individual bodies, psyches, or social relations, but only when they are rationally adjudicated by others. Privacy rights so posited, even if advanced to secure agent autonomy, bring agents' preferences under public scrutiny. Indeed, such rights are self-immolating. They make of irremediably private acts, like dying and procreating, public spectacles. Thereby, they intrude public authority into particular bodies, psyches, and social relations, which are then voided of any independent moral substance or worth in their privacy. Agent preferences become, rather, in the vernacular of the cult of life, mere arbitrary preferences, whereas they remain, for the cult of rights, impediments to full-fledged autonomy. This vanishing self, however, leaves it as unintelligible both how such private preferences could imperil or enhance our own or others' inviolable dignity, and what our inalienable autonomy might actually be good for.

For both cults, importantly, that absolute worth imposes itself upon us such that we owe ourselves and others either respect as autonomous ends, or love as dignified souls. But respect or love, wholly divorced from persons in their particulars, license us to ignore and even to extirpate those particulars, setting in their place goods of our own devising, ostensibly for their own good. On these counts, the apparent contrast between the cult of life's unrestrained paternalism, and the cult of rights' ostensible resistance to that paternalism, is precisely that, apparent only. The cult of life advances its paternalism under the premise that our lives are not our own but God's. The cult of rights insists instead that some persons should not be impressed into the service of others' values, particularly against the formers' will. Yet the right of persons to such self-determining liberty, like the right to life, is not a private but a public good. This point is obscured by the unfortunate distinction some ethicists draw between negative rights, which forbid us from harming those to which they attach, and positive rights, which enjoin us to assist those who bear them, even against the latter's will. The cult of rights would seem a natural candidate to advance negative rights, to insist that we may do whatever we choose as long as we do not violate others' rights to do the same. To claim such rights, however, as they indicate in positing a limited right to PAS, we must be deemed rational by qualified arbiters, who alone may identify whether we are acting as ourselves.

Against such limited rights, the cult of life immediately objects that we must oppose all such prospects as violating the agent's right to life. In situations ranging from anencephaly to advanced Alzheimer's to PAS, respect for persons or love of human life must trump private preferences to the contrary. This endeavor, involving action on behalf of others, even against their will to secure their own good, is of course the great seducer of bioethicists of all stripes.

It proffers the twin enticements of doing good for others while ensuring one's own virtue. Historically, similar reasoning was a prime moral rationale for slavery, as slaves, who were seen as being akin to non-rational animals, could scarcely prove self-determining but required others to direct them to their distinctive goods. This sort of justification has, of course, fallen out of moral favor with ethicists. Yet its operative logic, that some are better suited to direct the lives of others, for the latter's own good, endures. For the cult of life, my right to life strictly entails neither liberty nor responsibility on my part. I am enjoined instead to cede that life's entire disposition to God, or those who claim to speak for God. I have, that is, less a right to life – since neither I nor others can do anything to affect that life – than an inexplicable duty to live. Thus my right to life can be neither negative, insofar as it is inviolable in principle, nor positive, since its empirical conditions are irrelevant to its worth; it requires nothing of myself or of others.

As a gift from God or divinely authored nature, our lives can scarcely be claimed as a right and retain their status as gifts. Moreover, if they are entirely under God's disposition, we are no more enjoined to extend them (as for example, in anencephalic infants) than we are precluded from dispensing with them (as in PAS). The purported right to life, that is, yields no substantive content. In that right's negative guise, we deprive persons of nothing of substantive import if we kill their bodies, or truncate their minds, or embroil them in degrading social conditions. At the same time, persons neither need anything, nor need to do anything in particular, as persons, to sustain their moral worth. For the cult of life, practices such as PAS violate persons' right to life even if solicited by the person whose suicide is thus aided. On their own account, however, persons are not their bodies, or their minds, or their social relations to specific others. Nor are they essentially qualified by their own agency: persons need not be agents at all to qualify as persons, nor can their moral acts or omissions qualify their moral worth. Indeed, this position renders unintelligible its own presumption that any person who commits suicide thereby somehow violates his or her right to life. Not only can we not really kill ourselves, or be aided in such acts by others, but such acts destroy nothing of substantive worth metaphysical or moral import. Simply put: nothing they terminate matters.

For the cult of life, tellingly, the primary issue here is not the individual act of suicide, but its status as a referendum upon the value of human life. Similarly, for the cult of rights, the issue is less one of a particular act, than of whether that act secures individual autonomy, as publicly defined. As such, just as the cult of life's opposition to PAS is inconsistent with its operative theology, so too is the cult of rights' limited support for PAS inconsistent with its operative metaphysic. To qualify as truly autonomous, after all, such actions would have to prove entirely independent of any bodily or psychic or social impingements. They could not be legitimately predicated upon claims to intolerable pain, or a terminal condition, or guarantees that the agent is psychologically healthy, as all such considerations are extrinsic influences upon the will. Indeed, the cult of life opposes PAS on these grounds as well, insisting that we can never ensure that persons considering PAS are acting as themselves, given their distress. For the cult of rights, however, the issue is precisely not that persons must act as themselves, amid those constraints, but rather that they must act autonomously. We can have perfectly generic criteria for determining whether persons are so acting, because they are not acting as themselves – with their arbitrary whims and preferences – but as rational, autonomous, self-.determining ends. Yet on that standard, the very criteria they have thus far proposed, particularly that persons be terminally ill and experiencing intractable pain, preclude persons from making autonomous decisions. Anyone meeting those criteria would seem by definition to be precluded from making decisions that the cult of rights would deem rational.

As a matter of consistency, the cult of rights should assert an unalloyed right to suicide, to dominion over one's own life. Instead, it arbitrarily identifies some contingent conditions under which we may rationally deem our lives unlivable, and thereby renders PAS a matter of public morality. Our autonomous decisions must be rationally transparent to other agents, that is, to be definitively ours. They cannot, conversely, prove to be legitimately private at all. Many cult of rights defenders, of course, object vehemently to the cult of life's insistence that our lives belong not to us, but to God. At the same time, they reassign ownership and moral authority over individual lives not to particular persons, but to persons as instances of a type, autonomous ends. Against divine authority, they posit not individual assertions of will or preference, but the authority of autonomous reason as they envision it. The liberty of individuals to act is defined by their unfettered capacity to distance themselves from bodily, psychological, and social impingements, that is, to be not themselves at all. Emptied of private, arbitrary, or subjective motives, rather, they prove agents of autonomous reason, and all alike mutually transparent, as their inducements to act are entirely generic, entirely public, shorn of any opacity. Only on such a basis may a position that ostensibly advances individual liberty assert in that liberty's defense a moral paternalism that extirpates individual agency while seamlessly substituting its own moral authority in the former's place.

This seamless substitution of an alien agency for one's own poses a paradox. Both cults ostensibly join forces n refusing to render persons as means to others' ends. Yet they both do just that, by imposing upon individuals an alien public morality they may not share. Both cults reject not only that our lives are own, but that they embody any private goods – in bodily interiority, psychic subjectivity, or individual agency – that warrant moral protection. The very idea of such private goods would prove on both accounts nonsensical. Bodily pleasures and pains, psychological feelings, individual preferences and whims – none of these yield knowledge about us as persons or the world we inhabit, nor offer any normative guidance in how we ought to live. To the contrary, both accounts depict distinctively human life as entirely divorced from such contingencies. More strikingly, such views of human agency cannot admit of legitimate private interests or goods – of body, mind, or social relations – as rightful constraints upon the intrusion of public moral authority. Those particularities, rather, can be extirpated with no moral harm done to the person. Only in their utter public transparency as persons, after all, are persons subject to moral protection; only, that is, insofar as they are entirely identical to others, as ends or as souls.

Both cults' paternalisms, predicated on the twin assertions that we can know how others should live, and have the moral authority to impose that knowledge upon them, are thus legitimated on the same basis: that moral claims by definition trump individuals' preferences. Moreover, it may then seem sensible that both cults construe beginning and end of life issues, which most directly affect those immediately involved, as if they have grave moral import for all of us, implicating generic rights to life or liberty. These rights, however, have nothing to do with me or to you as individuals. Yet both cults advance the dubious presumption that in choosing for ourselves we directly affect others, such that, for example, in debating PAS we are enacting a referendum on human dignity or human liberty in their entirety. So construed, even to countenance PAS embroils us in an exercise in public moral agency. For the cult of rights, persons act autonomously only when they rationally deliberate upon their situations sans any influences of fear, pain, depression, social dependence or the like. The individual's situation as thus constrained, however, is precisely the problem. For the cult of rights, encroaching paralysis or dementia are in themselves not sufficient justifications for seeking PAS. Yet what of those who consider PAS on the basis of their own perceived loss of autonomy, their inability to continue the activities that underwrite the value of their lives to themselves?

For the cult of life, such considerations are irrelevant because we're enjoined to value human life or human dignity per se even as our own dissolves from within. That loss of value to an individual, as body and psyche unravel, leaves that life's essence untouched. As such, our empirical lives are not valuable, and our interior states have no moral claim; indeed, selves as selves have no moral worth, and so afford no basis for exercising moral agency. At the same time, for both cults, one central consideration in PAS situations is guarding against persons acting on depressed moods, or withdrawing their valuation of their own lives in contingent circumstances. Yet one task of dying is precisely that, to reconcile one's self to the dissolution not of human life in the abstract, but of this life in its particulars. The sheer intimacy of the dying process, not of persons but of specific individuals, should give us great pause in deciding for others the value of their own lives to them. Yet the cult of life does precisely the opposite, negating this process of any intrinsic worth while simultaneously depicting it as a public referendum on the sanctity of human life in its entirety. To couch some individual's wish to die, to withdraw from a particular life, as devaluing human life in its entirety asserts not only that the dying is at most incidentally his, but equally that it belongs essentially to persons as persons, such that the practices governing such dying require public approbation.

For the cult of rights, too, the death of any particular autonomous end is rendered a bafflingly public process. While for the cult of life the value of my life *to me* is of no moral import, such that I cannot seek PAS, for the cult of rights it assumes import only if I can make rationally transparent how it has lost that value to me, by demonstrating how it might do so for others. The absurdity of strangers deciding if I am acting as myself – and if my life is unlivable *to me* sans reference to the constraints that might make it intolerable to me, but not to another – escapes defenders of this position. So too does the absurdity of defending personal privacy in medical decision making, by subjecting individuals' intimate estimations of their own interior lives to public scrutiny, evaluation, and debate, and their decisions about the value of their own lives, to them, to external public authority. Indeed, both cults make of my dying a public affair, precisely by making my empirical life irrelevant. Selves, on both accounts, are not sources of valuation; nor do they bring anything of value into being in themselves which warrants moral surety. To say that I have a right to privacy is doubly false. Not only do I, as me, have no rights, but my privacy so construed defends not my particular exercise of my autonomy per se, but my capacity to act as everyone else. To say that I have a right to life is equally vacuous, as nothing valuable about my life may be imperiled; indeed, it is not my life that is valuable at all, but human life per se wholly apart from my own particular fortunes.

7.4 The privacy paradox

This double-speak echoes from both cults' paternalisms, because while they concur that private choices can exact public costs, they only rarely assess when public choices exact private costs. That over-sight is deliberate, as for both cults, public demands imperil no private goods and thus impose no morally relevant private costs. For such theorists, the primary challenge ethical principles face is our need for human dignity or autonomy, against which merely private interests or preferences must give way. In idolizing such public goods, however, both cults systematically degrade the private preferences and interests and valuations apart from which we have no basis for respect or love of persons in themselves. The persons both cults valorize, rather, are entirely impersonal, transcending any bodily, psychic, or social particulars. To be moral objects, objects of respect or of love, persons must on these accounts prove identical to their depersonalized souls or their autonomy. They secure their status as moral subjects on the same basis, as agents either of an inalienable human dignity or an inalienable autonomous capacity. As previously indicated, however, persons so construed are subject neither to others' agency, as their worth is inalienable, nor their own, insofar as nothing they do diminishes or enhances their worth as persons.

The paternalisms that both cults advance are thus doubly confounding, because we require moral protection neither from others nor from ourselves. For the cult of life, we require such protection because our actions thereby imperil not just our particular lives, but the sanctity of human life in its entirety. For the cult of rights, we require such protection lest we act at the behest not of our unfettered wills, but of alien impulses of body or mind or social pressure. Conversely, we are enjoined to accede to such protection precisely and entirely as bearers of this inalienable worth. The moral subject thus protected, however, is not only wholly depersonalized but shorn of any agent capacity. For the cult of life, the agent's valuation of his or her life is entirely irrelevant to its moral worth. For the cult of rights, the agent's valuation of that life is entirely subject to public adjudication. For the cult of life, the only such valuations that matter, morally, are ascribed to that life *a priori* and from without; for the cult of rights, the only such valuations that matter, morally, are ascribed to that life through rational, wholly public assay. On neither account, then, should the empirical passage of a particular amalgam of bodily and psychic and social affects matter morally. Put bluntly, they should be as indifferent to my particular life and death as I apparently should be.

Both cults, however, subject the passages of such selves or subjects to relentless moral scrutiny. The cult of life, for example, regards all PAS as murder writ large, whereas the cult of rights sanctions PAS only insofar as persons act as themselves –, that is as wholly impersonal, wholly rational, wholly impartial and autonomous agents of their biological deaths. The dignity or sanctity of human life, however, is invulnerable to murder, and persons who act entirely at the behest of public authority are at most numerically or incidentally acting as themselves. To the contrary, in advancing these proscriptions both cults perpetrate murder by other means, hollowing out the bodily and psychic interiority and agency that mark distinctively human lives, that is, distinctively human selves, and replacing them with transcendent ideals. To love the sanctity or the dignity of human life is precisely not to love human persons in their particulars; to respect autonomous ends is precisely not to respect human persons as self-determining agents. Both accounts, rather, dismantle from within the bodily interiority and psychic subjectivity, the personalized privacy, apart from which persons bear no substantive moral agency. In voiding persons of that metaphysical and moral privacy, they substitute in its stead inalienable properties or ideals – of human sanctity or dignity or autonomy – that bear no human reference, nor authorize love or respect for persons in their particulars. Depriving the latter of any metaphysical or moral value, rather, they authorize us instead to render persons entirely subjects to public censure and direction, as means to ends entirely of others' choosing.

It may seem harsh to depict such subjection as a species of murder. Perhaps calling it slavery instead – the subjugation of the entirety of one person's life to another's wholly apart from the formers' will – would be more palatable. It would prove so, however, only for those who maintain that depriving persons of their biological lives is somehow worse, morally, than depriving them of their agency, a point the cult of rights might otherwise contest. It would prove so, moreover, only if depriving persons of their biological lives truncates the dignity or sanctity of their lives more blatantly than does depriving them of their liberty, a point the cult of life should reject insofar as both actions leave persons per se unaffected. Neither account, in fact, may consistently advance any intelligible moral proscription against murder, whether at one's own hand or by another. Dissolving our bodily interiority and psychic subjectivity is incidental, and even required to define us as transcendent souls or ends. As the sanctity or dignity or autonomy of such persons is wholly depersonalized, it is in its essence as a moral object invulnerable to human agency, and in its essence as a moral subject entirely fungible, enacting a merely numerically distinct agency. We then cleave into self-subsistent souls or ends which warrant love or respect, and transitory selves hovering beyond the penumbra of our moral orbit. Hence the paradox of personal privacy that both cults raise: they demand moral love or respect for transcendent ideals that obtain wholly apart from human agency, while precluding moral love or respect for the specific individuals who ostensibly embody these properties or ideals.

Many bioethicists, to be sure, lament the *metaphysical* dualisms that continue to confound contemporary accounts of human personhood.[2] Yet they pay less attention to the *moral* perils of this grand philosophical legacy. It is perhaps easier to love human life in its idealized transcendence, or to respect autonomous ends standing in place of the more obdurate human individuals we meet in practice. Yet that may prove among the starkest challenges we face in dealing with matters bioethical: loving those whose valuations we do not share, and respecting those whose valuations we may not be able to countenance. I raise this prospect because, despite their disagreements, both cults make nonsense of the human dignity and human autonomy they purport to defend. Depicting them as properties borne by self-subsistent souls or ends, they render morally epiphenomenal both the contingencies of particular persons – of bodies, psyches and social relations – and their subjection to others' agency. They thus render vacuous the injunctions that we should love or to respect persons in their persons, because we may neither dignify nor degrade them thereby. Those injunctions bear moral weight not if they attach to inalienable properties, but only if they embody social practices whereby we bring others into being – in their bodily interiority and their psychic subjectivity – in ways that dignify or degrade them. We degrade persons, I suggest, when we bring them into being, as both cults do, entirely as objects of our design, negating their particulars. Conversely, we dignify persons insofar as we stoke the interiority, subjectivity and privacy that alone render them agents of their own lives.

Previously, I've suggested that such regard for evoking human persons as ends in themselves – that is, not as transcendent souls or autonomous agents, but as distinctive novel centers of bodily interiority, psychic subjectivity and agency – is the animating moral import of our procreative capacity. I wish here to reiterate that that procreative capacity extends well beyond parenting to include those practices of personal privacy through which we dignify or degrade others. To love or to respect persons as either cult requires precludes such practices. The love the cult of life enjoins negates need, desire, feeling, impulse, motive, interest, and the like as objects of moral concern, voiding human subjects in their particulars of moral consideration. Moreover, to impose such love upon them against their wills signals not generosity but sheer self-love, as it values them not at all in themselves, but only insofar as they are the objects of our grand ideals. To render them moral patients in this way voids not only their subjectivity, but also any metaphysical or moral constraint upon our judgments of them. In reducing individuals to their souls, that is, we do not announce an inviolability that we apprehend as an insuperable constraint upon our action. Quite the contrary, we undercut any such constraint by obliterating its bases, not in their possession of a transcendent property, but in their irreducibility to any such quality, in the insistent agent subjectivity that inhabits them. Only as thus embodied are human persons subject to dignifying or degrading practices; conversely, only such mutual vulnerability makes any sense of human love as morally operative, that is, as charged with bringing value into being.

For the cult of life, only divine love, finally, proves procreative in any moral sense. Yet in commending to human persons an entirely passive role in the process, the cult of life drains human love of any moral efficacy. In demanding such love or parents, for example, it directs it indifferently to persons as persons, and imposes it upon them sans any reference to individuals' response. The cult of rights might concur with that analysis, depicting human love as finally an egoistic animal emotion, a projection of one individual's preferences and ideals and valuations upon another. Indeed, love can bear no moral force on this account not only because it imposes one's preferences upon another: it remains, moreover, entirely private and arbitrary. In conveying nothing about its object, but only about its subject, it neither espies value in nor adds value to its object. On both accounts, love is morally impotent. For the cult of life, human love attaches to all indifferently as our recognition of their inalienable dignity; yet neither conferring nor withdrawing that love qualifies that dignity. For the cult of rights, human love is finally an animal sentiment, and threatens to embroil both its subjects and its objects in human preferences and desires, imperiling thereby – however unintelligibly – human autonomy.

Moreover, what then, do we respect, in respecting an agent's autonomy? The same thing we love in loving dignified human life – a transcendent end. It cannot be a person's bodily interiority, their distinctive pains and pleasures and tastes and preferences, as these are animal constraints upon our capacity to act autonomously, that is, to acts as ends in ourselves, that is, to act as ourselves. Nor can it be any psychic subjectivity, any interests or hopes or projects or desires or emotions, as these too constrain our capacity to act as ourselves. Nor can it be any substantive agency, any prospect of identifying and selecting individual ends or goods. Such goods would escape rational public assay, and prove not to be goods at all. We can have no legitimate interest in or for other persons as particulars. Their particular preferences thus lack not only metaphysical but also moral import. Accordingly, on this account, in acting for or on behalf of other persons we neither disrespect them nor imperil their autonomy even if we entirely abrogate those bodily and psychic and social particulars, precisely because they pose no moral constraint upon our public moral authority. Conversely, the very ideas of private agency, or of moral privacy, or of private interests, are all alike self-immolating, as we have no real self from which to act, and no real values to realize thereby.

While the cult of rights identifies our autonomy with our moral status as ends in ourselves, then, we might just as well conclude that such formulations portend the end of selves, and the end of persons as moral agents. This conclusion may seem counter-intuitive, given the cult of rights' out-sized effort to secure human autonomy against all potential perils. The autonomy it defends, which is metaphysically and morally secured *a priori*, is not mine at all though. I am, to the contrary, its greatest threat, precisely insofar as I am me. It does not attach to my decisions, but to my decision-making capacity; it does not attach to my valuations, but to my transcendence of them in principle; it does not attach to the content of my agency, but only to its form. The respect it secures for me thus does not qualify me at all, insofar as I am a specific self. Nor does it preclude others from deciding, for me, the worth of my biological life, to me, or of my valuations, to me, or of my life in its entirety, to me. To the contrary, it authorizes others, in respecting my autonomy, to defend me from the impingements of my body, my psyche, and my social affects. My autonomy, after all, is not a private good attaching to me at all, but a public good to which those bodily and psychic and social impingements must give way. Lacking any private good of their own, as publicly defensible goods, they admit rather of endless public scrutiny and moral assay. Despite the cult of rights' pretensions that it respects personal privacy, it nonetheless dismantles any basis – metaphysical or moral – for it. Persons, after all, are in their autonomy transparent to others, and retain their worth only insofar as they are shorn of any bodily or psychic or social interiority, that is, of any opacity that might obtain beyond others' moral reach.

The privacy paradox that I'm proposing here thus has two elements: the moral implication that persons are valuable only insofar as they are not human individuals, and the metaphysical implication that the source of human worth is an inexplicable special creation either at divine behest, or at the behest of an *a priori* transcendent property or capacity of mysterious reason. As a metaphysical matter, both cults depict persons as self-subsistent substances of non-natural origin. Yet they wish to draw from this premise the moral conclusion that how persons treat each other proves dignifying or degrading, as befitting, or not, their inviolate worth. In this they get their analyses precisely backwards. Only if persons are not self-subsistent but affected in their persons by others' agency may they be objects of substantive moral regard. M-oreover, only if persons' worth is not secured *a priori* but created in and through valuative practices may we regard persons as substantive moral agents, as bringing into being or effecting such moral valuations in and through such social practices. Self-subsistent substances can neither be objects of moral love or respect, nor be subjects of their own or others' moral agency. As such, love and respect have no metaphysical or moral substance, that is, they have no power to bring novel valuations into being. Both cults, then, in dispensing with the bodily interiority and psychic subjectivity that individuals embody, secure persons from any animal constraints – that is, secure their dignity or autonomy – at the price of rendering them invulnerable to nature or to time or to others' agency. The cult of life thereby depicts a love of persons void not only of sentiment and preference, but equally of mutuality and subjection to substantive harm. The cult of rights, conversely, depicts human love as a creature of unfettered will, wholly fungible, wholly self-involving.

For both cults, to root human love in private sentiment or preference, in private need or dependence, both animalizes it and degrades its objects. Yet a love so conceived is humanly inconceivable, insofar as human love is ferociously particular, and morally monstrous, insofar as it reduces its objects to specters of our fevered moral imaginations. Both cults oppose love of particular persons as particulars; the cult of rights because such private preferences constrain our rational agency, the cult of life because such private preferences undercut the respect of human dignity owed equally to all. Yet on neither account do the objects of such love pose a private interiority or subjectivity or opacity that should be respected or loved, as an object of our moral regard, or as a constraint upon our own will and agency. On neither account is love or respect personal or personalizing, or volitional or pro-creative; human love, rather, as either cult conceives it, like human life itself, itself conceives nothing, creates nothing, and brings nothing of value to world through its activity. Here, both cults maintain, human love and respect reach their highest moral issue: shorn of partiality, of private dependence and need and fear and hope, they allow us to value persons in themselves, not as particular bodies or personalities or characters, all of which are subject to the vagaries of biological nature and time and human will, but in their persons. But who are these impersonal persons we thereby love or respect, and more bluntly, what good are they, to themselves or to us, exactly, or we to them? In posing that question, I wish to consider not only what good persons are but also what respecting or loving that good requires of us morally. To depict human persons as ends in themselves heralds not only the end of selves, as objects of metaphysical or moral concern, but the end of ethics. If an absolute and inalienable worth already attends us, *a priori*, then that good requires nothing further of us. Indeed, human dignity and autonomy, on both accounts, cannot be objects of moral maintenance, as they pose the inviolable boundary conditions against which we cannot impose our wills upon others. So conceived, however, even the respect and love of persons owed to persons bears no substantive moral task. To the contrary, I suggest, they may do so only if such dignity or autonomy are not *a priori* properties, but are embodied in persons in and through social practices that dignify or degrade them. Only as such may we lend moral content to the injunctions to respect or love persons, that is, only insofar as we are enjoined to secure not inalienable properties, but the personal interiority, subjectivity and privacy through which particular persons bring distinctively novel valuations to the world as the hallmark of human moral agency and procreativity.

Both cults, of course, insistently contrast moral love or respect with any preferential regard for particular persons, the cult of life insisting that we properly love not bodies or minds or personalities but persons, and the cult of rights insisting that we love not others in their inalienable transcendence but only our own idealized conceptions of them. Both thereby make of embodied human love, most especially in its procreative intimacy, not an exemplar of moral relation but an intractable moral problem. Self-subsistent ends or souls, after all, have no intelligible relation even to their own bodies, much less to other persons whether embodied or not. It is perhaps unsurprising, then, that both cults enjoin us to love or to respect neither human persons as human persons, nor particular persons as particular persons, but rather metaphysical properties. Alas, such properties neither procreate, nor age, nor ail, nor die; nor do they in any intelligible sense qualify as human persons. Nor can they, from their transcendent surety, dignify human persons in their human particulars. To the contrary, only embodied human practices – aimed at personalizing persons, in their subjectivity and in their agency – can secure that end. Only on that basis, moreover, may we love human life and respect human autonomy for what they are, rather than for what we wish them to be, or worse, for the idealizations of them that we seek to impose upon our fellows – albeit for their own good.

8
A Culture of Living

Remember Gardasil? A vaccine against Human Papillomavirus (HPV), its initial claim to fame was its potential inoculating role against cervical cancer. Alas, it targets a virus communicable through sexual contact, and therein lies the rub. Recommended initially for prepubescent girls, its introduction met with predictable opposition. The cult of life, while granting its prospects as a life saver, decried the apparently equally compelling prospect that its use might sanction premarital promiscuity among those vaccinated. Sexually transmitted diseases, this position implies, are in fact goods, at least instrumentally, as fear of acquiring them may discourage indiscriminate sexual activity. The operative moral logic of this position, i.e. better dead than sex unwed, would seem incongruent with the claim that human life is an absolute good. Yet it reflects the extent to which the life that this cult valorizes is not only wholly divorced from the human body in any biological sense, but is defined in opposition to that body, which bears neither natural, nor instrumental, nor intrinsic goods. For the cult of rights, the use of such vaccines is a matter of parental rights. At the same time, this cult holds that parents should not impose such decisions upon their children. As previously indicated, both cults suffer from the same insuperable challenge: whatever we do, through our actions and even inactions, imposes some future upon our children, whether we like that or not.

8.1 What good is happiness?

The introduction of the Gardasil vaccine illustrates one of the great laws of contemporary bioethics debate: For every potential good that some new medical or biotechnological intervention offers, bioethicists of both cults will identify a vast range of moral concerns. While

Murphy's Law predicts garden variety disasters, bioethicists' fears augur mass extinctions, dystopias, and even the stray apocalypse or two. What would happen, they gravely murmur, if some strains of cancer were eliminated? Would life become too easy, would we all live too long, would we – gasp! – cease to be human, if we no longer bore these diseases of our ancestors?[1] For the cult of life, such diseases are not only natural goods, as elements of a divine creation, but instrumental goods, because they enjoin us to accept God's will. More strikingly, as inexplicably necessary elements of the human condition, they must prove, like humanity itself, intrinsically valuable.[2] For the cult of rights, while we may make of these diseases whatever we choose, they are neutral in themselves, neither valuable nor disvalued. As such, while we may decide for ourselves how to evaluate these diseases, we cannot decide for future persons, for example, that a life without some form of cancer would be better than a life with that disease. On neither account can we say either that biological health or function is a natural or instrumental or intrinsic good, or that such health is a proper end of medical intervention. Yet both cults seek to do precisely this: to identify the moral scope and limits of medical practice.

For the cult of life, medicine's proper ends are therapeutic and life maintaining, but not life enhancing; for the cult of rights, medicine's proper ends are defined only by autonomous wills. Yet the same arguments that the cult of life advances against medical enhancements apply equally to all therapeutic interventions. All such efforts – from heart surgeries and antibiotic use to vaccines – contest the dominion of nature, and prefer some biological states to others. All of them, moreover, enhance natural bodily capacities, and all insert human will into natural processes. No more patently is this the case than in the cult of life's bizarre insistence that machine-dependent PVS patients be kept alive for the course of their natural lives, as if such machine dependence constitutes a natural state, until they expire of natural causes. That this form of medical intervention is deemed natural and morally necessary, whereas some vaccine uses are deemed unnatural and *verboten*, indicates not mere conceptual confusion but the cult of life's wholesale inability to identify medicine's proper ends. It simply cannot do so because neither the human body nor its health nor its function is, on their account, a moral good. To the contrary, human goods are defined wholly in and through our capacity to transcend those bodies. For its part, the cult of life contrasts itself with the cult of rights on precisely this point: against the latter's insistence that we may make of our embodiment what we will, and so can use medical enhancements to serve individual wills, the cult of life asserts instead that we should not exercise such liberty because the body imposes natural and thus moral limits upon us. Yet do those limits necessarily include polio, small pox, and all manner of cancers against which medicine has waged such concerted battles?

The cult of life wishes to insist here that maintaining life is one thing, enhancing it quite another. But such claims presuppose the point they deny: that some measure of human biological health or function is normative, that is, provides a functional baseline that medical interventions may properly seek to maintain, but not enhance. Only on such an account can they resist the cult of rights' insistence that, precisely because there is no functional baseline that is morally normative, medical interventions may properly serve whatever ends individuals choose. The cult of life rejects such a functional baseline *a priori*, because it asserts that all lives are by definition equally good. At the same time, the cult of rights rejects such a baseline on analogously *a priori* grounds, on the insistence that self-creating persons decide for themselves the value of bodily or functional states. On neither account can biological health or function prove to be a natural good, because bodily pleasures or pains or enjoyments or displeasures bear no value in themselves. Nor may they prove to be intrinsic goods: for the cult of life, they are neutral until ascribed value; for the cult of life, any biological state is equally good. Nor, importantly, are biological health or function instrumental goods. For the cult of rights, biological states cannot impinge upon our autonomy. For the cult of life, conversely, biological sates have no bearing upon the worth of our lives. On neither account, then, do our biological estates enhance or impede our capacity to realize value in our lives, because such valuations transcend them.

Were either of these accounts true, however, the great medical mystery would be not what interventions to allow, but why we would bother seeking to intervene in our biological estates at all. These positions, after all, do not simply deny that health is a good, but render it wholly irrelevant to the value of our lives. Their ensuing conflicts, moreover, do not pose rival accounts of medicine's moral provenance, but deny that any such account is possible, precisely because health is not a good at all. Yet what then can philosophical bioethics study, if the human good wholly transcends human embodiment and human health and function? For their part, defenders of both cults reverently cite the ancient injunction of Hippocrates. To medical practitioners they enjoin in unison, first, do no harm. The persons, or better, the ideals of human dignity and autonomy that they aim thereby to defend, however, transcend harm; so too do they transcend help or enhancement, absolving us of all responsibility to or for them.

This result is too convenient, because bioethicists of both cults apply that ancient injunction only to others. Never do they ask of themselves if the moral ideals or practices they promulgate do harm; nor do they inquire whether such ideals of or practices forestall substantive goods. That they cannot even conceive that last prospect illustrates the moral as well as the intellectual bankruptcy of much of contemporary philosophical bioethics. Nowhere is this more evident than in disputes over quality of life and life enhancement measures. For the cult of life, just as we have no normative standard of human health or function, neither may we identify any substantive basis for gauging the relative quality of human lives. For the cult of rights, conversely, qualitative decisions are individual. On neither account, importantly, is quality of life per se an overriding moral consideration within medical practice or the development or use of new biotechnologies. To the contrary, the cult of life explicitly precludes such concerns in making moral decisions. In cases like those of PVS patients or severely compromised infants, for example, the quality of the affected person's life is deemed wholly irrelevant to the worth of that life, to that person or to others. The cult of rights instead refers these cases to the individual choices of parents or guardians. Neither cult formulates the most basic question: what human good is served in and through the perpetuation of such lives?

Both cults decree that we are not here trafficking in mere biological organisms, but in human persons. Yet that objection gets the moral matter backwards, because if we were not the biological organisms that we are, we would face no bioethical decisions. Previously I've suggested that it is only insofar as we are affected by others, in our persons, that we bear any substantively moral relations to those others. We are, I've maintained, in our bodies, our psychic interiority and our agency, both products and producers of those others. That we are, in our persons, thus spatially and temporally extended is beyond doubt: we embody the genes of our ancestors, and no less, of our successors; we grieve those who precede us in death, and envision the futures of those who will out-live us; we embed our moral inheritances in our social practices, yet aim simultaneously to redirect those practices, to leave things, as the trite saying goes, better than we found them. Cliché or not, that phrasing announces a generic human orientation: an aspiration not merely to live, but to live well, and better in the future than we do at present. Such is the obverse of the technological imperative decried by bioethicists of both cults. They espy in considerations of quality of life the markings of Brave New Worlds of human fashioning, all of which degenerate into horrific dystopias. Yet what is so wrong with the Brave New Worlds they prophesize? That question is raised explicitly in Francis Fukuyama's *Our Post-Human Future*, which foresees for us, particularly in contemporary neuropharmacology, a future of drug induced and thus slavish happiness.[3] We may desire easily attained happiness, he holds, but only happiness secured through human effort and struggle bears moral worth. That pleasure and happiness are not natural human states but must be earned through moral effort is, of course, an ancient theme among philosophers. Some, like Aristotle, grant that they are legitimate human ends, but only when rightly attained. Others, like Kant, deny that they are moral ends at all, and depict them instead, in their motive force, as potential impediments to our autonomy. That latter prospect underwrites Fukuyama's suggestion that chemically induced happiness is slavish, as it originates not in the human will but in the human body. Instructively, on all of these accounts, happiness or pleasure secured by biochemical means does not reflect distinctively human activity, which issues entirely from the will and not at all from the body. More strikingly, Fukuyama maintains, far from chemically inducing happiness, we should instead *willingly* endure pain, and despair, and debilitating disease, because these are part of the human condition.[4]

In depicting that human condition, philosophers have made a cottage industry of human unhappiness. Whether as precursors of the cult of life or of the cult of rights, they have largely rejected the seductions of human living, the fleeting pleasures and pains that attend mere animal existence. Instead, they have insisted that humans persons are not, finally, part of a natural world. This assertion of human exceptionality underwrites Western philosophical ethics, whether secular or religious, and with predictable results. Our happiness is not to be found in this world, by mere animal means, by a simple preponderance of muted pleasures and satisfactions. The happiness to which human persons aspire must be of a different order. So it is even with Huxley's *Brave New World*, which sates our biological nature, but extirpates the enduring unhappiness which is, apparently somehow the crown of our humanity. As such, we might naturally enjoy health or pleasure, but if we did they would prove dehumanizing, merely animal or slavish pursuits. We might eschew ill-health or pain or biological dysfunction, but only by surrendering our true humanity. On this view, any efforts to minimize pain, or to remedy dysfunction, or to enhance biological health or pleasure, would elevate the good of the body over the distinctively human good, which resides rather in the illness, pain and debility that essentially – and should properly - define the human condition. That may seem a stark conclusion, i.e. that on both cults' accounts, we should retain even preventable ills as a condition of our moral worth. But it follows directly from the twin insistences that mere animal desires must give way to transcendent moral goods, and that human goods reside only in our capacity to resist our arbitrary preferences. Such inducements, after all, are easily satisfied, whereas human happiness, these positions insist, is a much more arduous pursuit. If, however, happiness transcends our biological nature, then how could inducing it chemically pose a moral challenge? For Fukuyama, licit drug use may properly treat clinical depression, but may not enhance human happiness beyond a normal range. Importantly, happiness is identified here not as a natural good, but as an inducement to immorality: In taking happiness per se as our end, we extirpate our distinctively human displeasure. That point, however, would hold equally for dispelling clinical depression. Indeed, we can on this position identify no difference between the two states: no bodily state is good or normative *vis-à-vis* any other, after all; nor is inducing any bodily state a legitimate moral end. To the contrary, if our distinctive human good resides in illness and debility and depression – and most pointedly, in our permanent struggle to endure them – then medical interventions would have a moral mandate only to bring those states into being. If medical intervention has any inherent moral logic, that is, it is not to preserve biological health or function, or to minimize pain or suffering, but to cultivate the latter.

Strictly speaking, that last imperative would finally founder on the same grounds as does its obverse: we cannot, and should not, use biological modifications to bring about moral ends. So conceived, it makes little sense to assert simultaneously that we ought not to do what we in fact cannot do. If all biological states are equally good, it would seem to matter little which states we pursue or how we do so. Nor would those efforts at all affect, much less effect, our happiness. If, however, we can enhance human happiness by chemical means, that prospect challenges our ideas not only about what human happiness is, but about what human persons are. Indeed, Fukuyama's primary concern here, like that of many bioethicists, is less with the practical outcomes of such technologies than with their intellectual implications. For Fukuyama the challenge couldn't be starker, as the prospect of chemically induced or enhanced happiness imperils not only the idea that happiness should be earned through moral labor, but more broadly, the insistence that human moral agency transcends human biology. In the

Brave New World Huxley paints, Fukuyama espies a society sans ethics and character, wherein no link obtains between one's willed activities and the pleasure or happiness one attains. Yet the puzzle remains: if persons have what they naturally desire, then why would the absence of human willed activity diminish it? It can signal a moral loss only if human willing per se adds worth to the happiness or pleasure attained. Were that the case, however, we could scarcely maintain that human nature, in itself, constitutes the human good in total, sans any moral effort on our part.

At the same time, such activity could scarcely be subject to bioethical norms if human biology per se harbored no distinctive goods. Simply put: if we cannot improve ourselves, in and through our own efforts – if we are already good enough as is – what possible moral task could we face? We would have no such task, that is, if no gap obtained between what we are at present and what we could or should be. This fatal flaw confounds philosophical bioethics. While current debates endlessly assay the specter of human enhancement, they bury a more potent concern, that of whether the ideals and practices they authorize are life enhancing. Bioethicists of both cults wrangle endlessly over the moral imperative that medicine should first do no harm. In that vein, Fukuyama, for example, laments the prospect that medical interventions might yield longer life but with reduced mental capacity. That eventuality, however, which we are already witnessing, would not follow from a medical mandate enjoining us to pursue the optimal well being or health or function of human persons. It follows instead from their insistences, against all biological or empirical sense, that all human life is equally valuable, that all human life must be sustained as long as possible, and that the quality of a particular human life is entirely irrelevant to the value of that human life. These ethical injunctions, and not the technical capacity to extend human life, are the primary threat to human well being that bioethicists should concern themselves with – not because these prescriptions aim at enhancing human life and well being, but because they aim in precisely the opposite direction.

Bioethicists of both cults identify that impulse toward life enhancement and the technologies that may serve it as creatures of a technological imperative which aims, at its worst, to liberate us from our nature. Yet their own accounts – of an astoundingly unnatural human nature – authorize a Brave New World of their own making: PVS patients warehoused for decades, as they enact their "natural" deaths; children deliberately born with crippling, life-negating debilities that might have been prevented; persons outliving their mental faculties.

While both cults wildly envision grave future terrors, present persons have more immediate concerns. Will they be kept alive, in some vague biological sense, against their wishes? Will potential remedies or meliorations be forestalled by the affected moral niceties of bioethics busybodies? Will medical interventions continue to be directed mindlessly toward preserving life sans any reference to its quality, and that too not at technical but at moral behest? It's instructive that even those few bioethicists who lament such eventualities attribute them less to groundless and life-denying moral bromides than to a technological imperative of obscure origin, or to a medical commitment to sustaining life at all costs, as if the latter itself did not bear the imprimatur of bioethicists. It is even more instructive that those bioethicists most exercised about restraining technological imperatives are least capable of offering any coherent account of human health or happiness or pleasure as distinctive goods, such that we could identify what human ends those technologies might properly serve.

8.2 Feeling too good?

To offer anything akin to a philosophical bioethic, we require a substantive answer to that simple question: what good is human health? Yet that query decisively redirects bioethics inquiry away from the imperative that biological modifications do no harm, toward the imperative that they prove life enhancing. If medical interventions have any moral implications, they must traffic in distinctive goods, either thwarting or enhancing them. Both the cult of life and the cult of rights deny that prospect, maintaining that biological health or function are neither instrumentally necessary to human life, nor valuable as natural goods on the basis of simple enjoyment, nor ends for their own sake. We have then, dispensed with all bioethics controversies, not by reaching consensus on a moral guidelines, but by eliminating medical interventions in their entirety. They have, after all, no purpose. Both cults deny that conclusion, insisting instead that such interventions should prove life or health maintaining, but not life or health enhancing. Such interventions may seek to minimize pain, but not eliminate it; they may seek to combat clinical depression, but not to enhance natural happiness.

Here, the term "natural" embeds a covert normativity that both cults otherwise explicitly deny. They may mean by natural a happiness that falls within the statistically normal range of human psychological states. But depression, even in its clinical states, is no less natural for its comparative infrequency. We can no more say, on either account, that clinical depression is a lower quality psychological state then we can say that limb paralysis is a lower quality functional state, as all are or can be equally good through assertions of human will. Indeed, disease states are as natural as are health states. Any differentiation between healthy and diseased states must thus prove arbitrary, and all medical interventions in them equally illicit if aimed at enhancement. For both cults, the problem here is not merely the hint at a biological normativity that would tie persons to their animal nature, but their shared insistence that chemically enhanced happiness, or even eugenics, whether with therapeutic or ameliorative intent, would not reflect the enhanced person's agency or self but merely their biochemistry. The happiness so produced, they maintain in unison, would prove too easily attained, and wholly artificial. That consideration, in turn, underwrites a sprawling range of objections to any potential enhancement practices, from gene selection, to steroid use, to cosmetic surgery.

The latter have become among the most prominent enhancement prospects to occupy public debate, and among the least intelligible.[5] Opponents of steroid use in sports maintain, for example, that using steroids – but not nutritional supplements – artificially enhances physical prowess. They imply equally that using steroids somehow shortcuts the work involved in strength or endurance training, as if pills or shots alone suffice, sans any further effort on the takers' part. Recourse to steroids is cheating, they intone, because it extends human prowess beyond its natural limits, as if steroids are not in fact chemical components of all human bodies. Opponents of such usages cite equally the potential damage done to athletes' bodies, as if extreme sports were not in themselves perilous to life and limb. Strangely, moreover, while baseball players who take steroids to enhance their bat speed are deemed cheaters, those who consult sports psychologists to enhance concentration or motivation, or those who elect to have eye surgery to enhance their vision, or knee or elbow surgery to extend careers otherwise naturally finished, are applauded for their dedication and determination. In none of these latter cases are we plainly dealing with therapeutic rather than with enhancement measures. Quite the contrary, we have patently no dividing line between the two. So why the outcry about steroids, but not about surgeries or sports psychologists? Why are pitchers who return successfully from ligament replacement surgery lauded, while players who use steroids are vilified? Like bioethicists, baseball fans are a largely conservative lot, beholden to cherished ideals about how the grand old game should be played. But the weight of tradition aside, the question remains: If we can enhance our capacities, shouldn't we?

That query should strike philosophical bioethicists as bizarre in the extreme, as ethics has no more generic orientation than the injunction that, however we are at the moment, we should be better in the future – or at least, we should try to be so. The great paradox for bioethicists, of course, is that in answering no to that query, they void medicine of any moral import, and bioethics of any moral substance. Medical interventions may bear such import only if they aim to secure or imperil distinctive goods, among them bodily health and function. Bioethicists of both cults deny that we can identify no any such goods, and cite as evidence their endless wrangling over how health and optimal function might be defined. Those disputes, however, presuppose that we cannot consult our biological nature for natural norms. Moreover, they are beholden to the *a priori* ethical presupposition that all biological states are equally good. Cells, organs, organisms, populations, however, all have natural constraints of time and space and resource use, and their natural functions are relatively easy to identify. Blind eyes, deaf ears, and paralyzed limbs simply do not work properly, biologically speaking. Bioethicists' efforts to make virtues of the necessities these constraints impose upon the bodies of their bearers cannot change the biological facts.

From that contrary premise, however, follows not only bioethicists' rejection of eugenics, but also their insistence that all lives be valued equally. That last coda warrants closer attention, as it asserts not that all lives are equally valuable because we so value them, but that all lives are equally valuable in themselves. Were that the case, of course, ethics would have no normative task. Its historical trajectory took as its primary task the work of defining the human good, and thereby, of gauging the comparative worthiness of human lives. Alien to the vast sweep of Western philosophical ethics are any assertions that all lives are equally good. Aristotle, of course, rejected that last coda out of hand. Only a very few had the requisite capacities to achieve such a life, and even of those, few would succeed. For Kant, too, our task was to refashion ourselves, to make us, in his famous formula, better than nature made us. Even Mill, while content to identify human happiness with pleasure, *pace* Aristotle, insisted that we pursue human rather than merely natural or porcine pleasures. Whatever the merits of these approaches, they bear an operative intentionality, a moral imperative no less striking than the technological imperative that bioethicists so often decry. They insist that we aspire to a worthy or valuable life that we may secure only through our own efforts. Bioethicists who dismiss eugenic projects out of hand, then, deeming the very term itself one of moral scorn, would be well served to recognize the extent to which such ostensibly technological imperatives – aimed at re-engineering the human species in light of deliberately selected ideals or goods or values – bear distinctly ethical roots.

They would be equally well served to consider the dangers not of mindless technological imperatives, but of baseless moral imperatives. So eager are they to defend human transcendence that they wholly ignore that grand ideal's impact upon the realities of human living. The practical implications of this problem are staggering. Insisting *a priori* that all human lives are equally valuable, and indeed equally human, they enjoin precisely what they claim to disavow: the potentially ceaseless maintenance of human biological life; the creation of PVS chimeras, part biological organism, part machine, with no natural dividing line; the insistence that every possible person be born, sans any reference to population constraints; the insistence that all lives, at every stage, at every level of function, are all alike equally worthy of the full range of medical resource investment; the implication that we should not prevent costly, life crushing debilities, whatever their scope: the wholesale inability, that is, either to define an optimal range of human health and function and well being, a medical good, or to espy thereby both the proper scope and the limits of our medical interventions. The utter vacuity of so much of contemporary bioethics discourse exemplifies these points. What are we to do, the case study books cajole, with the 97-year-old patient with advanced dementia and pneumonia who now needs intestinal surgery? Sans any reference to human health, or to biological function, or to quality of life, or to the reality of a natural life-cycle, to what can we appeal in addressing such queries, apart from bioethicists' insistence that human life in any and all forms is an absolute good? Wholly proscribed from this discussion from the outset, after all, is any appeal to the distinctive goods of human living, the first-person identity, interiority and agency that ostensibly embody the value of such living in the first place, and which might provide ready answers to what such persons need.

Defenders of quality of life considerations within the cult of rights might well concur with that latter suggestion. Yet they would still refer those judgments either to the individuals affected or to mysteriously qualified specialists. For opponents of any such considerations, those judgments recur instead to absolute values mysteriously intuited. On neither account do human bodies per se pose any norms, nor do they claim any moral attention. Even amid standard quality of life assessments, after all, we need not defer to evaluations of pain or pleasure or function or health. We are rather to make bioethics decisions while denying that human bodies bear any goods. As indicated previously, the case for such denial is airtight: pleasure and pain are merely subjective states, we're told, i.e. private preferences inadmissible in a public forum. They are animal impulses, befouling our wills and inducing inherently selfish behavior. They may even lead us, falsely, to see the value of our own lives, to us, as diminished, lest we guard against such transitory impulses at every turn, or have others do it for us if we cannot. We are not, after all, our bodies, or our preferences, or our hopes or fears or desires, all subjective epiphenomena arbitrarily corralled within the contingent biological organisms that we inexplicably seem to occupy. Yet, what do we then preserve morally with the injunction that every human life is equally valuable, if we mean by that term not any particular life but the occurrence of one instance of a type? That is, after all, the central implication of the claim that the life of an anencephalic infant is equivalent to that of a ninety-year-old PVS patient, a healthy five-year-old child, or thirty-five-year-old adult.

Put differently, that is a central implication of the insistence that human health and biological function are wholly irrelevant to the value of human life. The issue here isn't simply that such moral injunctions leave it as unintelligible how we might frame elementary bioethics quandaries, such as how we might best distribute finite health care resources. Nor is it even that such approaches devalue particular persons by rendering distinctive capacities such as the first-person identity, interiority, or agency inessential to human worth. The more immediate practical problem, rather, is that they by definition divorce medical interventions from any considerations of a distinctively human good. Simply put, if such interventions can serve that good, they may do so only if health and biological function are valuable, and themselves offer norms to which bioethicists must attend. If the latter is not the case, bioethics has no distinctive good. Such is plainly the case for approaches which enjoin, at bottom, goods that no embodied living person could aver, the goods that underwrite our human capacities to pursue anything beyond what we are merely born as. If it is just as well that we be born, or conceived, blind and deaf and without brains or limbs, insensible to the world we inhabit it, and to die a week, or a month, or a year later, at incalculable cost, we can lend no substantive moral meaning to the value of human life even if that life transcends its mere biological occurrence. This may seem a paradoxical suggestion, that the absolute valuation of human life drains it of all moral worth. Yet that conclusion follows directly from the animating logic of Western philosophical ethics, which locates human worth not in a mere species markers alone, such as rationality or free will, but no less in what we make of ourselves through our distinctive capacities.

At the same time, if we are to improve ourselves – as this moral tradition enjoins us to – we require those distinctive capacities of first-person identity and agency and character – which make us moral agents in the first place. To make of human health or biological function thereby at minimum an instrumental good is not at all to arbitrarily select a range of capacities for mere preferential valorizing. If we are to admit bioethical norms at all, the human good must include some biological states that are naturally normative, and which are conducive to that good. It must alike designate some states as dysfunctional, either as not conducive to or as contrary to that good. To identify these norms, moreover, we must refer not to disembodied ideals but to the human organism per se, with its life-cycle orientations toward growth, maturation, decay and death, and likewise its preference for pleasure and its disavowal of pain. I mean here to advance the twin thesis that pleasure per se is a natural good because the biological organism enjoys it as such, and that pain per se is a natural disvalue because the biological organism opposes it as such. I mean here equally to advance the claim that health per se is a natural good, an index of normative biological function, and that illness and debility are natural disvalues, an index of biological dysfunction. In designating these as natural goods, moreover, I deny that they are instrumental goods alone, useful in some circumstances where health or biological function are needed to secure desired ends, but worthless in themselves. To the contrary, I suggest that bodily health and function and pleasure are not only valuable in themselves when enjoyed as natural goods, nor even only for their use in pursuit of other ends, but are in fact intrinsically valuable as moral ends, as underwriting the bodily interiority, first-person subjectivity, and agency apart from which human organisms could not value distinctively human lives at all.

To affirm that last point would deny the most basic premise both bioethics cults assert: that human persons wholly transcend human biology. More pointedly, it would locate the moral worth of human persons not apart from but within the interstices of our biological organisms. As a natural good, pleasure may well attend all animals. Indeed, that's a prime reason why many ethicists preclude it as an element of the human good. Yet what identifies it as intrinsically valuable for persons is its subjective entertainment, its lining of a particular bodily interiority distinctive to one individual. Such, of course, is the second grave objection that philosophical ethicists traditionally pose to pleasure as a potential human good – that it inhabits a mute sea of preferences inherently private, and inherently incommunicable. They extend here from the demands of epistemology that our reasons must be publicly assessable, to the broader metaphysical assertion that all of our experiences must qualify as publicly available to prove real or objective or true in any substantive sense. From this dubious assertion arises most such bioethicists' tendencies to dismiss others' pains or pleasures as fungible, as inadmissible to public discourse, as imposing no moral constraints upon others unless and until they can be made publicly assessable. Yet with these tendencies, as suggested earlier, comes also the sustained attack, within contemporary bioethics, on anything akin to personal privacy, to the integrity of individuals' own bodily experiences. Yet to withdraw from pleasure and pain any substance such as natural and intrinsic goods, drains from those organisms their bodily integrity, the good of human biological living, from within. It leaves that body a worthless integument, evacuating it of the subjective interiority that animates it.

Those subjective valuations, after all, are precisely what qualify that individual as the individual he or she is, anchoring him or her, however, in a locus inherently socially permeable because that embodiment permits shared pleasure or pain, initial entries into others' interiority. That we cannot feel precisely what others feel as precisely as they do may be indisputable. But while that may prove an epistemic problem for philosophers, it equally exemplifies the extent to which the privacy they concern themselves with inhabits the biological body. Simply put, were human persons the transparent rational psyches many philosophers idealize we would face no epistemic constraints, either *vis-à-vis* the world or each other. That we do face such constraints may restrict our knowledge of others and the world; yet it simultaneously sustains the types of persons that could exhibit bodily interiority and psychic privacy or subjectivity. For most philosophical ethicists any such ties to the human body, to pleasure and pain, to subjective valuations of such pleasures and pains, distract us from our pursuit of the human good. Such seductions, however, do not simply progressively inscribe us within the confines of our bodies; nor do they simply permit imperfect, incomplete *communiqués* with at most a few other such persons. Rather, amid these processes, they permit us to develop our agent capacity, to entertain and to assess competing desires and ends and to select among them. Disembodied, fully transparent agents, as soul or autonomous individuals, require no such agency, as they're enjoined to bring into being no goods in addition to their own occurrence as instances of a type, as functions of impersonal rational judgment.

In contrast, I suggest, we may exhibit substantive human agency only if we bring such goods into being in and through our activities. Seeding that process is our bodily entertainment of pleasures and pains, of natural goods and disvalues, which takes them up and transmutes them into intrinsic goods insofar as we pursue and enjoy them for their own sakes. Their intrinsic worth, I suggest, resides not in their public but in their private character, in their lining of the bodily interiority and intentionality of distinct individuals. At the same time, for that intrinsic worth to underwrite moral norms, it must prove an object of moral consideration and restraint such that it can underwrite distinctive agent capacities – in bringing into being an irreducible center of bodily interiority, subjective privacy, and agency. Human health and biological function are not mere instrumental but intrinsic goods, insofar as bodily interiority and subjective privacy inhabit an organic body as conditions of each individual's irreducible intrinsic worth and agential capacity. At the same time that agential capacity must be enacted, must harvest some goods, to sustain that worth as a process, not a state. Such a proposal, in turn, poses two broad implications for philosophical bioethics. First, for persons to be moral objects, they must exemplify the bodily privacy and psychic interiority and subjective agency that alone bring human transcendence to human life, such that that bodily privacy must prove in itself both a moral good and a constraint upon others' moral agency. Second, for such goods to underwrite substantive bioethical norms, the latter must take the good of the human body, including its optimal health and enhancement, rather than the simple maintenance of human biological life, as the over-riding good of medical interventions.

8.3 Bringing transcendence to life

Why, after all, even set broken bones, or develop vaccines, or pursue grievous potential cures, or conduct dangerous medical experiments, if these activities serve no good? Why celebrate physical prowess in sports, and grieve illness, disability, and loss of physical function? For most philosophical ethicists, such pursuits are at best distractions from our true good, indulgences in the seductions of physical nature. The pleasures and pains of human organisms are subjective wisps of experience:

mute, incommunicable, inherently self-absorbing and self-absorbed; they bear neither metaphysical reality, nor epistemic truth, nor moral value in themselves. Circumscribed within a particular body, they bear no public connection to the world, nor do they pose to that world any moral or epistemic or metaphysical reality. The transcendence of human persons, after all, resides precisely not in their bodies but in eternal souls or unfettered autonomous wills, metaphysical specters that elide the grasp either of the natural world or of other agents. So secure is this transcendence, in fact, that it escapes human life, in its familiar biological and social guises, entirely. At the same time, however, we witness no signs of that transcendence, either in ourselves or in those other would-be selves we encounter, as we cannot identify it in particular bodies, or psyches, or social relations. Indeed, for such ethicists the infamous "problem of other minds," as philosophers have labeled this inconvenient metaphysical quandary, is insoluble. Insofar as transcendent persons are shorn of all such particulars, they are not merely transparent to one another, but invisible, and indistinguishable from each other. For any person to transcend my grasp, however, that person must bear a precisely contrary nature: irreducibly opaque, ensconced within a body and a psyche I cannot fully penetrate, an obdurate social reality whose transparency forever escapes me.

Philosophical ethicists thus rightly insist, I suggest, that our bodily interiority is irremediably private and that our subjective psychic states are not wholly communicable. Yet these attest not to the unreality of our particular subjectivities, but to the reality of our transcendence both of nature and of others. We may not be, as these accounts suggest, simple organisms whose senses render fully and faithfully the sensate deliverances of our environs. Yet the complexity attributed to human organisms thereby follows precisely from such private or subjective overlays, from the modulations and interpretations of such experiences that human organisms are. Moreover, however private or incommunicable such bodily experiences may prove, that privacy ties us irremediably to the natural world we inhabit and only thereby remake. That interiority with its social and linguistic tinges, which is ours and ours alone, more primitively even than our psychic subjectivity, renders us irremediably, irreducibly opaque to others, who simply cannot feel what and as we do. At the same time, only insofar as we are essentially such bodies may we be affected in our persons through their treatment. Many philosophers throughout the Western philosophical tradition have maintained the contrary point, that other persons cannot cause us to feel pleasure or pain, and that neither our bodies, nor the world we inhabit, nor others, can induce feelings sans our rational or volitional or subjective consent. The Stoics, in particular, took our assertion of wholesale control over such feelings as a primary moral task, as a measure of our virtue or character.

In asserting the potential transcendence of our autonomous will over our animal impulses, the Stoics brief writings, formulated over a millennium ago, continue to cast a towering shadow over contemporary theorists, both philosophical and theological. Transcendent persons, however, as conceived by such theorists, could scarcely prove their moral mettle in such fashion, if they elide such impingements by definition. Nor do these theorists make plain how we may evaluate, morally or factually, responses which are deemed by metaphysical fiat to be wholly private. Even if we ignore such epistemic puzzles, moreover, the greater moral challenge seems plain. If we cannot induce pleasure or pain in others, we cannot harm other persons, or ourselves, regardless of what bodily states we induce. If those responses are at any rate wholly subjective and private, and bear no causal connection to an external world, we can neither predict what affect our actions will have on them, if any, nor can we project their preferences, for example, for pain or pleasure. We cannot even lend public meaning to those terms, which describe wholly private states. An analogous analysis holds equally for psychic states. If we alone induce our experiences as we will, then we can lend no content, epistemic or moral, to the injunctions that we should help and not harm others. Moreover, as wholly opaque agents we could not predict how we might affect others, anyway, since we can know nothing of their preferences, their motives, their aspirations, or they of ours.

Such persons, moreover, could scarcely prove particular subjects any more then they can prove moral agents. Epistemically, their bodily interiority and their psychic subjectivity escape us; metaphysically, they elide us; and morally, they bear no good that they or we can affect through our actions. If they are to bear such goods, rather, they must harbor them not simply as they are *a priori*, but in and through their own and others' actions. Those goods cannot, that is, flow necessarily but only contingently from such persons' natures. They must, moreover, be subject to the vagaries of such natures, to biology, to sociality, to time. They must, then, be brought into being in and through human agency, as objects of deliberate cultivation. That human persons are such objects, I suggest, is evident even in how they are brought to life: through the commingling of biological bodies, of genetic and social inheritances, of physical and psychic and social intimacies and practices. Bioethicists of both cults are enamored of virgin births. Whether through divine creation or the equally mysterious self-creation of autonomous agents, persons are made not of persons but of metaphysical properties. Persons are thus neither affected nor effected in their persons, either by the actions of their progenitors, or by their social inheritances; or even, vitally, by what they make of themselves through their own self-directed agency. Such accounts are all but inevitable, given both cults' insistences that persons are not animals, and that only in what they are not do they secure their transcendent moral status.

Yet nowhere is the disembodied transcendence of human persons that both cults posit more precisely turned inside out than in sexual procreation. From the commingling of two bodies, two psyches, two personal and social histories, springs forth an equally opaque body, an equally irreducibly distinctive psyche, and a novel personal and social history in the making. Philosophical bioethicists of both cults lament the prospect that such a merely physical account of human reproduction will rob the process of its mystery, and its humanity. But their own accounts of human procreation, shorn of substantive human agency, dehumanize the process by draining it of any substantive personal investment or moral import. On their accounts, human parents contribute genes, contingent bodies, from which fully formed persons mysteriously issue, sans any intimate personal or social engagement. Persons so conceived are, of course, not conceived at all, in any intelligible sense; they need not be, as their relations to their own bodies and psyches and social relations, much less to those of their parents and children, are wholly extrinsic to them. That sexual procreation is a normative element of person-making is for both cults a confounding prospect. The cult of life famously asserts that sexual procreation alone properly issues in human life, such that human cloning and like prospects are morally *verboten a priori*. Yet transcendent souls attend these creatures, they grant, deferring the matter to God's grace. Reproduce however you will, insists the cult of rights, and you will leave the persons so conceived untouched in their autonomy. Unless, alas, you select their genes deliberately, in which case you will have mysteriously truncated that autonomy at its root.

The transcendence they posit, and so desperately seek to defend, slips through their fingers at every turn, as both cults espouse a biophobia that refuses to locate human transcendence at its source. Defenders of human dignity, of human autonomy, of natural or inalienable human rights, nervously scan the heavens, seeking out souls, or essences, or Platonic forms, or autonomous specters – any transcendent property that might under write their favored moral claims. Alas, the transcendence they seek inhabits us, but only contingently, and in ways that require constant moral maintenance. The claim that other persons transcend us has neither metaphysical nor moral substance unless it implies equally that they inhabit themselves, that they embody a distinct bodily interiority and psychic subjectivity, and that they thereby have metaphysical and moral reality as distinct persons. Yet that particularity harbors moral freight only if is in itself a good, and an object of moral cultivation, both in itself and by others. That last coda underscores the logical limit of both cults' conceptions of transcendent persons, who are invulnerable both to biological or psychological influences and to others' agency. Their ideals, after all, are animated more by their shared biophobia, their distaste for human life and its contingency, than by any love of human life or human liberty as we know them.

The cult of life aspires to be the standard bearer of our love of life and the architect of a culture of life. But it cannot bear human life in its contingency, and refuses to love its embodied constraints. Its defenders assert the precise opposite, of course: that in equally respecting or valuing all wisps of human life, it affirms its absolute value. But the life it thereby valorizes, often twisted beyond recognition, precludes our finding any intrinsic good in health or pleasure or biological functioning. More strikingly, it precludes our finding any such good in the specific persons we encounter in their particulars, or in their agency, or in their capacities or achievements or preferences or aspirations, or in anything pertaining to the contingencies of human living. Only shorn of their specifics, rather, are persons absolutely valuable. That insistence insures us against all eventualities, and yet does so at a pernicious moral cost: the cognate insistence that we have, really, nothing to lose, when illness and debility and grief and death come for us, when what we love most and what we most value are most directly imperiled. A love thus invulnerable to such vagaries may well befit divine beings. But it bears no consort to human love, forever shadowed by the contingencies of nature and time, and of grief, of life as we know it.

Nor does the transcendence the cult of rights envisions for us bear any resemblance to our most enduring experiences. As far as we know, illness, debility, and grief come for all of us, and insisting that this is not really the case, or that ill-health is good, or that we may make of our experiences whatever we wish, is not merely a biophobic but indeed a life denying premise, however disguised. Both cults, in their eagerness to secure our transcendence, seek also our surety, our security against all contingencies, against which we need neither human medicine nor human agency. As a basis for bioethics, such approaches founder, driving transcendence from life and life from transcendence, and counterposing the two in irremediable opposition.

The task of our medical and bioethical practices, however, should be precisely the opposite, not only to enhance the quality of human living but to bring transcendence to human life.

This suggestion that human transcendence is brought about through human labor, the mutual making or personalizing of persons – would prove anathema to both cults, for whom persons are not born of persons at all but of transcendent ideals. If we are not person makers, however; if our moral agency lends no substance either to our own or to others' persons, then that moral agency finally has no object, no end whatsoever. Whatever our intentions or character, whatever our actions, whatever our hopes or desires or aspirations, these all dissipate *vis-à-vis* our inviolable and inalienable surety. Such accounts secure us both against interior moral failure and external assault, beyond which we reside, at once untouched and untouchable. Yet what then remains of human living in its particulars, of bodily and psychic and social comportment, if the entirety of such lives' comportments are alike equally valuable and in fact, in their value, wholly indistinguishable one from the other? Both cults begin from what they take to be not merely a noble moral premise but the *sine qua non* of our moral capacity: the assertion that all human lives are equally valuable by definition. But these assertions drain human moral activity of any substance, and render unintelligible how any particular variant of human living can prove valuable, in any sense, in its particularity.

On both accounts, the moral perils of valuing such particularity are incalculable. If we attend to the particulars of others' bodies, or of our own, we fall prey to all manner of animal inducements, beauty and desire and lust, vanity and hedonism, raw passion and animal excess. If we attend to the particularities of psychic interiority, we fall prey to mere pathological affections and loves, of persons not in themselves, but insofar as they are appealing or useful to us. If we attend to persons' characters, to their choices and personalities, we substitute our arbitrary valuations of particular traits for the respect or love owed to all as persons. In all three venues, we illicitly objectify those others, making them means to our ends and objects of our use. The first problem with these analyses, of course, is that we can make no sense of persons in themselves apart from such particular features. We may attend to particular persons, rather, only insofar as their particulars, of bodily interiority, psychic subjectivity and moral agency become objects of our deliberate and sustained attention. At the same, they may become objects of our moral attention only if they both transcend us, retaining an opacity beyond our reach, and still prove available to us such that we may do those particulars – of body, psyche and character – and thereby their bearers, good or ill, in their persons. That mutual transcendence may prove a substantive object of our moral agency only if it is a product of mutual agency.

Both cults would deny any such prospect, insisting that human dignity or autonomy precede human agency, such that persons cannot prove objects of others' moral agency, much less moral construction. Nowhere are these insistences more evident than in their twin objections to making persons sexual objects. Such objectifications, they maintain, reduce those others to their bodies, and thereby to objects of our wills. Human bodies, however, as most ethicists lament, are rarely so easily subdued, whether by one's own or by another's will. The seductions of biological living could scarcely prove such an enduring object of moral condemnation were that not the case. Indeed, given how much of moral life, as these ethicists conceive it, involves contesting such impulses, it is unclear what tasks would remain to our moral agency if we succeed in subduing them.

The agency they depict poses a patent paradox. It presupposes bodily impingements for its exercise, yet takes its utter transcendence and independence of such impingements as the basis of its worth. But what good is that agency, if it *a priori* secures its purported task, wholly apart from human effort? In insisting that the absolute value of human life transcends the human body and the quality of human empirical living, both cults intend to assert the moral equality of persons. They do so, however, not by maintaining that specific persons warrant such moral regard, but by insisting that persons per se bear such worth because they transcend all such animal, and individualizing, accouterment.

For both cults, we illicitly objectify others whenever we attend to them as the specific individuals they are. As such, neither human bodies, nor psyches, nor characters, can be objects of moral love or respect. But there is nothing more particular about human persons than their loves, their attachments to particular persons in their particulars, apart from which love of persons, and even love of human life, prove at most vague slogans.

That point might occur to us most vividly when we are in the clutches of an acute grief; when, to put the matter bluntly, the absence of one particular person renders the presence of billions of others a matter of comparative disinterest. For the cult of life, such responses would signal our pathological affections, which cloud our judgments of the others' absolute worth. For the cult of rights, we may still make of this absence what we will. On the first account, we are neither diminished nor even changed in our persons, essentially, by this absence; on the second account, whatever changes we may undertake *vis-à-vis* this event are entirely at our behest. On neither account, strikingly, does this absence impose itself upon us. It cannot, because the absence of one particular agent, in his or her particulars, can scarcely affect another. Neither the former's death, nor his or her empirical life, attaches to either in their persons.

If those particulars lack metaphysical or epistemic or moral substance, however, so too does the entirety of human living in its familiar empirical guise – its pleasures and pains, feelings and preferences, desires and fears, hopes and aspirations. Previously, I've suggested that we may refer(?) to the human body's functional capacities to identify some natural goods, such as pleasure or health, which pose indelible constraints upon our wills. I've maintained also that some substantive goods inhabit individuals as such. I mean here to claim more generally that only if human living may be cultivated through human agency do we have any substantive basis for bioethics. That point is flagrantly denied by the cult of life, which insists, for example, that the life of an anencephalic infant is as good as any other, such that even if we could prevent anencephaly, we should not. Nor should we hasten the passage of fatally compromised lives. Some defenders of the cult of life may even admit that such love seems to pose a stark moral challenge, particularly to would-be parents, constrained as they are on all sides by animal impulses, by egoistic fears and hopes and subjective preferences. I suggest instead that the love they counsel, shorn of particulars, is metaphysical nonsense and a moral abomination, as it precludes in principle the work of parental human love in dignifying persons, in personalizing them, in making them visible in their particulars.

That account deprives human love of any moral task, not only by dehumanizing it, and attaching it instead to a transcendent specter beyond its reach, but also by negating its procreativity. The work of human love, after all, is inversely proportional to its distance. Subject to a pathological gravity, its prime moral challenge is not to extend indifferently to all at the behest of their dignity, but to dignify a few by cultivating the particulars of body, mind and psyche. Such parental responsibility arises, that is, only if they are charged with a substantive procreative task: with embodying, and personalizing and thereby bringing into being a distinct, novel center of valuation irreducible to the conditions of its origins. For both cults, of course, a distinctive feature of human agency is that persons entertain an open future. Yet that prospect remains open only insofar as persons are metaphysically procreative, bringing into being in and through their agency not identical centers of absolute value – an endless succession of fungible persons – but new persons, with distinctive bodies and psyches and characters, and both subject to and objects of substantive moral valuation in their persons. I add that last qualifier to stress the second major point identified above, not only that human persons harbor distinctive goods in their particulars of bodies and psyches and agent characters, but that these goods are cultivated – or thwarted – in and through human moral agency.

This relation is perhaps most clearly exemplified in parenting – in parents investing not only their genes but their personalities and characters into the deliberate cultivation of new lives, and in being mutually transformed in the process. For both cults, such relations are unintelligible. Parents should not, they insist, impose their preferences upon their children. Yet they cannot avoid doing so, and are, even in that initial and deceptively simple subjection to time and to biology, moral patients as well as moral agents. Whether ceded by choice or by design, parents impose a genetic inheritance upon their children; however selected, by tradition or by rebellion or by default, parents impose a valuative inheritance upon their children. The insistence that the latter is malleable in ways the former is not simply begs the critical question. Given that human parents cannot help but impose a range of potentials upon their children, the issue is not how they may avoid doing so, but how they may do so in dignifying ways. Nor, more vitally, is that consideration restricted to relations between parents and children, as we can no more avoid objectifying at least some others, and thereby mutually constituting them in turn.

We cannot, that is, avoid person making, whether we wish to or not.

9
The Triple Helix: Time, Love, and Memory

Bioethicists of both cults delight in discourses over what some term "human life at the margins". While they decry clones and chimera and similar byproducts of the medical technologies they lament, however, their writings teem with extra-corporeal embryos, PVS patients, and like products of their moral imperatives. The latter in particular, after all, are less the creations of biotechnology than of the moral insistence that human life be sustained regardless of its empirical quality. That imperative exhibits how both cults aver such technologies for the maintenance of human life, but not for its enhancement. Both cults, despite the ostensible culture wars so often associated with them, are nearly unanimous in their opposition to eugenics, for example – maintaining instead that human persons are not only good enough in their biological estates, but absolutely good as persons. Any efforts at human enhancement, then, moral or material, would prove not merely practically impossible, but morally nonsensical. Moreover, our bodies' fortunes no more qualify the empirical quality of our lives than do our moral characters qualify our moral worth. Their goodness, rather, resides in the bare fact of their existence, and can neither be augmented nor diminished through human agency.

From this assertion of the absolute moral equality of human lives, in turn, issues the corollary that the ostensibly variable quality of human lives is illusory, and at any rate, bears no relation to the value of such lives, whether to others or to the particular persons in question. Yet from these shared premises, both cults draw confounding conclusions: first, that we should not aim to enhance the empirical quality of human lives, lest we imperil their inalienable goodness; and second, that we should make sustaining human life as we currently know it the overriding end of our moral endeavors.

Both cults lament proposed enhancements – to biological health or bodily function or even mood maintenance – which imperil human life as we know it. These accounts, however, render unintelligible what ends any medical interventions properly serve, moral or medical. If they aim neither at enhancing the empirical quality of human life nor at making persons better than they are at present, what purpose could they serve? One great challenge traditional moral aspirations pose to both views is their temporal trajectory: their underwriting of our ability to project our aspirations into the future, and to redirect our activities in light of them, recreating ourselves in the process. If, instead, we are already, *a priori*, all that we should be, then we can no more improve our moral capacities than we can our physical capacities. To the contrary, we should pursue neither prospect.

9.1 What wondrous love is this?

Perhaps nowhere are both cults more united than on this point, in their shared assertion of the timeless value of human life. Yet that assertion drains both time and life, and indeed, particular life-times – of their distinctive human worth. To maintain instead that the value of human life is essentially time sensitive affirms two premises that both cults deny: first, that the value of individual lives, to the persons who embody them and to others, is variable over time, from birth to maturation to death; and second, that how we use the time we have essentially conditions the worth of particular lives. The cult of life affirms these points in maintaining that how we die matters morally. Yet it denies these points in insisting, bizarrely, that the life and death of an anencephalic infant is equivalent, in value and quality, to that of a healthy seventy-year-old, as if those seventy years add nothing of value to the particular life in question, and as if we should love both lives equally. Despite the familiarity of the phrase, however, we do not love life in itself, neither in its vast riotous teeming across the planet, in plants and people and penguins and piranhas, nor in as a bare logical category.

Our loves, like our lives, are more local, irremediably attached to some persons and some experiences, apart from which we can quite literally make no sense of the terms. Indeed, while human life has suffered gravely at the behest of bioethicists who refashion it into a grand abstraction, human love has fared worse. Its absence shadows the endless disputes over our practices of procreating and living and dying, all undertaken in the service of human persons who, as both cults depict them, are neither needful nor capable of love. It is no surprise, then, that references to individual loves hold no purchase on their accounts of how we should live, or procreate, or die, nor that what little love bioethicists counsel is directed not at specific persons, but at the mysterious metaphysical properties that haunt them, and into whose service they must be impressed, for their own good. In service to its love of life, the cult of life may deem sexual intimacy or procreation not acts of generosity offered to particular others, but duties owed to this life we love in their stead. They may equally demand of us that we endure an endless dying, lest we imperil this life that they love, and indeed, which they love infinitely more then us. We may even demand of future persons that they endure preventable maladies for us, lest we love other apparent goods, like health or happiness, more than we love life itself.

The very great mystery of love of life so conceived, however, is not merely how life, but indeed how love is understood. Among its most traditional depictions is also the most straightforward: to love someone or something is to take that object's good as our own end. So we might ask here, what good do we do to human living, or to the love of human life, by in demanding that it be created as a duty, or sustained as a testament to our endurance of it? Such prescriptions void both life and love of human reference, precisely because they dissolve the integral link between them. What we know of human life we know in its particulars: bodies and psyches, hopes and fears, drives and ambitions, enjoyments and sorrows, failures and successes. These alone, these qualifications of body and psyche and character, render human life distinctively human. Yet it is these very qualities that both cults deem inessential to our persons, rendering them worthless precisely because they are creatures of human living, and not of transcendent metaphysical properties. How we live and how we die, however, matters at all, morally or metaphysically, only if we inhabit the bodies and the psyches and the social relations that we do. These experiences embody human living, our capacity to value our own experiences for ourselves, apart from which our lives could be neither subjects nor objects of any moral valuations.

When we make of procreating a morally laden activity we acknowledge precisely this point: that it brings into being not human life per se, but a particular new life, with its distinctive goods, real and potential – and it thereby evokes a range of responsibilities. When we mourn the passage of such a life, we grieve not for human life in itself, but for the end of a distinctive center of value. When we lament the loss of health and impending disability, we devalue not human life in its entirety, but a particular future less open than one we might have once envisioned. To insist in each of these cases that the particulars matter not at all, that whatever prospect we face is equally good, announces not love of life, nor even a maniacal biophilia, but its precise opposite, a biophobia that refuses to value all that is transitory and fragile in human experience, lest we lose it. That charge may seem incongruous when leveled against the cult of life, which demands that we love all human life as such. But distinctively human life is neither timeless, nor ageless, nor invulnerable to biological and psychic and moral vagaries. Against these forces, it simply cannot prove inviolable, however else we might wish otherwise.

For both cults, those particulars, of body, and psyche, and character, do not signify human life in itself, not only because they are irremediably private, but equally because they are transitory. But then what do we protect, exactly, in defending persons, if nothing valuable about them can be imperiled? I suggest instead that it's precisely because these personalizing elements of persons are transitory and fragile, that human persons require moral provision. If persons are fungible, valuable only in their inalienable worth, then they are interchangeable. Despite both cults' enduring exhortations, however, we remain no less stubbornly in the grips of our mere animal passions: our valuing of some specific persons over others, the narrowing of our loves to an intimate few, and our preference for health and happiness, over their absence. For the cult of life, such valuations are a grave affront to the love of life owed to all persons and all bodily and subjective states equally.

But the love they thereby counsel has neither a moral task nor any moral issue, as it brings nothing of value into being. Worse, it takes as its primary object not the love of any particular persons, but of a life that transcends them and their own valuations, over- writing the latter with those authorized by the cult of life itself. Not only are we not enjoined to love all others in their particulars, then we are equally licensed to substitute our own valuations of their lives for theirs, in service to our purported love of their lives. Yet what are we then valuing? Not their particulars, which may include practices and attitudes contrary to our own, nor their aspirations or hopes or fears or pains or pleasures, all of which must give way to our own valuations. Yet, what then is left to their lives, if we have hollowed out their interiority and privacy, their own valuations, and replaced them with our own, in and through our love of their lives? That the love of life ethic, advanced absolutely, may prove fatal to those so loved may seem a paradox. But that ethic poses no less mortal peril to persons than does the cult of rights' defense of human autonomy, and on the same counts. The autonomy they secure, after all, is no more recognizably human, or particular, than is human life per se as the cult of life conceives it, alike in its transcendent splendor.

What makes the term "human person" a moral category, in contrast – what makes human persons subjects and objects of moral valuations – is not the second word but the first; not the possession of a timeless metaphysical property, personhood, that is, but the empirical conditions under which human persons are brought into being and pass away. To suggest that we dignify or degrade eternal souls, or that we imperil the rights of disembodied autonomous ends – in and through human practices of procreating and living and dying – announce mass metaphysical muddles. We may dignify or degrade persons only insofar as they are objects of our valuations as persons, and thereby, are brought into being as subjects in and through those valuations. Only if their interiority and privacy are partly accessible to us, that is, only if they are real, and only insofar as their attendant particulars of body, psyche and character are valuable in themselves, by the subject and potentially by others, may we make of those persons, in their persons, moral objects.

On that account, to overwrite that privacy and interiority with our own valuations, to redirect that other's bodily interiority and psychic privacy and agency to serve ends entirely of our demand not only degrades that other or violates an abstract right, but imperils that person as a moral subject. To demand of others, for example, that they sustain their lives contrary to their own valuations insists not only that they continue living – whether that holds any value to them or not – but that they affirm such public value regardless of their own private valuations. Moreover, that demand requires such persons to assert that the life they bear, perhaps another month or two in intractable pain or debility, is as good as every other, warranting neither grief nor suffering. Conversely, those who love this other are commended to love instead human life in itself, and to urge ceaseless endurance of this life. The cult of rights, of course, advances a more restricted case, that such persons may seek an early terminus for their dying, provided they can prove, on an autonomous basis, that such a life is unlivable. The autonomy demanded here, however, like the love, is unfettered by time and place and circumstance, and bears no resemblance to any agential capacity that might be deemed distinctively human.

The love the cult of life commends here, like that demanded in dealing with anencephalic infants, is generic, impersonal, and offered as a duty, without cost or issue. It should prove alien to anyone who has witnessed a particular loved one die, and moral nonsense to anyone who has grieved such a loss. I introduce the term moral deliberately here, to underscore the extent to which it is less the timing and manner of the dying than the grief that ensues, that embodies our moral relations. Despite both cults' pretensions, our capacity to make of our deaths what we will is quite limited. The cult of life rails against PAS, as if persons in the last weeks or months of their lives seek death entirely independently of the dying process imposed upon them biologically. The cult of rights insists that we may dignify our death through our choices, as if the dying process might not rip them from us. The cult of life insists that we not exercise our agency in the face of natural necessity, yet it denies that we are subject to such necessity at all. The cult of rights locates the dignity of our death in that agency, as if in acquiescing to or protesting against our death we somehow make it entirely a function of our will. At the same time, both cults' efforts to subject our dying to others' supervision underscore how powerless we are in its stead. Worse, in that supervision, both cults sharpen its power: while our bodies dissolve from within, both cults work feverishly from without, substituting their valuations for our own, in an unacknowledged species of moral murder.

Again, if either cult's operative assumptions about our status as persons were true, no particular dying process would exercise us. Yet they've managed to make of dying a public project, a spectacle wherein the choices of our fellows, whether intimates or strangers, somehow directly implicate the value of our own lives. How can the private dissolution of one particular life implicate the worth of human life per se, and thereby invoke public moral scrutiny and authority? It can do so only if individuals, as individuals, have no such authority over their own lives – if, that is, those lives have no distinctive worth to themselves, but only insofar as they are authorized by others. Only on such a basis may "we" demand that others endure intractable pain and suffering on our behalf, or love an unlovable life, lest ours mysteriously become unlovable, too. We may love human life at its zenith, and may cherish it such that we endure even lengthy rough patches with equanimity. Some may even cling to it under any conditions. But what about those for whom this distinctively animal impulse passes? For the cult of life, any refusal to value human life absolutely signals a moral failure, and a mere preference which must give way to the timeless value of human life in itself.

So too, the grief that attends dying, not simply the physical decline but the loss of an open future, of familiar social relations and valued projects, of freedoms once taken for granted, must prove morally suspect, and be resisted. A similar analysis holds, moreover, in the case of anencephalic infants, whose truncated futures leave their human lives, in themselves, unaffected. In both situations, the cult of life depicts grief as devaluing the absolute worth of such lives, precisely because it implies that alternatives would be better. For the cult of rights, conversely, while dying persons may make whatever they choose of their deaths, they should not direct their dying process at the behest of fear or pain or grief. Instead, they should make whatever they wish of their death, but may do so only if they can act autonomously, that is, independently of those contingencies. To prove to be capable of acting as themselves, they must wholly transcend any such bodily or psychic impingements. Similarly, they must ignore any social or economic or psychic costs their dying process might pose to others, to mitigate any extrinsic influence upon their self-determining will. To act autonomously *vis-à-vis* their dying, that is, they must act as if they are not dying, or grieving, or countenancing the loss of the life they ostensibly value. They may earn the right to act as themselves, that is, only insofar as they are not themselves but instantiate unfettered human autonomy in itself.

In this, the cult of rights not only undercuts the transcendent autonomy it aims to defend, but, like the cult of life, makes utter nonsense of distinctively human agency, and indeed, of distinctively human lives. If a frozen embryo, an anencephalic infant, a healthy forty-year-old physician, a PVS patient, and a cancer riddled ninety-year-old in the last hours of life all bear equivalent worth, to themselves and to those around them, they can do so only if their bodily and psychic and social particulars add precisely nothing of value to them. If, conversely, we can make of these lives entirely what we will, that can be the case only if what those persons make of their own lives, for themselves and for others, adds nothing to their worth. Such assertions alone underwrite both the cult of life's insistence that such lives retain their absolute worth even if they are not valued by those who must endure them, those dying agonizing deaths, for example, and the cult of rights' insistence that persons can act as themselves only insofar as they may completely divorce themselves from such contingencies. Such assertions authorize the cult of life's assertion that parents of anencephalic infants should not wish that their children were born healthy, and also the cult of rights' insistence that our valuations are ours only when they are rationally intelligible to others. Persons as either cult conceives them, that is, are not themselves at all in their particulars, insofar as they are persons; indeed, human persons are persons precisely insofar as they are not human at all.

Both cults offer moral theodicies, assurances that we are in our persons secured not merely from biological or social impingements, but from time itself, from the very life beginnings and life endings that they so hotly contest. But human persons, in their particulars, do not enjoy eternal splendors. Perhaps partly for this reason, philosophers have long counseled love not of specific persons, but of timeless ideals or mathematical truths or undying wisdom, – of anything except life as we know it. Perhaps equally for this reason, they have so eagerly exhorted us to replace our private preferences with eternal verities. So arises the fine Stoic sentiment, voiced by Epictetus and echoed by his cult of life heirs, that the passage of particular human lives is nothing to us, and should occasion no grief. Our deaths, after all, are divinely authored, and such grief would prove at most a futile protest against natural necessity. That a human propensity for grief *vis-à-vis* such events in invariably a losing proposition may be true. Given any attachment to matters temporal, hopes for futures we cannot conjure entirely through our own efforts, regrets for a past we cannot change, fear of an impending death that we cannot forestall – all such responses may prove ineffectual and tortuous. Epictetus' advice bears sound common sense. Asserting the goodness of what we cannot change, and foreswearing efforts to change what we cannot, may be the recipe for a contented life. But do we then call "good" a life that aims entirely at contentment with divine decree, or with natural necessity, or with how we choose to see the matter?

For both cults, that conclusion is inescapable. Human souls or human wills, and thus human persons, are *a priori* what they ought to be, wholly independently of human agency or moral labor. Nor can human bodies or human characters, or anything that traffics in such temporal ephemera, qualify that goodness, or elicit moral labor on their behalf. The human condition in its entirety both cannot and should not be modified on these accounts, such that nothing we can affect through our agency bears any moral import. Conversely, to mourn the loss of our own life or our own capacities wholly misconstrues our relation to those ephemera. These particular attachments, like their objects in those specific others, are finally unreal. However vividly our own, or others', bodily interiority and psychic privacy and moral character may seem to qualify us, or them, they do so not at all in our persons. Persons, rather, on both accounts cannot constitute one another in their persons – not only because persons so qualified would prove irremediably private and distinct from one another in that privacy, but also essentially temporal. At the same time, however, if persons are inviolable in their persons, and timeless, the conditions under which they come into being and pass away – conditions at the margins of human life – should be matters of moral indifference to us, since persons neither are born, nor live, nor die.

Both cults, however, take these ephemera as their stock in trade. In defending future persons, for example, both cults presuppose that what we do to embryos not only affects them in their persons, influencing their quality of life or health status, but also effects them, changing them in their persons. To say that modifying the genetic potentials of a person thereby changes that person announces not only that persons are their genotypes, at least in part, but equally that they are subject to others' choices, to others' actions or omissions, in their persons. Moreover, if affecting the bodies or the psyches of persons changes them, essentially, then persons are essentially embodied, in their status as moral objects. Indeed, I suggest, not only do such selections, or omissions, affect persons, but persons are constituted – in and through time – by persons, in their particulars. For both cults, of course, future persons are an oxymoron, because persons are timeless. The cult of life, however, asserts simultaneously that all embryos embody lives equally complete and valuable to every other human life, and that they should be brought to term – as if doing so could add anything to their lives, and as if leaving them eternally frozen could in any way diminish those lives. Similarly, the cult of rights rejects genetic modifications – for example, to forestall disease or disability – as imperiling future persons' autonomy. Yet that autonomy, like the dignity ascribed to human persons by the cult of life, is not only unconstrained by human embodiment, but by definition disembodied.

Both cults refuse, in their parlance, to reduce persons to their genes, to the mere biological unfolding of the famed double helix. But in asserting a wholesale human independence of that genetic inheritance, they undercut any intelligible basis of human transcendence amid our lives as we know them, amid what we might term a triple helix – of time, love and memory. Only if persons are products of their genetic inheritances can potential modifications of our genetic prospects prove matters of metaphysical or moral import. Yet even to grant that point, and with it the premise that the empirical ephemera dismissed by both cults in fact essentially qualify persons, understates the extent to which we may speak of potential or future persons, of persons made through human labor. Parents who mourn the birth of an anencephalic infant underscore this point, that some goods which might have arise in and through their specific investments in that particular child will not be brought to life, and that some potential goods have been lost. We may speculate endlessly about the metaphysics of the matter, and might even follow the cult of life in insisting that the child was the complete person he or she was meant to be. Yet we may do so only if we dismiss as unreal the parents' loss – of hopes and dreams and expectations – and the child's loss of a more open future – as temporal ephemera that leave them mutually unaffected as persons, and which properly evoke no grief.

Ethics, however, like grief, and much of human life, is an exercise in counterfactuals, in what is not yet, but should be; in what is good or bad or could be better; in what once was, and should or should not be again. Lost in the previous paragraph, for both cults, is precisely this texture: the parents' anticipation of a shared future, their willingness to invest in this particular child, the love they countenance for him or her, a future unexpectedly foreclosed, an enduring grief occasioned not by loss of human life in itself, but of a particular life that could have been but was not. This very prospect, that we might mourn such unrealized futures, such unknown persons, is unintelligible from both cults' perspectives, under which there are no unrealized futures, and no unknown persons. Nor is such grief of metaphysical or moral import. Yet metaphysically, grief teaches precisely the opposite. It endures, because human persons are socially and thereby temporally extended. Amid such intimacies, persons invest their work and their futures – their hopes, their fears, their aspirations, their regrets – into each other. Nor is this a metaphorical matter, but strictly literal. To hold, for example, that parents whose children have perished are no longer parents is no more intelligible then to say that children whose parents have died never had those parents to begin with. Rather, these temporal relations, forever intertwined, essentially condition, that is, essentially personalize persons in their particulars, no less than do their genetic inheritances.

Indeed, only insofar as persons are brought into being, physically, psychically, and socially, can we lend moral content to the claim that our actions may dignify or degrade or love or respect or in any way affect them in their persons. Only insofar as persons pass away, trailing substantive grief in their wake, may we ascribe any metaphysical import to human mortality, and moral import to how we use the time between life's beginning and its end. Only, that is, as such an intertwining of time, love, and memory, may we make of human persons objects of moral regard and subjects of moral agency. If human lives bear any dignity or autonomy, that is, those cannot be timeless ideals, but must be practices through which we personalize and thereby dignify or degrade persons. Only as such may they attach to distinctively human persons, and only as such may what is distinctively human about human persons bear any moral worth. To that end, instead of asserting the absolute, timeless worth of all human lives, we need instead a life-cycle bioethic that serves not eternal verities, but embodied human life as we know it. We need a bioethic, that is, which is animated not by a love of life or rights – a love of transcendent ideals – but of living, and indeed, not of living per se, but of living persons in their particulars. We need, in short, a bioethic aimed not at making human life artificially transcendent, but at bringing transcendence to human life as we know it.

9.2 A life cycle bioethic?

However involved the details of its applications, such an ethic embodies two simple principles: first, that a bioethic suited to human persons must affirm that the body underwrites some natural goods, such as health, pleasure, biological function, and happiness, apart from which we cannot determine medicine's and biotechnologies' proper uses; and second, that the adjudication of these goods, because they arise amid bodily and psychic states – admits an irreducible privacy which must remain ineradicable, morally, as a condition of those goods being embodied in particular lives. That first premise, that the human body authors some distinctive goods, contravenes the vast bulk of the Western philosophical heritage. It also contravenes the vast bulk of literature in contemporary bioethics, bent as both cults are upon insisting that human persons are not their bodies but transcend mere animal nature as a condition of their outsized moral worth. The second premise, that the bodily and psychic interiority or privacy of particular individuals is in itself a substantive moral good, bears an even more tenuous relation to that tradition, for which such subjectivism is an enduring barrier to truth, knowledge, wisdom, and goodness. That tradition has long maintained, to the contrary, that we must extirpate such individual taints to validate our judgments and perceptions – that is, to make them publicly assessable. While this demand animates traditional epistemic prescriptions, it even more forcefully underwrites our moral judgments or evaluations, which must be authorized by recourse to public goods – whether to transcendent ideals or ends, generic human faculties, moral intuition, conscience, reason in itself, or to God's will.

Nowhere is the moral carnage wrought by these presumptions more evident than in the demands posed by both cults that we love life, or love rights, in complete disregard to the particular individuals who bear them. For the cult of life, that love is directed at persons neither embodied, nor mortal, nor personalized amid human practices, nor even needful of others. This cult enjoins, for example, that every human embryo be brought to term. As embryos, however, they are already complete persons, with complete lives, and can neither gain nor lose worth through human agency. At the same time, other persons are enjoined to bring such embryos to term, in the service to love of human life in itself. Here, the patent logical problem that bringing the embryo to term adds precisely nothing of value to it, gives way to a more striking moral challenge: the moral impotence this cult ascribes to human love. That dismissal has long been advanced by philosophers of all persuasions, who locate in human love's subjectivism, its privacy and partiality, its sheer animal obduracy, its unsuitability for any moral task. Love's capacity to bend the vaunted human will, to flummox esteemed reason, to tie us to narrow private interests, has long exercised moral philosophers bent on disinterestedly serving public goods, and so of purifying human love of any subjectivist taints to serve those ends. Indeed, the love of human life commended here is entirely impersonal, directed not at specific persons but at human life in itself. At the same time, the public demand that all embryos be brought to term impresses particular bodies and psyches into service to this public good, regardless of and even in direct opposition to the private valuations of particular persons.

For the cult of life, for example, even an unwanted pregnancy signals a gift, a gift, however, that one cannot refuse, because one must love human life in itself. Human life in itself, however, transcends human agency, as do embryos, all of which are complete persons apart from their empirical fortunes. The love of life that this view demands of potential parents does not attach to particular embryos at all; nor, importantly, does its presence or absence affect those embryos. So self-subsistent are they in their complete persons that they gain nothing through human living, and lose nothing if they are not brought to term. To make of cultivating this gift a publicly imposed duty, of course, implies precisely the contrary point – that is, that human parents substantively affect these embryos through their agency. If that's the case, however, to make of such parental investments not even a public duty but a matter of natural necessity voids procreativity of its distinctive worth, reducing persons in their particulars to mere conduits of transcendent public goods. For the cult of life, unwanted pregnancies, like insufferable deaths, must be endured both in service to a public good – human life in itself, and for the good of the pregnant person, even if the latter identifies no such goods, or even potential harms, in her own private experience. To secure transcendent human life in itself, that is, we must extirpate its distinctively human guises, the bodily interiority and psychic privacy and moral agency apart from which persons, as persons, are indistinguishable from and invulnerable to each other, secure in their inviolable worth.

While the cult of life, in defense of human dignity, unleashes thereby a full scale assault on human liberty and agency, the cult of rights, in its defense of transcendent autonomy, unleashes a full scale assault upon the bodily interiority and psychic privacy which underwrite that autonomy. Both cults seek through their paternalisms to out-source our moral judgments, forcibly substituting public for private assessments. Thereby they not only coerce individual decisions or actions, but also draining them of any moral worth. I mean here to defend not simply unfettered liberty in procreating or dying, but what is the lone basis for regarding human life or human love or human agency as embodying any distinctive worth at all: the interiority and privacy of individuals in their particulars. If human love has any moral power in human procreation, that can only be so if it affects persons in their particular persons. Precisely for that reason, it cannot be demanded or proffered as a public duty. It must instead be offered to particular persons by particular persons; it must equally be freely chosen if it is to admit of moral prescriptions at all, and not just prove a matter of natural necessity. Similarly, if human autonomy has any moral power, and any moral task, that can reside only in bringing into being specific individuals in their particularity. For both cults, such persons are at most epiphenomena, and valuable only insofar as they harbor transcendent properties and enact the prescriptions those properties commend, as identified by their respective cults.

On both accounts, respect or love for persons is finally nonsensical. Under the banner of love of human life in itself, we are enjoined to turn medical practice, however unintelligibly, to serve the bare extension and reproduction of human life as the cult of life idolizes it, and to deliberately retard efforts to enhance the quality of that life or to manage that reproduction. Under the banner of human autonomy, the cult of rights licenses rights bearers endlessly to assess and supervise others' reasons and valuations, rendering all manner of private valuations matters of public assay. Indeed, the cult of rights is now one standard bearer in contemporary bioethics' full scale assault on human agency, as every proposed expansion of human choice – in genetic enhancement, or a right to die, or psychopharmacology – breeds its own public debate and leads persons to intrude their own valuations into others' private decisions. This ethics creep, the gross incursion of public debate and supervision into our private lives, is patently an effort to engineer persons, not through genetic selection but through public coercion. Yet it goes unnoticed by both cults because it extirpates only what they both deem mere human ephemera: the bodily interiority and psychic privacy and substantive moral agency apart from which we can identify neither intelligible bioethical norms nor proper constraints upon the scope of public authority in particular persons' private lives.

For both cults, that scope is limitless; the entirety of embodied human living, in its particulars, may be forcibly impressed into service to their timeless ideals – if need be, against individuals' wills. As persons, the cult of life insists, we must love human life, so much so that we can be coerced to do so for our own good. To forestall imperiling human life in itself, a fanciful prospect on their own account, they thereby perpetrate a greater evil: impressing into public service the bodily interiority and psychic privacy of particular persons whose intimate investments are inexplicably owed to future persons, wholly apart from their own valuations. To forestall imperiling human autonomy, the cult of rights will protect persons from their own agency, ensuring that persons act as "themselves," that is, as rational persons, as the cult of rights defines them. Here, of course, both cults would protest that the relentless expansion of bioethics is less a deliberate effort on their part to colonize individuals' private lives, than a concerted effort to protect human persons from the relentless growth of biotechnology and of medical practice. They would have us believe, then, that public discourse over matters like PVS patients and clones and living wills and PAS is driven by, and a necessary response to, the occurrence of medical practices which pose previously unimagined moral quandaries.

Even the technologies involved in sustaining PVS patients, however, are no more fraught with moral implications than are band aids or wheelchairs or thermometers. Their use, after all, exhibits not a technological but a moral imperative. Long-term use of such technologies is hardly the necessary byproduct of their original purpose: to keep persons alive temporarily, while they recover from illness or injury. The demand to use such interventions in cases where they have no patent purpose, and no natural terminus, arises not from efforts to enhance human life but from the insistence that human life in itself must be idolized, wholly apart from its quality. Bioethicists of both cults, however, while endlessly fascinated by the potential unintended consequences of new biotechnologies, show no comparable inclination to assay the disastrous consequences of their cherished ideals. In the case of PVS patients, for example, many bioethicists will be quick to point out that we thereby have unprecedented liberty in deciding, essentially, whether someone lives or dies. "We", however, are deciding no such thing. Left to its own devices, that body – the human body as we know it – will continue its relentless dissolution. Thwarting that process does not restore biological health or function, but creates a human–machine hybrid entirely a creature not of technological but of moral imperatives – that is, of the injunction that human life in itself must be sustained, even if no distinctively human living is in evidence.

Despite bioethicists' protests to the contrary, the moral dilemmas arising in such cases have nothing to do with the technologies available, and everything to do with their timeless conceptions of the absolute worth of human lives, concepts far removed from human life as we know it. To be sure, these transcendent ideals secure the vaunted moral equality of human lives that both cults assert. They do so, however, not by affirming the goodness of empirical human living – amid the transience of its goods – but by insisting, finally, that there is no good in human living. Only insofar as we foreswear our animal attachments to these ephemera – to pleasure and health and happiness and function, to our preferences and valuations – may we maintain the transcendent goodness of human life in itself. Indeed, our primary moral task is not only to resist those attachments but to extirpate our private preferences and valuations, and to substitute the public authority of such ideals in their stead. As such, persons are licensed neither to act upon their interior preferences nor even to ascribe those preferences moral weight. Nor, vitally, are persons authorized to act upon the deliverances of their bodily interiority, the distinctive pains and pleasures and preferences that they embody as individuals. To the contrary, they are enjoined in both cases to resist any private impingements, either because they undercut their moral agency or autonomy, or because they must give way to greater goods.

9.3 Bringing transcendence back to life

That transcendence of embodied human living might liberate us from human constraints – from illness and aging and debility and grief. But it does so not only by insisting that human life is not as we know it, but but by depicting that life, in its distinctive elements, as in itself degrading and dehumanizing. For both cults, after all, our human worth resides precisely in our capacity to transcend our human nature. Both cults pose this transcendence as the lone bulwark against degrading and dehumanizing technologies. I suggest, instead, that the ideals they valorize leave us in the clutch of degrading and dehumanizing ideals. Instead of locating any distinctive human worth, or any distinctive human good, in the particulars of human embodiment, these ideals require that we wholly transcend our empirical nature as a condition of our moral worth. We must dehumanize ourselves, that is, by clearing away all human taint, any hint of which degrades us not by what we do, but in what we are. These ideals not only recreate human persons in their favored images, but insist that we are, in those idolizing conceptions, precisely what we should be, inalienably and inviolably. They enjoin us, then, not to enhance human living or human persons, but to perpetuate human dignity or human autonomy or life in itself in perpetual moral stasis.

Among the most pernicious implications of these ideals is that static character. Both cults insist at once that the human essence is timeless and transcends nature, and that it should not be modified, as if the first premise doesn't render the second superfluous. On neither account, moreover, do human persons evolve biologically, since the essence of a human person transcends mere human being. Free of nature's and time's dominion, it should prove a matter of moral indifference where we've come from and where we are going, biologically speaking. That both cults insist instead that biotechnological changes to human bodies somehow affect persons could be dismissed as an insuperable logical or metaphysical muddle properly consigned to the musty tomes of philosophical discourse. That confusion, however, underwrites a sustained attack upon efforts to use biotechnologies to enhance human living as we know it. As indicated previously, the bulk of the Western philosophical tradition which both cults issue from aims systematically to disembody and to depersonalize persons, to correct for and to liberate us from our bodily interiority and psychic subjectivity. For the most part, philosophical bioethicists follow in their wake, negating any prospect of a distinctively embodied human good.

Unlike those traditional philosophers, however, bioethicists ostensibly traffic daily in precisely confounding events – in births and ailing and debilities and deaths – that belie human transcendence at every turn. They traffic equally in occasions of grief or joy, in occasions that embody in human living a natural order we cannot elide. To affirm any moral theodicy, any insistence that the human good abides only sans any reference to this order, drains not only human living but human agency of any moral tenor. That tenor arises, rather, in and through our efforts – moral and material – to make of our lives something better then what they are at the present moment. Only such aspirations lend moral shape and value to our lifetimes and their finite capacity to embody distinctively human enjoyments, and thereby, distinctively human goods. These aspirations alone, in their uncertainty, in the fragility of their attainment, allow us to harvest what we can from those lifetimes: achievements and failures, satisfactions and regrets, joyous gains and crushing losses. They alone permit us to distinguish and to evaluate individual life times, and to assay our own life times as well or poorly spent. Not only do they individuate and personalize specific persons, but they also bind persons together: in shared pasts, in diverse futures, in common projects, in distinctive lifetimes substantiated in and through how we use our time, which is to say, how we use our lives.

This proposed texture of human living, however, leaves us irremediably subject to time's dominion. The transcendence this position posits, after all, is not metaphysical or moral, but merely human. We transcend our finitude, the limited confines of our own personalized experiences, not by eliding time, but by investing our lifetimes, that is, our selves, into projects and persons which, like us, perish. We do so, that is, by respecting or loving human lives as we know them, in their transience. To be sure, the cult of life holds itself up as an exemplar of such love. It idolizes all that is unlovely in human living: grave illness, debility, and physical decay. Yet it does so by demanding that we espy in them life's eternal, invariant goodness. Indeed, it portrays any efforts to forestall them, as through genetic enhancement, as failures to love human life in itself. It demands instead that we offer such love indifferently, to health and illness, to pleasure and pain, to biological function and dysfunction. We are not, this is, to enjoy that living or to enhance our own or others' enjoyment, but are merely to endure it as it is. Nor may we find in the particulars of this life anything of value to cultivate. Such love, rather, is morally impotent: it brings nothing of value to life, but simply entertains transcendent ideals which obtain securely sans any reference to particular times or places or persons.

In this self-imposed impotence, the cult of life precisely mirrors the cult of rights, which insists both that our will can make of our biological nature whatever it wills, as a condition of our unfettered autonomy, and that we ought not to make of transcendent future persons objects of our empirical designs. That we cannot improve the empirical life prospects of such persons through genetic enhancement is undeniable on this cult's operative assumptions. Not, however, because we cannot identify what preferences they might have, but because such modifications leave them untouched. To hold that we should not modify future persons' genotypes assumes precisely the contrary point, that such actions do affect their autonomy, and thereby their persons. On that account, it is nonsensical to assert that in choosing some such modifications for them we impose our choices illicitly, whereas in refusing such modifications we make no similar impositions. More strikingly, to assert that we do not attenuate future persons' autonomy if we could prevent them from suffering crushing physical maladies is equally nonsensical, unless we assume that human autonomy wholly transcends the empirical conditions of human life.

At bottom, these demand no moral labor from us. The cult of life insists that we love human life in itself, such that we need make no decisions about how to enhance that life. The cult of rights insists that we respect human autonomy, to the point of refusing to consider whether a life without preventable illness or debility might be preferable, in itself, to its opposite. Both accounts make moral good of natural necessity. In the process, they undercut their own criticisms of biotechnology. If medical practices can dignify or degrade persons, they may do so only insofar as human dignity and human autonomy are not transcendent ideals, but are quite literally embodied in human persons. Any bioethical considerations are intelligible, that is, only if such medical practices are generative of human persons, personalizing them in their bodily interiority and psychic subjectivity and agent capacity. At the same time, to evaluate whether such practices are dignifying or degrading, we can refer only to human living as we know it; only, that is, to how well or poorly those practices cultivate health or pleasure or function – as distinctive human goods – across the human life-span. Both cults would reject the implication that pleasure and health and function are human goods, since they alike regard human goods as by definition disembodied. Both would equally reject the implication that human goods can be time sensitive, with more being available at some life stages then others, since both regard the goodness of human life as timeless. Indeed, to take enhancing pleasure or health as distinctive human ends would both degrade and dehumanize us, befitting us – in Mill's famous formulation – for merely swinish lives.

If those are not legitimate moral ends, however, then medical practices have no moral purpose, and admit no moral norms. The timeless sanctity of human life is scarcely imperiled by deaths however untimely, or by intractable pain or illness or debility. To the contrary, we serve no good by ameliorating disease or forestalling death. If all lives are equally good, rather, we should proscribe all medical practices, since we should prefer no biological states to others. Similarly, the transcendent autonomy of persons can make of those biological states whatever it wills; as such, nothing we do to our bodies should matter, morally. Instead, I suggest, only if human persons are essentially human, that is, essentially embodied, can medical practices harbor any moral content. Moreover, only if life enhancement, rather then simply life maintenance or disease amelioration or health restoration, is an end of medicine, can it have any distinctive moral trajectory. To sustain life for the sake of sustaining life is a vacuous imperative unless any and all health states are equally good. Yet if we grant that latter point, health cannot be morally preferable to illness, including terminal illness. To resist the latter would be no more authorized then would seeking health enhancement. To depict medicine's moral imperative instead as simply restoring or sustaining, but not enhancing, health, implies that we have some normative standard of biological function, a point both cults alike reject. On none of these grounds, in fact, does medical practice have any substantive moral authorization.

The cult of life, rather, should proscribe medicine in its entirety, as preferring some biological states to others; the cult of rights should license all medical practices as equally assertions of human will. Both positions, however, are finally unintelligible, and on the same grounds: on neither account is human health a distinctive human good that might be morally imperiled. Health is, after all, transitory, and contingent, irremediably subject to nature and to time. Worse, if it is an empirical condition of some other human goods, like pleasure or enjoyment, then human living can surrender its worth, to some particular agents, amid such bodily dysfunction. Against those premises, both cults assert that the quality of human living is, finally, wholly immaterial to the worth of human life in itself. Were that the case, however, any medical interventions would prove not merely amoral but pointless. We would be, rather, not only already as good as we are supposed to be, *a priori*, but as healthy (or not) as we should be, on the same basis. This insistence makes utter nonsense not only of medical practice, but of human morality as well. Goodness, like health, is simply not a static, transcendent property that we bear by definition. They are both aspirational ideals, asymptotically approached. Both presuppose, as conditions of our realizing them, a gap between what we are and what we might be, and continual effort on our part to traverse that gap.

They presuppose, that is, substantive human agency charged with bringing these goods into being. We do not, I suggest, cull health, or any other human good, simply by forbearing its opposite. We do not secure health merely by diminishing disease and fending off death any more than we cull goodness merely by eliminating evil. The ideals posed by both cults, in their transcendence, are not life enhancing – precisely because they assert that human persons, and the empirical conditions of human living, are already as they should be, and inviolably so. Indeed, human life in itself neither requires nor even admits of empirical or moral enhancement, such that we should preserve it precisely as it is. Even ignoring the logical tangles such positions pose, their moral challenge is starker. Just as we cannot improve our biological fortunes, nor may we improve our moral worth, which is already absolute. But what good are such moral ideals, if we have, finally, no moral task? We must, the cult of life demands, love life as they do – exactly as it is, and we will be forced to do so, if need be, for our own good. We must, the cult of rights holds, respect human autonomy as exercised amid their oversight, for our own good. We are emphatically not enjoined to love others in their particulars, particularly if their own valuations grossly diverge from our own. Similarly, we are emphatically not enjoined to respect particular persons with their own preferences, but only their autonomy.

To the contrary, at the behest of human dignity and human autonomy we may well license astonishingly life-hating and life-disrespecting practices – for example, enjoining those for whom living has become irreparably burdensome to endure their dismay, and those with no desire to procreate to do so. That latter injunction, issued by the cult of life, ignores the extent to which human procreating is generative, is charged with personalizing its issue through love and through service that simply cannot be summoned through impersonal duties owed impersonally to persons. To make of this love and service a moral demand publicly imposed, and to which all must submit, degrades precisely what segregates distinctively human procreation from animal reproduction – its spontaneity as a freely willed offering. To make of this love a duty dehumanizes and devalues its practice, undercutting its potential issue: the personalizing of a novel individual, in and through specific bodily and psychic and social investments. To be sure, this process poses moral perils because it has the capacity to dignify or degrade the particular individuals thereby personalized. Those moral evaluations are possible, however, and procreation morally momentous at all, only if it poses a substantive challenge to human agents: to bring something of value into being through their efforts, or to fail to do so.

Like the cult of life, the cult of rights denies that moral prospect, insisting that we should not do what we cannot do: truncate other agents' autonomy. At the same time, it undercuts that autonomy in every direction. We should not, it insists, impose our choices on future persons – as if we can avoid doing so. We should not, it demands, impose our choices upon dying persons, unless their choices differ from our own; then, they must be seized from them for their own good. The value of particular human lives, moreover, on both accounts is degraded not only in their inception and in their passage, but at every point along the way. Persons, after all, are timeless, whereas the biological organisms they mysteriously haunt are mere ephemera. The common denominator for both cults is familiar: we should ignore the quality of empirical human living across the entirety of human life-spans. That conclusion follows almost inevitably from the insistence that private, subjective human experiences bear neither substantive metaphysical nor epistemic nor moral worth. To that extent, not only can individuals, as particular individuals, exercise no substantive moral agency, but their bodily and psychic affects pose no goods that we might enhance, or thwart, through the biotechnologies both cults excoriate. For both cults, we should not seek such enhancements, precisely because they would thereby serve private, subjective interests sans public assay, and so imperil public moral authority. Absent such private goods, however, we are left defending not the worth of individual human lives, but rather of metaphysical properties which transcend those lives, and which the latter must serve.

We are left, worse, with technological and moral practices directed not at enhancing those human lives as we know them, but at paying homage to idealized self-conceptions which dehumanize and degrade human lives at every turn. To hear bioethicists of both cults tell it, those properties face grave perils at every turn: cloned children, transgenic human hybrids, spare parts harvesting, and designer people. Yet those prospects, attention grabbing as they may be, leave human persons as both cults conceive them serenely unscathed. They also pale in comparison to more mundane fears that we will outlive those we love, or our own faculties, or our own capacity to value our lives as we see fit. These fears, despite all the bio-hype surrounding emerging biotechnologies, are not the progeny of new medical practices. They are born, rather, of antique moral ideals that have long outlived their usefulness, and of the enduring human propensity to demand that others live according to our own valuations – whatever they might wish for themselves – for their own good. That this paternalism has new weapons in the unending battle against human liberty is indisputable. But that it is the technologies, rather then their would-be authorizers, that are our primary peril is a myth perpetuated by bioethicists to serve ends entirely of their own design. In the purported interests of human dignity, or of human autonomy, partisans of both cults join forces in resisting any efforts to enhance human living or dying, lest we imperil the timeless worth of human life. Yet human ideals, like human children, bear our mortal nature: they are born, they age, they die, and the life-cycle properly begins anew, charged not with recreating what was, but with making of human living what we can, while we can.

Notes

1 The Wages of Grief

1. MacIntyre, Alasdair. *After Virtue: a Study in Moral Theory.* Indiana: University of Notre Dame Press, 1981. Cf. for example MacIntyre's broad discussion of rational incommensurability in contemporary ethical discourse, pp 1–22.
2. Cassell, Eric. J. "The Schiavo Case: A Medical Perspective," *Hastings Center Report* 35, no. 3 (2005): pp 22–23.
3. Nuland, Sherwin. *How We Die: Reflections on Life's Final Chapter.* New York: Random House, 1993.
4. Kaufman, Sharon R. ...*And A Time to Die: How American Hospitals Shape the End of Life.* New York: Scribner, 2005.

2 Getting Too Personal?

1. Moreland, J.P & Rae, Scott B. *Body and Soul: Human Nature and the Crisis in Ethics.* Illinois: InterVarsity Press, 2000.
2. Jonas, Hans. *The Imperative of Responsibility: In Search of an Ethics for the Technological Age.* Chicago: University of Chicago Press, 1984.

3 Where do Bioethicists Come From?

1. Sartre, Jean-Paul. *Being and Nothingness.* New York: Washington Square Press, 1956. Cf. Sartre's discussion of bodily constraints, pp 506–511.

4 Invasion of the Body Snatchers

1. Roochnik, David L. "Metaphorical Immortality: Some Platonic Reflections," in *If I Should Die*, Leroy S. Rouner, ed., Indiana: University of Notre Dame Press, 2001, pp155–69.
2. Peck, M. Scott. *Denial of the Soul: Spiritual and Medical Perspectives on Euthanasia.* New York: Harmony Books, 1997.
3. MacIntyre, Alasdair. *Dependent Rational Animals: Why Human Beings Need the Virtues.* Illinois: Carus Publishing Company, 1999.
4. Kass, Leon. *Life, Liberty and the Defense of Dignity: The Challenge for Bioethics.* San Francisco: Encounter Books, 2002, p. 248.
5. Locke, John. *Second Treatise of Government.* Chapter II: Section 6. Cited in *Classics of Moral and Political Theory*, Steven M. New York: Oxford University Press, 2002, p. 462.

5 Are We Good Enough?

1. Garreau, Joel. *Radical Evolution: The Promise and Peril of Enhancing our Minds, our Bodies – and What it Means to be Human.* New York: Random House, 2005, pp 158–159.

6 Engineering Bioethics

1. MacIntyre, Alasdair. *After Virtue: A Study in Moral Theory.* Indiana: University of Notre Dame Press, 1981.
2. That term "tragedy of the commons" was popularized by Garrett Hardin to describe environmental commons, such as oceans and other ecosystems, plundered to the verge of destruction because no one in particular bore any specific moral responsible for them.
3. McKibben, Bill. *Enough: Staying Human in an Engineered Age.* New York: Henry Holt & Co., 2003.
4. Garreau, Joel. *Radical Evolution: The Promise and Peril of Enhancing our Minds, Our Bodies – and What it Means to be Human.* New York: Random House, 2005.
5. Kass, Leon. "The Wisdom of Repugnance: Why We Should Ban the Cloning of Human Beings." *The New Republic,* June 2, 1997.
6. Burger, A.J. ed. *The Ethics of Belief.* Roseville, CA., Dry Bones Press, 1997.
7. Callahan, Daniel. "When Self-Determination Runs Amok." *The Hastings Center Report* 22, 2 (March–April 1992).
8. Callahan, Daniel. "Reason, Self-Determination and Physician-Assisted Suicide," in Foley, Kathleen, and Hendin, Herbert, eds., *The Case Against Assisted Suicide: For the Right to End of Life Care,* Maryland: Johns Hopkins University Press, 2004. pp 52–69.
9. McKenny, Gerald. *To Relieve the Human Condition: Bioethics, Technology and the Body.* New York: State University of New York Press, 1997, p 171.
10. Miller, Franklin, G., et al. "The Oregon Death with Dignity Act," in *Biomedical Ethics,* 6th edn, Mappes, Thomas A., and DeGrazia, David, eds., New York: McGraw–Hill, 2006.

7 Who Do Bioethicists Think They Are?

1. For an overview of some of the more exotic prospects, cf., Naam, Ramez. *More Than Human: Embracing the Promise of Biological Enhancement.* New York: Broadway Books, 2005.
2. For an overview of the relevant philosophical issues, cf., George Lakoff & Mark Johnson, *Philosophy in the Flesh: The Embodied Mind and its Challenge to Western Thought,*, Basic Books: 1999. Cf., also Antonio Damasio, *The Feeling of What Happens: Body and Emotion in the Making of Consciousness.*Mariner Books, 2000.

8 A Culture of Living

1. Cf., for example, Bill McKibben's lament about the fate of humanity in a bioengineered world in *Enough: Genetic Engineering and the End of Human Nature.* BloomsburyPublishing, 2004.

2. Cf., for example, Michael J. Sandel's discussion of contemporary eugenics in *The Case Against Perfection: Ethics in the Age of Genetic Engineering*. Belknap Press (Harvard), 2009, pp.63–85.
3. Fukuyama, Francis. *Our Post-Human Future: Consequences of the Biotechnology Revolution*. New York: Picador Press, 2002.
4. Fukuyama (2002), pp 6–7.
5. For an extended discussion of steroid use in contemporary sports, cf., Julian Bailes, *When Winning Costs too Much: Steroids, Supplements, and Scandal in Today's Sports World*, Taylor Publishing, 2005.

Bibliography

Bailes, Julian. *When Winning Costs too Much: Steroids, Supplements, and Scandal in Today's Sports World*, New York: Taylor Publishing, 2005.
Burger, A.J. ed. *The Ethics of Belief.* Roseville, CA: Dry Bones Press, 1997.
Callahan, Daniel. "When Self-Determination Runs Amok." *The Hastings Center Report* 22, no. 2 (March–April 1992).
Callahan, Daniel. "Reason, Self-Determination and Physician-Assisted Suicide," in Foley, Kathleen, and Hendin, Herbert, eds, *The Case Against Assisted Suicide: For the Right to End of Life Care,* Maryland: Johns Hopkins University Press, 2004.
Cassell, Eric. J. "The Schiavo Case: A Medical Perspective," *Hastings Center Report* 35, no. 3 (2005): pp 22-23.
Damasio, Antonio. *The Feeling of What Happens: Body and Emotion in the Making of Consciousness.* New York: Mariner Books, 2000.
Fukuyama, Francis. *Our Post-Human Future: Consequences of the Biotechnology Revolution.* New York: Picador Press, 2002.
Garreau, Joel. *Radical Evolution: The Promise and Peril of Enhancing our Minds, our Bodies – and What it Means to be Human.* New York: Random House, 2005.
Jonas, Hans. *The Imperative of Responsibility: In Search of an Ethics for the Technological Age.* Chicago: University of Chicago Press, 1984.
Kass, Leon, et al. *Beyond Therapy: Biotechnology and the Pursuit of Happiness.* New York: Dana Press, 2003.
Kass, Leon. *Life, Liberty and the Defense of Dignity: The Challenge for Bioethics.* San Francisco: Encounter Books, 2002.
Kass, Leon. "The Wisdom of Repugnance: Why We Should Ban the Cloning of Human Beings." *The New Republic,* 2 June 1997.
Kaufman, Sharon R. *...And A Time to Die: How American Hospitals Shape the End of Life.* New York: Scribner, 2005.
Lakoff, George & Johnson, Mark. *Philosophy in the Flesh: The Embodied Mind and its Challenge to Western Thought.* New York: Basic Books, 1999.
Locke, John. *Second Treatise of Government.* Chapter II: Section 6. Cited in *Classics of Moral and Political Theory,* ed. Steven, M. New York: Oxford University Press, 2002.
MacIntyre, Alasdair. *After Virtue: a Study in Moral Theory.* Indiana: University of Notre Dame Press, 1981.
MacIntyre, Alasdair. *Dependent Rational Animals: Why Human Beings Need the Virtues.* Illinois: Carus Publishing Company, 1999.
McKenny, Gerald. *To Relieve the Human Condition: Bioethics, Technology and the Body.* New York: State University of New York Press, 1997.
McKibben, Bill. *Enough: Staying Human in an Engineered Age.* New York: Henry Holt & Co., 2003.
McKibben, Bill. *Enough: Genetic Engineering and the End of Human Nature.* Indiana: Bloomsbury Publishing, 2004.

Miller, Franklin, G., et al. "The Oregon Death with Dignity Act," in *Biomedical Ethics*, 6th edn, Mappes, Thomas A., and DeGrazia, David, eds., New York: McGraw-Hill, 2006.

Moreland, J.P & Rae, Scott B. *Body and Soul: Human Nature and the Crisis in Ethics*. Illinois: InterVarsity Press, 2000.

Naam, Ramez. *More Than Human: Embracing the Promise of Biological Enhancement*. New York: Broadway Books, 2005.

Nuland, Sherwin. *How We Die: Reflections on Life's Final Chapter*. New York: Random House, 1993.

Peck, M. Scott. *Denial of the Soul: Spiritual and Medical Perspectives on Euthanasia*. New York: Harmony Books, 1997.

Roochnik, David L. "Metaphorical Immortality: Some Platonic Reflections," in *If I Should Die*, Leroy S. Rouner, ed., Indiana: University of Notre Dame Press, 2001.

Sandel, Michael. *The Case Against Perfection: Ethics in the Age of Genetic Engineering*. Belknap Press (Harvard), 2009.

Sartre, Jean-Paul. *Being and Nothingness*. New York: Washington Square Press, 1956.

Index

Aristotle 19, 89, 183

Biofallacies, definition 129
  Aspirational Fallacy 131
  Blind Man's Bluff Fallacy 130
  Brave New World Fallacy 132
  Frankenstein Fallacy 134
  Future is Now Fallacy 134
  Galileo Gambit 133
  Inertial Fallacy 133
  Intentional Fallacy 129–30
  New Kid on the Block Fallacy 134
  Playing God Fallacy 135–6
  Principled Inaction Fallacy 133
  Seinfeld Fallacy 131
  Yuck Factor Fallacy 135
Biophobia 4

Callahan, Daniel 138–9
Cicero, 74
Clifford, William 136
Cult of Life
  love of life 61, 80
  metaphysical dualism 32–3, 34–6, 67, 80
  natural norms 40–1, 66, 79, 84
  persistent vegetative states (PVS) 24–7, 82–3
  personhood 31, 34, 41–3, 54–7, 62–3, 120
  physician assisted suicide (PAS) 112
Cult of Rights
  autonomy and liberty, 4–5, 10–16, 28, 37–8, 110
  reproductive liberty 38–9
  death, philosophical views on 20

Epictetus 19–20
Epicurus 18–19, 74

Fukuyama, Francis 183–4

Garreau, Joel 106–7

health, value of 51–2, 186–9, 193–9

Jonas, Hans
  Technological imperative 39–40
  future persons 99–100

Kant, Immanuel
  dualism 3, 35, 80–1, 183
  suicide 78–82
Kass, Leon 77, 135
Kaufman, Sharon 27

MacIntyre, Alasdair
  virtues of dependence 75–6
  incommensurable moral debate 126–7
McKenny, Gerald 75, 139–40
Medicine, purpose of 180–2
Mill, John Stuart 49–53

Nuland, Sherwin 26–7, 138

Plato 146–7
Philosophical Bioethics 9–10
  current state of 8–9, 47
    demise of 4–6, 45, 104–6, 147–51, 122–30, 169–71, 182–6, 189–91, 217–18, 202, 216, 220–3
    future persons 101–3, 107–8, 153
    love and grief 24, 64–5, 72, 156–8, 177–8
    persons 6, 11–15, 57–8, 136, 158–9
    purpose of 154–6, 171–5, 200–2, 205–8, 211–12

Roochnik, David 74

Sartre, Jean-Paul
  self-consciousness 18–19, 63, 68–9, 158–9
  human nature and freedom 112–13
Socrates, 19, 74–5

Triple Helix
  Life cycle bioethics 212–16, 220
  subjectivity and agency 58–60
  time and sociality 5, 13–17, 22–3, 203–5